Integral Pluralism

INTEGRAL PLURALISM

Beyond Culture Wars

FRED DALLMAYR

UNIVERSITY PRESS OF KENTUCKY

Copyright © 2010 by The University Press of Kentucky
Paperback edition 2015

Scholarly publisher for the Commonwealth,
serving Bellarmine University, Berea College, Centre College of Kentucky,
Eastern Kentucky University, The Filson Historical Society, Georgetown
College, Kentucky Historical Society, Kentucky State University,
Morehead State University, Murray State University, Northern Kentucky
University, Transylvania University, University of Kentucky, University of
Louisville, and Western Kentucky University.
All rights reserved.

Editorial and Sales Offices: The University Press of Kentucky
663 South Limestone Street, Lexington, Kentucky 40508-4008
www.kentuckypress.com

The Library of Congress has cataloged the hardcover edition as follows:

Dallmayr, Fred R. (Fred Reinhard), 1928–
  Integral pluralism : beyond culture wars / Fred Dallmayr.
    p. cm.
  Includes bibliographical references and index.
  ISBN 978-0-8131-2571-8 (hardcover : alk. paper)
  1. Cultural pluralism. 2. Intercultural communication. 3. Philosophy,
Comparative. I. Title.
  HM1271.D37 2010
  305.8001—dc22   2009045426

ISBN 978-0-8131-6633-9 (pbk. : alk. paper)

This book is printed on acid-free paper meeting the requirements of the
American National Standard for Permanence in Paper for Printed Library
Materials.

Manufactured in the United States of America.

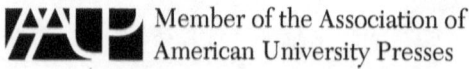 Member of the Association of
American University Presses

For Keegan Jeremiah
and for the 100th anniversary
of the birth of Merleau-Ponty

If ever there was a house of civilization divided within itself and against itself, it is our own today.
—John Dewey

The human world is an open and unfinished system and the same radical contingency which threatens it with discord also rescues it from the inevitability of disorder and prevents us from despairing of it.
—Maurice Merleau-Ponty

Confrontation does not divide unity, much less destroy it. ... It is a gathering (logos).
—Martin Heidegger

Contents

Preface xi

1. Integral Pluralism: Holism and Difference 1
2. The Concept of the Political: Politics between War and Peace 23
3. The Secular and the Sacred: Whither Political Theology? 45
4. Postsecular Faith: Toward a Religion of Service 67
5. Religion and the World: The Quest for Justice and Peace 85
6. Hermeneutics and Cross-Cultural Encounters: Integral Pluralism in Action 103
7. A Man for All Seasons: Mahatma Gandhi's Integral Pluralism 123
8. Reason and Lifeworld: Two Exemplary Indian Thinkers 143

Appendixes

A. Return of the Repressed: Merleau-Ponty Redivivus 167
B. Disclosure and Critique: Critical Reason and Its Horizons 175
C. On Love with Distinction: A Chinese Debate 185

Notes 191

Index 223

Preface

These are perilous times; the issue of war and peace hangs everywhere in the balance. Despite an unexpected recent upsurge of political goodwill, structural constraints and ingrained habits of rivalry may well tip the balance against it. Behind the habits of ill will and distrust, deeper fissures lie in waiting—fissures (we are told) demarcating cultural or civilizational "fault lines" and rendering our age prone to civilizational "clashes." According to some observers, clashes of this kind—often disguised (and mislabeled) as "terror wars"—are likely to persist for decades and perhaps even centuries. Quite apart from these civilizational conflicts, however, there is another, no less profound fissure affecting Western, especially American, society today. In the view of competent analysts, the latter society has rarely been so radically split asunder. The split here runs along cultural, religious, and socioeconomic lines. A common term for such divisions is "culture wars."

To be sure, culture wars of this sort are not new in Western societies, although they have reached a particularly acrimonious stage today. As people with historical memory will recall, Western culture wars go back basically to the French Revolution, when that country was divided into the forces of the "Red" and the "Black." In that context, the color red designated those forces seeking social progress, democracy, and individual freedom, whereas black symbolized the forces of "reaction," those seeking to restore order, traditional authority, and discipline. The division also carried religious implications, with one side extolling Christian, especially Catholic, faith and the other tending toward secularism, perhaps atheism. Culturally and politically, the Blacks stood for compact French unity ruled by traditional elites, while the Reds favored a degree of social pluralization (and sometimes a transnational cosmopolitanism).

Under somewhat changed auspices, the phenomenon of culture

wars emerged in Germany during the Bismarck era and later, with even greater vehemence, during the Weimar Republic. As earlier in France, the conflict (called *Kulturkampf*) raged between more forward-looking and more backward-looking forces, between defenders of traditional order and champions of liberty and emancipation. (To some extent, one might claim that the National Socialists used or abused the "progressive" agenda of popular mobilization for the purpose of reestablishing absolute unity and sovereignty.) During the later part of the twentieth century, the conflicts and fissures of the Weimar Republic were transferred to American society—where, due to the absence of buffering elements (such as old-style British conservatism), they quickly spawned streamlined and aggressive ideologies, pitting unitary and triumphalist Americanism against radical individualism or anarchism. The high point of the controversy came after September 11, 2001, when neoconservative ideologues blamed the national debacle on the disintegrating and demoralizing effects of liberal postmodernism.

Although often voiced in more subdued terms, the sentiments giving vent to this controversy still persist and fester. On a more sophisticated philosophical level, what is hidden behind heated culture debates are issues that cannot and should not be easily dismissed or sidelined: questions regarding the priority of unity over diversity, of the "one" over the "many," of holism over particularism, of shared virtues over individual (or group) freedom. Although these issues are in a sense perennial, they have acquired particular relevance and urgency in our time of democratization, multiculturalism, and global pluralization. Under the label of "integral pluralism," this book hopes to contribute to the clarification and perhaps softening of the ongoing culture wars. Actually, some steps in this direction can be discerned today on many levels. As we know, religious faith has made a comeback and is no longer the exclusive prerogative of reactionary authoritarians; rather, we see a newfound "postsecular" religiosity endorsed by many progressive democrats. In the same manner, "virtue ethics"—previously the monopoly of conservative Aristotelians—is being rediscovered by pluralists and multiculturalists as an asset for democracy and as a bulwark against rampant abuses of political, especially executive, power. Far removed from "fundamentalism" and "moral majoritarianism," the core of "civic virtues" is found here in a generous openness to diversity and a solicitous care for, and service to, others (especially underprivileged or marginalized others).

Together with William James, I believe that we live in a "pluralistic universe" and in an age of steady pluralization. Together with him (and many others), however, I also believe that there are emergent connections and concatenations linking all the elements of the universe in what Merleau-Ponty called the "flesh of the world" (beyond appropriation and control). In writing this book I am distantly indebted to James as well as Merleau-Ponty. In fact, the book is meant as a small contribution to the 100th anniversary of Merleau-Ponty's birth in 1908. Other thinkers inhabiting the pages of this book are Martin Heidegger, Hans-Georg Gadamer, Charles Taylor, William Connolly, Raimon Panikkar, Richard Falk, and Jonathan Sacks. As always, I owe a great intellectual debt to such friends as Calvin Schrag, Hwa Yol Jung, Eliot Deutch, and Chandra Muzaffer. No line in this book would have been written without the caring solicitude of my wife Ilse and our children Dominque and Philip. The book is dedicated in part to our grandson Keegan Jeremiah.

South Bend, October 2008

1. Integral Pluralism
Holism and Difference

In traditional terminology, the world was conceived as a "cosmos," that is, as an appealingly structured ensemble endowed with internal coherence and a high degree of intelligibility. In conformity with this conception, human societies were seen as small replicas of the cosmic order, replicas whose constituent elements were integrally related, with each fitting harmoniously into a preordained pattern. Since the onset of Western modernity, this orderly vision has been increasingly sundered or thrown into disarray. In large measure, the trajectory of modernity can be construed as a series of steadily deepening dualisms or polarities. In the course of this development, human beings have been progressively segregated from both external nature and the (ontological) backdrop of the divine—a segregation matched by the steadily more competitive and even hostile relations between individual agents as well as larger human societies or states. In sociological and anthropological literature, this proliferating process is often discussed under the labels of "differentiation" and "disenchantment."[1] In the vocabulary of contemporary astronomy, one often speaks of the upsurge and veritable explosion of "Nova," that is, the emergence of new planetary constellations that do not seem to fit any previously known pattern of phenomena. The question remains whether these and related developments necessarily imply a negation or rejection of "cosmos" in the sense of a coherently holistic pattern.

This, in any case, is the question raised in this chapter and in this book as a whole. In my view, the issue is not only of purely theoretical or metaphysical significance but has clear practical implications. On the assumption of a radical lack of cosmic coherence, individual human lives likewise become incoherent and unintelligible—outside the pursuit of purely private agendas or projects. In the social and political domain, the same assumption lends credence to the Hobbesian "war of all against all," a formula rendering the traditional notion of the "good life" hopelessly obsolete or apocryphal. To a considerable extent, contemporary "culture wars," both in the West and elsewhere, revolve around this issue. For some, the ongoing process of pluralization or dispersal requires a resolute reaffirmation of integral holism, even at the price of restoring traditional autocracies and social hierarchies. For others, the ongoing proliferation of differences and dispersed identities is an unmitigated boon—a view often bolstered by a benign neglect of the looming prospect of Hobbesian warfare and "clashes among civilizations." As it seems to me, these two options are far from exhausting the range of available avenues; speaking more concretely, neither coercive autocracy nor social atomism is compatible with a viable sense of democracy.[2] For both philosophical and political reasons, I want to explore here another alternative: what I call an integral (or holistic) pluralism. Seen under these auspices, holism is not a preordained structure or pattern but rather something that emerges laterally or in tandem with the upsurge of Nova, the rise of frequently unexpected new initiatives, constellations, or events. I proceed in three steps. First, I discuss the pervasive appeal of pluralism and pluralization. Next, I review efforts to mitigate or complement this appeal along more integral or holistic lines. Finally, I offer an overview of subsequent chapters that, in different ways, articulate this alternative view.

Pluralism and Pluralization

Late modern and postmodern times are marked by growing attentiveness to processes of social as well as metaphysical and even theological pluralization and differentiation. In the West, successive waves of Reformation have led to the proliferation of the traditional unity of Christendom into a variety of denominations, sects, and religious communities. At the same time, both medieval hierarchical patterns and the uniform structure of the modern absolutist state have been forced to give way under the impact of revolutionary and semirevolutionary upheavals. Even the vaunted transparency and certitude of the liberal "law state" (*Rechtsstaat*) have been subject to the splintering effects of social movements and partisan ideologies. In the words of political philosopher Claude Lefort, it is precisely the distinguishing trait of modern democracy to entail the erasure of traditional "markers of certainity."[3] More recently, all these developments have been intensified by the rapid acceleration of globalization, a process thrusting familiar conceptions and worldviews into the disorienting maelstrom of multiple national or ethnic cultures as well diverse religious and ethical traditions. Needless to say—and as some observers have forcefully pointed out—globalization happens for good or ill: apart from enabling multiple contacts or interactions, the closer proximity of peoples can also lead to armed conflicts or clashes along civilizational fault lines.[4]

In the context of modern Western philosophy, probably the first major thinker to grasp the deeper implications of pluralization was the American pragmatist William James. In his 1909 study titled *A Pluralistic Universe,* James boldly sketches the vision of a dynamic universe—always expanding and proliferating—as a counterpoint or corrective to the conception of a static cosmos. Constantly changing and in the throes of novelty, such a dynamic universe may never be completely transparent or fully grasped by traditional conceptional categories. As James writes, in a stunning formulation: "The pluralistic view which I prefer to adopt is willing to believe that there may ultimately never be an all-form at all, that the substance of reality may never get totally connected, that some of it may remain outside of the largest [conceptual] combination of it ever made." In this passage, the importance of constitutive elements of the world—all endowed with a distinctive "each-form"—is highlighted in opposition to a totalizing conception—an "all-form"—imposed on elements from above. James's text is emphatic in denouncing the static "totalism" or "monism" that has dominated much of traditional Western metaphysics. In such a conception, he writes, the world is a "complete block-universe through and through"; that is, it is not a "collection" of elements but rather "one great all-inclusive fact outside of which there is nothing." An example of this view is "monistic idealism," a system in which the "all-enveloping fact" is represented as "an absolute mind that makes the partial facts by *thinking* them" and where "to be" means "to be an object for the absolute." When absolute or monistic idealism is given a religious or theological cast, God emerges as an unlimited ruler or potentate sanctioning in his totalizing nature all the blessings and all the miseries, all the good and evil happenings in the universe without discrimination.[5]

While opposing the totalizing ambitions of monism, James is equally pointed in critiquing all forms of static dualisms or dichotomies, especially those dualisms that have beleaguered modern Western philosophy—those between mind and body, between human beings and nature, or (in Cartesian terms) between "thinking substance" and "extended matter." One of the dualisms particularly singled out in the text is that between humans and God or the divine. In strong terms, James attacks the "two-worlds" theory prevalent in forms of traditional theism. "The theistic conception, picturing God and his creation as entities distinct from each other," he states, "still leaves the human subject outside of the deepest reality of the universe." In this view, God, seen as eternally complete, "throws off the world by a free act as an extraneous substance" and "throws off man as a third substance, extraneous to both the world and himself."[6] Basically, James lays the blame for the persistence of abstract dualisms at the doorstep of (Platonic and Cartesian) rationalism or what he calls "intellectualism." The "ruling tradition" in philosophy, in his view, has been the belief that "fixity is a nobler and worthier thing than change" and that "concepts, being themselves fixities, agree best with this fixed nature of truth." The remedy proposed by James for this kind of intellectualism is a "radical empiricism" that breaks through the barrier between mind and matter, between reason and external phenomena. In contrast to "sense-data" empiricism, this approach sees mind not as helplessly bombarded by random stimuli but rather as itself participating in the phenomenal world. In his words: "Reality, life, experience, concreteness, immediacy—use what word you will, exceeds our [internal] logic, overflows and surrounds it." From this angle, reality is "where things *happen*," an "all temporal reality without exception" in which things are "distributed and strung along" and in which "we finite beings" are immersed.[7]

Toward the end of his study, James rearticulates the crucial distinction between a static "intellectualist" worldview—whether monistic or dualistic—and the kind of dynamic pluralism he is inclined to endorse. Basically, he notes, the distinction boils down to the difference between a "top-down" essentialism embracing everything a priori and a "bottom-up" approach acknowledging the coorigination of diversity (or "the many"). In the former perspective, "everything, whether we realize it or not, drags the whole universe along with itself and drops nothing. The log starts and arrives with all its carriers supporting it." In the pluralist perspective, by contrast, "all that we are required to admit as the constitution of reality is what we ourselves find empirically realized in every minimum of finite life"—which means "that nothing real is absolutely simple, that every smallest bit of experience is a *multum in parvo* plurally related." The difference can also be explained by using the terms "all-form" and "each-form" (previously mentioned). James argues that under a priori intellectualism, especially in its monistic guise, "the all-form or collective-unit form is the only form that is rational," that it "allows of no taking up and dropping of connexions, for in the 'all' the parts are essentially and externally co-implicated." The pluralist approach, on the contrary, "lets things really exist in the each-form or distributively," which means that "a thing may be connected by intermediary things with a thing with which it has no immediate or essential connexion." With these formulations, James concludes, we arrive at a "plain alternative" of philosophical approaches or perspectives. In a nutshell, the issue boils down to this: is the "manyness in oneness" that characterizes our world "a property only of the absolute whole of things, so that you must postulate that one-enormous-whole indivisibly as the *prius* of there being many at all," or "can the finite elements have their own aboriginal forms of manyness in oneness," with each one of these elements "being one with its next neighbors and yet the total 'oneness' never getting absolutely complete?"[8]

Apart from articulating different philosophical perspectives, James's text also reflects on the religious implications of his discussion. "Let empiricism [in the Jamesian sense] become associated with religion," he states at one point, "and I believe that a new era of religion, as well as philosophy, will be ready to begin." The reason is that a pluralistic approach, sensitive to difference, is "a more natural ally of the religious life" than intellectualism.[9] With or without acknowledging Jamesian teachings, many contemporary philosophers of religion endorse and even celebrate a pluralistic religiosity. A prominent example is the Spanish-Indian thinker Raimon Panikkar. In one of his writings, titled *A Dwelling Place for Wisdom*, Panikkar remarks pointedly that, with regard to the diversity of religious traditions, "the time has come for a pluralistic attitude—for a head-first dive into the Ganges." As he elaborates, pluralism is not equivalent to sheer factual plurality or multiplicity. Although it is clear that there are many religions that cannot be reduced to sameness, genuine pluralism means "more than the mere acknowledgement of this plurality," namely, an ethical and religious engagement with religious difference. Paralleling James's critique of intellectualism, and especially of abstract monism, Panikkar asserts that pluralism "does not regard unity as an indispensable ideal"; nor does it cling to an "eschatological expectation" that "in the end everything will come to unity by itself." Philosophically, the approach has no room for system building, seeing that "a pluralistic system would be a contradiction in itself." In a Jamesian vein again, the approach "makes us aware of our contingency, our limitations, and shows us that reality cannot be fully comprehended." In the end, religious pluralism for Panikkar entails "a nondualist, *advaitic* attitude which defends truth's pluralism since truth itself is pluralistic" and "cannot be expressed in terms of either unity or multiplicity."[10]

Partly under James's influence, pluralism has also left its imprint on contemporary political theory and philosophy. The reason is not hard to discern: its open-ended vista is clearly more congenial than intellectualism to an age of democracy or democratization, with its corollaries of multiculturalism and the pluralization of identities. A prominent proponent of the approach is political theorist William Connolly, well known for a string of publications contesting forms of static traditionalism. In his book *Pluralism*, Connolly makes explicit reference to James's vision of a "pluralistic universe" composed of multiple elements and connections unable to be exhaustively mapped or grasped. By contrast to earlier—merely empirical or functional—forms of social differentiation, the book articulates the idea of a "deep" or "thick network" pluralism with quasi-ontological and even theological implications. As Connolly writes, the notion of a pluralistic universe testifies to "the highest hope that James invests in the world"—the hope or experience that, on the far side from monistic omnipotence, "a limited God participates as one agent in a larger world of imperfect plural agents of different types," a world reducible to neither a static universalism nor a chaotic relativism. The political repercussions of this view are pervasive. Pluralism of the kind envisaged in his text,

Connolly observes, "denies the sufficiency of a concentric image of culture to territorial politics"; it also alerts us "to eccentric connections that cut across the [closed] circles of family, neighborhood, and nation"—such as when ecologists in different parts of the world "align to put pressure on several states at once" or a cross-state coalition of citizens exposes and protests human rights violations in places such as Tibet, Palestine, or Zimbabwe. In these and other respects, pluralism reflects not so much fixed or predictable lines of development but rather latent possibilities inscribed in our democratic age: "To bypass pursuit of deep, multidimensional pluralism today would be to fail an elemental test of fidelity to the world."[11]

Though not always under Jamesian auspices, pluralism has also been strongly embraced by "postmodernists" or thinkers close to the "postmodern" persuasion. Under such labels as "difference," "otherness," "heterogeneity," and "rupture," pluralist premises have in fact been occasionally erected into firm doctrines or creeds. Carried to its logical extreme, this treatment tends to transform pluralism into radical fragmentation and grant separate elements a fixed, self-enclosed identity. This tendency is conspicuous in the work of one of the founding architects of postmodernism, Jean-François Lyotard. In his book *The Postmodern Condition,* Lyotard challenges and rejects all forms of traditional metaphysics, forms that, for him, are invariably marked by rationalism (or intellectualism), "logocentrism," and a monistic teleology verging on totalitarianism. According to his text, the metaphysical preferences of the past typically found expression in a series of "grand metanarratives"—from salvation history to Adam Smith's *Wealth of Nations* to Karl Marx's vision of a proletarian world revolution—all of which aimed to unify all possible knowledge and experience in a comprehensive synthesis. Rebelling against these synthesizing stories, postmodernism in Lyotard's account inaugurates a radical reversal or shift of priorities: namely, from unity to fragmentation, from Platonic-Cartesian *logos* to "paralogy," from homogeneity to heterogeneity, and from a common identity to the negation and dispersal of identities. Borrowing a Wittgensteinian motif, but with a postmodern twist, the text sees human language as dispersed into "language games" marked by incompatibility and incommensurability. In Lyotard's words, what postmodernism brings into view is not communication and consensual understanding but

8   Integral Pluralism

"a theory of games which accepts agonistics as a founding [foundational?] principle."[12]

Affinities with Lyotard's founding principle can also be found in an American thinker loosely associated with the postmodern agenda: Richard Rorty. One of the central motivations of Rorty's work has always been to challenge or debunk the traditional addiction of Western philosophy to "epistemology," the latter seen as a gateway to the acquisition of apodictic or indubitable knowledge of "reality." Having boldly launched this attack in one of his early writings (regarding the knowledge of "nature"), Rorty subsequently extended his deconstructive effort to cognitive assumptions in a variety of domains, including history, culture, and society. Once cognition is viewed as thickly embedded in varying historical and cultural contexts, the inevitable philosophical upshot is radical contingency and fragmentation—a basic theme of Rorty's *Contingency, Irony, and Solidarity*. Following the general postmodern agenda, the text on the whole endorses the primacy of particularity over universality, of heterogeneity over unity; paralleling and even further accentuating Lyotard's approach, it insists on the diversity and incommensurability of language games, on the absence of a shared or overarching linguistic idiom. In Rorty's words, there is "no final vocabulary" available to either philosophers or ordinary citizens, no "meta-language" through which cross-cultural arguments can be reconciled or adjudicated. More astutely than Lyotard, Rorty is aware of the danger of "performative contradiction," that is, the pretense of exempting one's own vocabulary from contingent relativity. The remedy for this danger is "irony," which, in a way, cancels all cognitive claims. Ironists, he asserts, are so "impressed by other vocabularies," vocabularies taken as final by other people, that they stop defending or taking seriously either their own or other people's arguments. On these premises, "the distinctions between absolutism and relativism, between rationality and irrationality, and between morality and expediency are [seen to be] obsolete and clumsy tools—remnants of a vocabulary we should replace."[13]

Integral or Holistic Pluralism

As the preceding discussion indicates, pluralism harbors a danger that, curiously, approximates it again to the monistic temptation.

Carried to the extreme of radical fragmentation or dispersal, pluralism—despite its protestations—shades over into an assembly of fixed and self-enclosed monadic units exhibiting the same static quality as its counterpart. For this reason, it seems advisable to differentiate, at a minimum, between genuine "pluralism" and empirical "plurality," where the latter signifies a mere juxtaposition of existing units and the former implies a measure of mutual engagement, interrogation, and relatedness.[14] Actually, more is involved than mutual relatedness (which still carries overtones of plurality). In many ways, it seems preferable to speak of a mutual embroilment, interpenetration, and contestation, of a differential entwinement without fusion or segregation. It is this kind of entwinement that I designate "integral (or holistic) pluralism." Using an image employed previously, one might say that, whereas in traditional monism (as well as dualism) the unifying structure is imposed from the top down, the linked quality of integral pluralism emerges from the bottom up—in a way that can never be fully predicted or exhaustively mapped.

At a closer look, James's *A Pluralistic Universe* illustrates the meaning of integral pluralism. Repeatedly he speaks of the differentiated elements of the universe as "distributed, strung-along, and flowing" in a stream. Remonstrating against the assumption of a radical rupture or discontinuity, he emphasizes "the stream's sensible continuity," adding, "No element there cuts itself off from any other element, as concepts cut themselves from concepts. No part there is so small as not to be a place of conflux; no part there is not really *next to* its neighbors—which means there is literally nothing between." Elaborating on this point, and opposing the notions of both static fusion and fragmentation, the text states: "Things are '*with*' one another in many ways, but nothing includes everything, or dominates over everything. The word 'and' trails along after every sentence; something always escapes." Seen from this angle, the pluralistic universe is "more like a federal republic than like an empire or a kingdom." However much may be collected or unified, "something else is self-governed and absent and unreduced to unity." In an intriguing passage toward the end of his study, James points to the practical and ethical implications of pluralism. Just because pluralism is always in danger of sliding toward either monism or fragmentation, human praxis is needed to keep it on an even keel: "The incompleteness of the pluralistic universe . . .

is also represented by pluralistic philosophy as being self-reparative through us, as getting its disconnections remedied in part by our behavior. . . . Thus do philosophy and reality, theory and action, work in the same circle indefinitely."[15]

As it happens, James's view of pluralism was shared in large measure by his fellow pragmatist John Dewey. Regarding the topic at hand, Dewey strongly endorsed James's opposition to a monistic intellectualism (as well as a fixed dualism), without embracing the alternative of "absolute" otherness and fragmentation. As one of his students, Raymond Boisvert, indicates, Dewey was strongly opposed to (what he calls) the "Plotinian temptation," the urge to reduce the manifold texture of the world to oneness. At the same time, he had no sympathy for rationalist "purification" (as found in Descartes and Kant), the tendency to strip the cogito from its inherence in "extended matter" and the lived body. "Dewey," Boisvert writes, "will have none of the bi-compartmentalization of human beings. His great enemy was dualism" (as well as static monism). All these inclinations prompted Dewey to endorse the perspective of pluralism—a pluralism predicated not on "isolated entities seen as raw givens of experience" but on "interpretation, conjunctions, reciprocating influences." From this pragmatic angle, Boisvert comments, a garden should be viewed not as a place populated by separate plants but as "a network of interconnections."[16] In one of his own writings titled "The Development of American Pragmatism," Dewey pays explicit tribute to James's vision of a pluralistic universe. In several of his lectures, Dewey states, James tackled "the philosophical problem of the One and the Many, that is to say of Monism and Pluralism," showing that monism is equivalent to "a rigid universe where everything is fixed and immutably united to others," a universe "which demands the sacrifice of the concrete and complex diversity of things to the simplicity and nobility of an architectural structure." Pluralism, by contrast, is revealed as leaving "room for contingency, liberty, novelty"; while "accepting unity where it finds it," pluralism does not attempt "to force the vast diversity of events and things" into a preordained and static mold.[17]

At a closer look, William Connolly in this respect follows in the footsteps of James and Dewey (rather than Lyotard and Rorty). Repeatedly his study points to the mutual embroilment and connectedness of elements in lieu of their fusion or separation. As indicated before, he describes his perspective as a "thick network pluralism" that exceeds both a shallow, empirical plurality and the idea of a compactly centered unity. At another point he invokes the Jamesian notion that "sensations, set in the protracted pulse of time in which they occur, arrive already equipped with *a set of preliminary connections.* There is no such thing as brute sense data or pure sensation." Significantly, Connolly draws out the ethical and political implications of mutual connectedness and engagement. As he writes: "Pluralism, particularly of the multidimensional, embedded variety supported here, requires a set of civic virtues—in fact, pluralist virtues—to sustain itself." This means that genuine or deep pluralism entails a "public ethos" that "solicits the active cultivation of pluralist virtues by each faith [or group] and the negotiation of a positive ethos of engagement between them." Using a slightly different vocabulary, he speaks of the "urgent need" in our time to cultivate something like a "presumptive" or "receptive generosity," or at least an agonal "respect," among people of different backgrounds. Such cultivation, he adds, proceeds in part "by mixing into faith-imbued practices of devotion secondary practices that prepare you to participate with forbearance and presumptive generosity in a larger ethos of pluralism." To be sure, the ethos or "ethic" thematized here is not an abstract morality imposed from the top down but a lived practice growing out of concrete engagements on the ground. In Connolly's words—again echoing James and Dewey—a pluralist ethos is "not derived in the way a conclusion is drawn from a set of premises"; rather, it implies a sensibility "infused into the interests, identities, and connections that help to constitute you, stretching them in this way and limiting them in that."[18]

In the field of religious studies, Panikkar's version of pluralism likewise does not sanction the mere juxtaposition of different faith traditions. In a text specifically devoted to interfaith relations, Panikkar insists on a certain relatedness among these traditions despite their evident distinctiveness or differentiation. In his words: "Any difference has meaning only within and over against an underlying connection." Like the idea of an absolute difference, an absolute change is "a contradiction in terms, for nothing would remain of what is supposed to have changed." In order to make headway in this terrain, his study emphasizes the need for a "crossing of the ways," for a cross-cultural dialogue and even a "dialogical dialogue." This dialogical dialogue, he writes, "which differs from a dialectical logic, stands on the assumption that nobody has access to the universal horizon of human experience, and that only by not postulating the rules of the encounter from a single side can humankind proceed toward a deeper understanding of itself and thus come closer to its own realization." In Panikkar's terminology, the upshot of this kind of dialogue is an embroilment or "syncretism" of traditions—a syncretism allowing for a relatedness of elements by virtue of which they "cease to be foreign bodies" and make room for "the mutual fecundation of religious traditions." As a religious thinker steeped in the traditions of both Hinduism and Abrahamic monotheism, Panikkar is also led to speculate about the conundrum of immanence and transcendence (which has troubled Western theology for a long time). Honoring the Abrahamic legacy, Christianity tends to uphold the "transcendent" character of divine mystery, whereas Hinduism as well as Buddhism on the whole favor the "immanent" quality of the divine. Drawing out the implications of his dialogical approach, Panikkar in the end embraces again a syncretistic embroilment, whereby the mystery resides precisely in "the intersection between immanence and transcendence."[19]

To some extent, Panikkar's comments on these issues are inspired by hermeneutical phenomenology and especially by the teachings of Martin Heidegger. As is well known, Heidegger from the start distanced himself from abstract rationalism—what James called intellectualism—by portraying human being not as a self-enclosed cogito but as a being intimately enmeshed "in-the-world." In this portrayal, human being (or *Dasein*) does not occupy an Archimedean point that would allow it to survey and master the world; rather, it is in part constituted by a world or worldliness whose complexity constantly exceeds or overreaches its cognitive grasp or control. Moreover, thoroughly pervaded by temporality, human being-in-the-world is a dynamic process whose course and future possibilities can never be fully or exhaustively charted; in Jamesian terms, *Dasein* is not imprisoned in a finished "block-universe" but is a participant in the ongoing fashioning, the creation and re-creation, of the world. Together with James, Heidegger's philosophy thus stands opposed both to a static or essentialized monism and to a fixed dualism, opting instead for a pluralism of elements whose connection exceeds the alternatives of fusion and separation. As in the case of the pragmatist thinker, a key term in Heidegger's thought is "with"—a term that, beyond identity and dichotomy, denotes the mutual embroilment among human beings as well as among humans, nature, and the divine. Although frequently sidelined or misread, Heideggerian "being-with" points not just to an external addition or supplement but to an intimate (though nonsynthetic) contiguity and concatenation. Perhaps the best source for understanding his view of basic connectedness is his text *Identity and Difference*. There, focusing on the relation between concrete elements (or "beings") and what allows these elements to be ("Being"), Heidegger emphasizes their mutual entwinement, stating: "The difference of Being and beings is, like the distinction between past and future, the tensional engagement (*Austrag*) of both."[20]

In a somewhat different idiom, Heidegger's insights have been complemented and further fleshed out by Maurice Merleau-Ponty. The preface to one of his first books, *Phenomenology of Perception*, strongly resonates with both Heideggerian and Jamesian teachings. Departing from Cartesian and Husserlian "idealism," the preface describes phenomenology as "a philosophy which puts essences back into existence," a philosophy "for which the world is always 'already there' before reflection begins, as an inalienable presence." Such a philosophical approach is "absolutely distinct from the idealist return to consciousness" found in much of modern Western philosophy; it is distinct because phenomenology posits a consciousness that is embedded in, and open to, a world that constantly overflows its cognitive grasp. Husserl's (correct) emphasis on the need to "return to the things themselves" should be seen as a call "to return to that world which precedes knowledge, of which knowledge always *speaks,* and in relation to which every scientific schematization is an abstract and derivative sign-language." In accord with Heidegger and James, *Phenomenology of Perception* later speaks of the "with" character of all beings, especially human beings, on the far side of fusion and rupture. "I am necessarily destined," we read, "never to experience the presence of another person to himself/herself. And yet: each person does exist for me as an unchallengeable style or setting of co-being, and my life has a social atmosphere just as it has a flavor of mortality" (or no-being). And here is another stunning formulation of this view: "The other-as-object is nothing but an insincere modality of others, just as absolute subjectivity is nothing but an abstract notion of myself.

I must, therefore, in the most radical reflection, apprehend around my individuality a kind of halo of universality or an atmosphere of sociality."[21]

In a posthumously published work, Merleau-Ponty elaborated on the embroilment of beings under such labels as "intertwinement," "chiasm," and "flesh of the world." Commenting on the inter-being of humans in a society, he notes that their connection brings into view an "anonymous whole [of beings] which through them unfolds" an "*Ineinander* [entwinement] which nobody sees and which is not a group-soul either, neither object nor subject, but their connective tissue." Using modified Hegelian language, his text speaks of "*Geist* as *Ineinander* of spontaneities, itself founded on the aesthesiological *Ineinander* and on the sphere of life as sphere of *Einfühlung* and intercorporeity." At another point, further exploring the theme of entwinement, Merleau-Ponty states that "perhaps self and non-self are like the obverse and the reverse," and "perhaps our own experience *is* this turning round that installs us far indeed from 'ourselves,' in the other, in the things." Continuing this line of thought, he adds, "Like the natural man, we situate ourselves in ourselves *and* in the things, in ourselves *and* in the other, at a point where, by a sort of *chiasm*, we become the others and we become the world." Still later, the meaning of "chiasm" is explained in terms of "reversibility," the discovery that "there is neither me nor the other as positive subjectivities"; what we find, rather, is that "there are two caverns, two opennesses, two stages where something will take place—and which both belong to the same world, to the stage of Being." In this context, the notion of the "flesh of the world" is also introduced and elucidated in terms of "dimensionality, contiguity, latency, and encroachment." As we read in one of Merleau-Ponty's memorable formulations: "My body is made of the same flesh as the world," and moreover, "this flesh of my body is shared by the world, the world *reflects* it, encroaches upon it and it encroaches upon the world . . . : they are in a relation of transgression and embroilment."[22]

Difference and the Good Life

On the basis of the preceding discussion, it becomes possible to draw some implications for the understanding of contemporary social and political life. Using Max Weber's device of "ideal types," it seems feasible to discern a limited number of broad configurations or constellations in the relation between the "One" and the "Many": integral or holistic monism, integral and static dualism, random dispersal or pluralization, and integral pluralism. In the first type, everything is unified in "oneness" under the aegis of a reigning metaphysics and religion, while the second type assumes an "essential" polarity (mind-matter, subject-object, self-other) seen as an internal division of "oneness." In the third type, unity is entirely abandoned in favor of a radical "manyness" and fragmentation—a dispersal remedied in the last type through attention to emerging linkages or connections. Without assuming a neat linear teleology, and taking into account all sorts of overlaps and detours, one can detect a certain parallel between this typology and Western social and political developments. While integral monism characterized broadly premodern imperial or monarchical regimes, integral dualism emerged as the trademark of Western modernity manifest in rational enlightenment and the nation-state (or "law-state"). Pluralization, in contrast, goes hand in hand with the process of democratization in late modernity, leading to the options of either dispersal or holistic recuperation. For both political and ethical reasons, I consider the last type preferable and find it intellectually most plausible. Subsequent chapters are written from the vantage of this preference.

Chapter 2 addresses the issue of the basic meaning of politics and "the political." The discussion takes its departure from Carl Schmitt's definition of "the political" as residing in the distinction between "friend and enemy"—a conception that has exerted a profound and, in my view, largely disorienting influence on contemporary political thought. As I indicate, Schmitt's definition was advanced mainly (though not solely) in support of the modern unitary nation-state and as a bulwark against tendencies toward progressive democratization and pluralization. In nearly Kantian fashion, his text predicated the political on a categorial dichotomy, a division he juxtaposed to other categorial distinctions (such as good and evil, ugly and beautiful). One of the merits of Schmitt's approach was his insistence on keeping the political separate from religious or ethical motivations—a quality that was purchased at the steep price of a rigid and essentialized dualism (between private and public, self and other, friend and enemy). Turning to Leo Strauss's comments on Schmitt, I show how Strauss basically endorses the latter's conception of the political but ultimately merges the friend-enemy polarity with that between good and evil (a move foreshadowing later notions of an "axis of evil"). After reviewing some of Schmitt's repercussions in recent French political thought, I present a radically different view of the political whereby it denotes not a rigid dualism but a shared space-time framework in which politics of different kinds can happen. Articulated mainly by the French philosopher Claude Lefort, the political emerges here as an ontological matrix (akin to Merleau-Ponty's "flesh of the world")—a place encouraging friendly, though possibly agonal, engagements in pursuit of the "good life," while relegating stark enmity to "extreme" situations.[23]

Chapter 3 takes up another dimension of Schmitt's work: his reflections on "political theology." The main emphasis here is on one of Schmitt's early writings titled *Political Theology: Four Chapters on the Concept of Sovereignty*. As the subtitle indicates, political theology for the author is anchored in "sovereignty," seen as supreme and absolute power. On the premise that modern political concepts are basically derived from (monotheistic) theology, the text presents genuine political theology as resulting from the translation of "the idea of the omnipotent God into that of the omnipotent law giver." In the terminology previously employed, this conception reflects an extreme version of integral monism. In contrast to the text on "the political," *Political Theology* gives vent to partisan and ideological rancor: late-modern liberalism and democratization are blamed for the steady decline of "political theology" and the ongoing slide into "nihilism and anarchism." To counteract this decline, Schmitt appeals to a movement wedded to old-style political theology: the movement spearheaded by such counterrevolutionary thinkers as de Maistre, Bonald, and Donoso Cortés. At this point, I briefly look at one of Schmitt's later writings, commonly known as *Political Theology II*, in which he defends his position against a radical Augustinian approach, driving a wedge between the "worldly" and "heavenly" cities. Taking the latter approach a step further, I highlight some versions of political theology sharply diverging from the premise of divine omnipotence (such as Latin American "liberation theology"). In terms of political theory, I place the accent, once again, on the work of Lefort, for whom the "theological-political" dimension is at best a recessed ontological underpinning that can never be stabilized or erected into a sovereign public power. (Raimon Panikkar's notion of a *consecratio mundi* points in a similar direction.)

Sharpening the distinction between political theologies (and resulting political theories), chapter 4 elaborates on a stark division between forms of religion or religiosity: a religion of mastery and dominion, on the one hand, and a religion of service, on the other. While the former reflects a monistic attachment to divine omnipotence, the latter stresses modes of lateral, pluralistic engagement. The chief focus of the chapter is on James's famous Gifford Lectures of 1901–1902 entitled "The Varieties of Religious Experience," together with recent comments by Charles Taylor. In his talks, James divided religious phenomena or the "religious field" into two branches: organized, institutional religion equipped with formal dogmas and rituals, and personal religiosity nurtured by inner feelings and experiences. In his comments, Taylor appreciates the stress on personal religiosity—a hallmark of the Reformation and modern individualism—while at the same time critiquing a tendency toward the "privatization" of faith, its seclusion in personal "inwardness." Taylor at this point introduces a broad typology of religious attitudes (which roughly replicates my earlier typological scheme): the sequence of "paleo-Durkheimian," "neo-Durkheimian," and "post-Durkheimian" dispositions—with the first corresponding to radical monism, the second to the modern public-private split, and the third to the process of rampant pluralization and dispersal. Suspecting James (perhaps erroneously) of favoring a neo-Durkheimian fragmentation, Taylor opts here for a more holistic, interpersonal outlook that, at least incipiently, points in the direction of a postsecular "religion of service."[24] To illustrate the meaning of this religiosity, I turn to the work of Paul Ricoeur as well as some recent restatements of the tradition of the "suffering servant." In our steadily shrinking world, I conclude, service has to be an interreligious undertaking promoting global justice, as articulated in some writings of Jonathan Sacks and Richard Falk.

Issues of a similar kind are discussed in chapter 5, though with less attention to typological distinctions. The basic question raised here is how, in our complex and multifaceted world, religion can contribute to the advancement of global justice and peace. Obviously, there are many factors obstructing this task, some of which have a nonreligious or purely "worldly" character, such as the lust for power, the striving for unlimited wealth, and the ravages caused by chauvinism, xenophobia, and genocidal mayhem. However, several obstacles can also be blamed on religion itself. I distinguish among three main factors obstructing religion's fruitful potential. One is the recruitment of religion for strictly worldly purposes, that is, its enlistment in the pursuit of power, wealth, and domination—possibly hegemonic or imperial domination. I call this the "politicization" of religion (a throwback to monistic agendas). The second factor involves an opposite move: the retreat of faith into a purely inward or "private" disposition, shunning all involvement in social affairs. This can be (and often is) called the "privatization" of religion (corresponding to the modern private-public bifurcation). The third factor is relevant especially in international politics and involves a quasi-Manichean division between good and evil, religious and nonreligious motives—in the sense that an ethical or religious disposition is narrowly confined to private life, while politics, especially international politics, is viewed as being entirely in the grip of "immoral" power politics. In the third area, special attention is given to "realist" teachings (especially those of Reinhold Niebuhr and Hans Morgenthau). By way of conclusion, I sketch a path leading beyond these obstacles, and especially beyond the pitfalls of utopian optimism and a realist-Manichean pessimism.

The path beyond these pitfalls is basically the path of ethical engagement and lateral embroilment—what I call in these pages integral pluralism. The concrete unfolding and elucidation of this engagement, in turn, are the work of dialogue and interrogation, where dialogue does not mean empty chatter but the exploration of the distinct "otherness" of interlocutors on the far side of assimilation and exclusion. The question raised in chapter 6 is whether dialogical interrogation—which is the heart of hermeneutics—can be transferred from textual readings to the domain of cross-cultural or intercultural encounters. Preoccupied with preserving the intrinsic difference of cultures, some scholars consider cross-cultural understanding impossible or futile, citing as reasons both the internal complexity and the basic incommensurability of "cultures" seen as "language games." Standing against this pessimistic outlook, other scholars—perhaps unduly optimistic—cite the need for cross-cultural interrogation on the assumption of a common, universally shared "human nature." Preferring the middle path, I first discuss the historical development and basic meaning of contemporary hermeneutics, relying chiefly on the work of Hans-Georg Gadamer. At this point, various practical applications of interpretation come into view, underscoring the close linkage between hermeneutics and "practical philosophy." Drawing on the insights of both Gadamer and some more overtly political thinkers, I next explore the relevance of hermeneutics for cross-cultural encounters, as an antidote to the "clash of civilizations." By way of conclusion, and in order to correct a purely mental or idealist construal, I turn to Merleau-Ponty, whose writings on dialogue insist on the close entwinement of understanding and concrete human embodiment and situatedness.

As should be evident from these successive chapters, the relation between religion, ethics, and politics is complex and needs to be viewed along integral pluralist lines. Clearly, religious and ethical teachings are bound to impact contemporary politics—not with the aim of solidifying a monistic power structure but with the intent of promoting human self-rule and responsible democratic agency, an agency that remains open to the demands (and plural interpretations) of ethics and religion. Differently phrased, the task of religion and ethics in our time is not to buttress but to contest or critique sovereign political power; for this reason, their locus of activity is mainly on the level of (what is called) "civil society" or the "public sphere" rather than that of government. Chapter 7 offers a concrete illustration by focusing on a prominent figure whose entire life turned around the contestation of imperial power but whose liberating élan never abandoned central teachings of ethics and religion: the Mahatma Gandhi. In many respects, Gandhi can be called an integral pluralist by virtue of his strong commitment to the democratization of India coupled with his equally strong attachment to such ethical standards as nonviolence (*ahimsa*) and "truth force" (*satyagraha*). The label "integral pluralist" can also be applied to Gandhi in light of his balanced pursuit of traditional Indian goals: happiness, mundane achievement (especially in politics), ethical rightness, and salvation. Here I rely on a recent study eloquently portraying this balanced striving: Anthony Parel's *Gandhi's Philosophy and the Quest for Harmony*.[25] Though basically endorsing Parel's emphasis on this quest (rendering Gandhi a "man for all seasons"), I conclude by highlighting a feature that should not neglected: unified harmony is bound to be accompanied by tension, disharmony, and struggle, a fact that is one of the hallmarks of integral pluralism.

The final chapter returns to the central theme of this volume: the notion of integral pluralism. As has become clear by now, the notion involves a calibrated relation between the one and the many, between holism and difference, between ordered coherence and dispersal. Other ways of characterizing the notion is to speak of the tensional linkage between reason and its precognitive underpinnings, between system and lifeworld, or else between critical rationality and innovative disclosure (of possibilities). To illustrate what is involved, I turn to two prominent Indian philosophers whose writings exemplify the issues involved: Daya Krishna and Ramchandra Gandhi (one of the Mahatma's grandsons). The former places himself squarely in the modern tradition of critical rational philosophy shaped by Descartes and Kant, while being distant from, if not dismissive of, large segments of traditional Indian spirituality. In a string of writings he celebrates the virtues of rational cognition and, partly inspired by Kant and the later Husserl, sketches the history of humankind in terms of the maturation of rational consciousness. In contrast, Ramchandra Gandhi takes his bearings initially from Alfred North Whitehead (and in part from William James), elaborating especially on Whitehead's distinction between "assemblage" and rational "system," where "assemblage" refers to the welter of precognitive experience that can never be fully captured by conceptual reason. In subsequent writings, Gandhi pursues above all the religious and political-theological implications of Whitehead's notion. In an effort to profile the relation of these two thinkers, I explore a number of formulas in the conclusion of chapter 8 but finally settle on the image of "figure and ground" as articulated by Merleau-Ponty. In this articulation, figure and ground are neither fused nor antithetical, but linked in a holistic difference.

The appendixes amplify or flesh out some of the main themes discussed in this volume. Appendix A reflects on the resurgence of a thinker frequently mentioned in this book who was a preeminent philosopher of integral difference and of both lateral and vertical pluralism: Merleau-Ponty. The focus is on a recent text by Diana Coole that presents him as supplying resources for the recovery of a differentiated political agency after the interlude of structuralism and poststructuralism. Appendix B returns to the issue of the relation between reason and experience or between critique and "disclosure." In this case, my focus is on a recent book by Nikolas Kompridis that explores this relation with particular attention to the tension between "critical theory" and Heideggerian ontology. Appendix C addresses a conundrum that has been troubling ethical thought in both the West and the East: whether it is necessary to give precedence to universal rational principles or to particular attachments and loyalties. Referring to an ongoing debate in contemporary Chinese philosophy, the appendix ponders the ethical legitimacy of filial piety and the special fondness for particular persons (called "love with distinction"). Drawing inspiration from the tensional entwinement characterizing integral pluralism, I counsel a contextual treatment of the ethical conundrum—a treatment steering a path between and beyond abstract holism and random particularism.

2. The Concept of the Political
Politics between War and Peace

Politica est ars consociandi.
—Johannes Althusius

The constants in the human problem indeed form a system, but a system of conflicts. The question is to know whether they can be overcome.
—Maurice Merleau-Ponty

A distinguished American senator and onetime presidential candidate not long ago delivered an important opinion by stating that America will not achieve peace "by being inoffensive." In the senator's view, several recent American politicians had brushed aside or forgotten about a basic international reality, namely, "the difference between America's friends and America's enemies."[1] In making this statement, the senator—knowingly or unknowingly—endorsed a crucial principle famously articulated by German legal theorist Carl Schmitt, to the effect that the core of politics—what he terms "the political"—resides in the "friend-enemy" distinction. The senator was by no means alone in lending his support to Schmitt's principle. In an even more emphatic or dramatic fashion, his endorsement had been preceded by President George W. Bush's repeated pronouncements that people everywhere had to choose between America and "terrorism," that is, between being America's friends or being its enemies. In the wake of these pronouncements, traditional warfare has been supplemented and deepened by the spread of seemingly unlimited "terror wars," by the upsurge of a Manichean and near-apocalyptic division of the world into supporters of "freedom" and devotees of an "axis of evil"—the latter styled as enemies of humankind (*hostes generis humani*).

In truth, the acceptance of Schmitt's principle antedates Bush's pronouncements by several decades, serving in large measure as the mainstay and ideological prop of the protracted Cold War between East and West. Notwithstanding its widespread effects and repercussions, however, Schmitt's principle has rarely if ever been the target of sustained questioning or contestation.[2] In fact, quite contrary to Schmitt's expectations, the maxim has become a simple truism for most students of politics. The school of international realism (so called) is strongly indebted to Schmitt's analysis (filtered through the writings of Hans Morgenthau, Henry Kissinger, and others). Most rank-and-file political scientists take it for granted that the essence of politics is the struggle for power, which is a somewhat sloppy and imprecise version of Schmitt's formula. Of late, animated by a certain anti-Enlightenment ressentiment, even left-leaning democrats and postmodern deconstructionists have come under the Schmittian spell—again, without any serious questioning or contestation of his principle. Such questioning is precisely the aim of the present pages. It seems to me that the friend-enemy distinction is far from being self-evident; in fact, I consider it untenable and highly misleading, except in extreme circumstances.

My presentation proceeds in four steps. First, I subject Schmitt's text to detailed critical scrutiny, pointing to some of its strengths and its equally glaring deficiencies. Next, I turn to Leo Strauss's well-known response to Schmitt's text—a response that, though introducing some corrections or modifications, never really departs from the basic friend-enemy polarity. In a third step, I briefly discuss Schmittian repercussions in some examples of recent French political thought. By way of conclusion, I turn to an alternative conception of "the political" articulated by French philosopher Claude Lefort, an alternative that treats the political not as a form of polarization but as an enabling space-time matrix of political life. Elaborating on this conception, I reinvigorate the Aristotelian notion of politics as the quest for the "common good," a conception in which enmity is considered not as the essence but as a "limit-case" of politics.

Schmitt's Concept of the Political

Schmitt's text was first written and published in 1932, on the eve of Hitler's fateful "seizure of power" (*Machtergreifung*) in Germany.[3]

Yet, despite the author's subsequent accommodation with the new regime, his text was not chiefly a defense of that seizure; in fact, as in his other writings of the period, his principal concern was to buttress the supremacy of the German president, who might well have thwarted the rise of a totalitarian movement. For Schmitt, however, the president was the sovereign representative of the German state (a role later transferred to the chancellor), and what mattered most to Schmitt was the unity of that state rather than the fortunes of a particular party. As George Schwab, the translator of the text, observes: the crucial issue for Schmitt at the time was "the modern European state" and its future. In dealing with this issue, Schwab notes, "he attempted on the one hand, to derive a model of this state, and on the other, to focus particular attention on the centrifugal forces within the state that were responsible for tearing it apart."[4] Commenting on his text several decades later, Schmitt himself remarked: "The decisive question . . . concerns the relation of state and politics. A doctrine which began to take shape in the sixteenth and seventeenth centuries, a doctrine inaugurated by Machiavelli, Jean Bodin, and Thomas Hobbes, endowed the state with an important monopoly: the European state became the sole subject of politics."[5]

It is important to keep these observations in mind because they help extricate Schmitt from the morass of narrowly ideological recriminations (of which there is no shortage). Although often embroiled in heated battles, Schmitt was primarily a lawyer or legal theorist, more specifically a constitutional lawyer concerned with the "constitutive" features of the modern state (seen as "the sole subject of politics"). Although repeatedly dabbling in such fields as existentialism and Christian theology, Schmitt did not present himself as a metaphysician or a trained theologian. His text *The Concept of the Political* exudes the cool sobriety of an expertly drafted legal brief. In this respect, it is not far-fetched to compare his work with that of another great legal theorist of the same period: Hans Kelsen. Although radically at loggerheads with each other, both thinkers shared the same hankering for conceptual rigor: paralleling Kelsen's "pure theory of law," Schmitt's text might be described as a "pure theory of the political," where "purity" means conceptual self-containment and large-scale independence from ancillary factors. In both cases, the argument proceeds relentlessly from initial premises to conclusions, carefully avoiding pointless detours or unnecessary obiter dicta.[6] As in Kelsen's case, the basic issue is whether such a pure theory is plausible and whether it is adequately sustained by its first principles. It is this assumption I wish to examine and contest in these pages.

Schmitt's "purist" or conceptual approach emerges clearly in the opening lines of his text: "The concept of the state presupposes the concept of the political," where "state" means "the political status of an organized people in an enclosed territorial unit." As he notices immediately, the formulation so far remains dubious and even circular, since it is not yet clear what "concept of the political" is presupposed by the state. Clarifying this point for Schmitt is all the more urgent, as recent centuries have led to a mingling of "state" and "society" in such a way that social phenomena have increasingly become "politicized" (in a loose sense). In his words: "The equation 'state = politics' becomes erroneous and deceptive at exactly the moment when state and society penetrate each other"; at that point, everything appears "at least potentially political." In Schmitt's view, this development is at odds with classical German political thought, which, under Hegel's influence, treated the state as "qualitatively distinct from society and higher than it." This qualitative distinction, however, was progressively abandoned during the nineteenth century for a number of reasons: under the impact of industrialization and democratization, society or the social domain steadily rose to prominence and finally asserted its superiority in the doctrine of associational "pluralism," according to which the state is at best "one association equal to other associations"—with the corollary that every individual "lives in numerous different social entities and associations."[7]

For Schmitt, the central question was whether—in partially sidelining the state—the social domain could also sideline and absorb politics in the sense of the political, or whether a new definition was needed that would recognize the state as a prominent though not exclusive example of the new concept. It is at this point that the well-known definition of "the political" is introduced, a formula that instantly lifts it out of the welter of social or associational relationships. "A definition of the political," Schmitt writes, "can be obtained only by discovering the specifically political categories." In contradistinction to all other social relations—be they moral, economic, or aesthetic—the political must display its own defining criteria and hence "rest on its own ultimate distinctions to which all action with a specifically political meaning can be traced." Thus, whereas the moral domain rests on the polarity between good and evil, economics on that between profit and loss, and aesthetics on the difference between beautiful and ugly, the "specific political distinction" must be found in the difference "between friend and enemy." As Schmitt immediately adds, the political is not simply another dimension that can be added to other social relations (moral, aesthetic, and economic). In fact, it is "independent" of existing relations, "not in the sense of a distinct new domain, but in that it can neither be based on any one [existing] antithesis or any combination of other antitheses, nor can it be traced to these." Rather than further pluralizing an existing social pluralism, the political introduces an entirely new aspect of qualitative intensity: "The distinction of friend and enemy denotes the utmost degree of intensity of a union or separation, of an association or disassociation."[8]

The intensity of the political contrast is often denied by well-meaning observers, and especially by devotees of such modern trends as liberalism or pacifism. Liberalism in particular, Schmitt notes, has attempted "to transform the enemy from the viewpoint of economics into a competitor and from the intellectual point into a debating adversary." From a strictly conceptual angle, however, such attempts are extraneous or beside the point; nor should the cogency of the concept be confused with private preferences or good and bad intentions. "The concern here," we read, "is neither with [empty] abstractions nor with normative ideals, but with the inherent reality and the real possibility of such a distinction." On the level of international politics, the persistence of the Westphalian system of interstate conflict was for Schmitt an incontestable fact: "It cannot be denied that nations continue to group themselves according to their friend and enemy antithesis, that the distinction still remains actual today, and this is an ever present possibility for every people existing in the political sphere." Yet, even when the accent is shifted to society and domestic politics, the intensity of the political can play its role. In that context, the political in the strict sense asserts itself "whenever antagonisms among domestic political parties succeed in weakening the all-embracive political unit, the state." If the state is basically undermined or destroyed, interstate conflict makes way for the brute eruption of civil war: "If one wants to speak of politics [or the political] in the context of the primacy of internal politics, then this conflict no longer refers to war between organized nations but to civil war. For to the enemy concept belongs the ever present possibility of combat. . . . War is armed combat between organized political entities; civil war is armed combat within an organized unit."[9]

As Schmitt makes clear, the reference to war and combat as crucial features of the friend-enemy distinction is not merely a metaphor or a figure of speech; what is involved is the reality (or actual possibility) of killing and physical destruction. In his words: "The friend, enemy, and combat concepts receive their real meaning precisely because they refer to the real possibility of physical killing. War follows from enmity; war is the existential negation of the enemy." This aspect is repeated and underscored in several poignant and eloquent passages. "The state as the decisive political entity," we read at one point, "possesses an enormous power: the possibility of waging war and thereby publicly disposing of the lives of men. The *jus belli* contains such a disposition." And a later passage confirms: "In case of need, the political entity must demand the sacrifice of life." To avoid misunderstanding and to guard against accusations of aimless warmongering, Schmitt's text soberly introduces a qualification (which does not in any way alter the basic meaning of the political): "It is by no means as though the political signifies nothing but devastating war and every political deed a military action. . . . The definition of the political suggested here neither favors war nor militarism, neither imperialism nor pacificism." In a still more (seemingly) conciliatory vein, the text continues: "War is neither the aim nor the purpose nor even the very content of politics. But"—and here comes the crucial point—"as an ever present possibility it is the leading presupposition which determines in a characteristic way human action and thinking and thereby creates a specifically political behavior."[10]

As a theologically sensitive (albeit not theologically trained) intellectual, Schmitt is, of course, aware that the equation of the political with the friend-enemy distinction runs counter to some time-honored biblical teachings extolling peace over war and love or friendliness over enmity. A particularly outstanding example is Christ's famous exhortation to his followers to "love your enemies" (Matthew 5:44, Luke 6:27). With a nimble dexterity testifying to his legal background, Schmitt at this point resorts to a piece of casuistry that older "schoolmen" might have envied and basically consists of separating religion from the political by radically privatizing religious faith. Erecting a sharp public-private divide, Schmitt locates the political distinction strictly in the public domain. In his words: "An enemy exists only when, at least potentially, one fighting collectivity of people confronts a similar collectivity. The enemy is solely the public enemy" and not "the private adversary." Turning to the biblical injunction mentioned above, Schmitt relies on a semantic distinction that can (possibly) be made in the Latin translation: that between *hostis* (public) and *inimicus* (private). "The enemy," he writes, referring to his friend-enemy formula, "is *hostis*, not *inimicus* in the broader sense." Following this construal, in Christ's exhortation, "no mention is made of the political enemy"—a conclusion supposedly confirmed by the fact that "never in the thousand-year struggle between Christians and Muslims did it occur to a Christian to surrender rather than defend Europe out of love toward the Saracens or Turks." The basic upshot of this line of argument is that Christ's injunction does not and cannot mean "that one should love and support the enemies of one's own people."[11]

Although supported by casuistry, Schmitt's comments on biblical teachings have at least one salutary effect: by privatizing faith, they guard against the temptation of conflating religion and politics (especially when the latter is construed in Schmitt's sense). As indicated earlier, one of the distinctive merits of his text is his sober "analyticity," his effort to present a "pure theory" of politics. One of the central dangers of conflating religion and politics is the impulse to "upload" religious beliefs or ethical convictions onto the friend-enemy distinction, thereby dehumanizing opponents and rendering warfare more destructive. The point of his differentiation of the political from other social domains (economic, moral, aesthetic) is precisely to prevent such a "totalization" of conflict. In his words: "The political enemy need not be morally evil or aesthetically ugly" (or adhering to different economic principles). What particularly antagonized Schmitt was the late-modern tendency to fight wars for ideological panaceas, in the name of humanity, or for the sake of "ending all wars." Taking aim at a certain liberal cosmopolitanism, the text states bluntly: "When a state fights its political enemy in the name of humanity, it is not a war for the sake of humanity, but a war wherein a particular state seeks to usurp a universal concept against a military opponent."

Deftly employed by designing politicians, the concept of humanity in this context becomes a "useful ideological instrument for imperialist expansion," while its ethical or moralizing tenor serves as a "vehicle of economic imperialism." The human costs of high-minded moralizing agendas are particularly stark: "The worst confusion arises when concepts such as justice and freedom are used to legitimize one's own political ambitions and to disqualify or demoralize [or demonize] the enemy."[12]

Needless to say, some of Schmitt's observations have a timely ring today, when wars are launched against members of an "axis of evil" and warfare is expanded into seemingly endless "terror wars." Schmitt's concept of the political is far removed from such totalizing recriminations. Reflecting on the rhetoric of some recent "liberal" regimes—where liberalism often serves as a screen for imperial ambitions—he writes that war and violence may be verbally "condemned," while "executions, sanctions, punitive expeditions, pacifications, international police, and measures 'to assure peace' remain in place." What happens under such liberal and "peace-loving" auspices is that "the adversary is no longer called an enemy but a disturber of peace [perhaps a terrorist] and thereby designated as an outlaw of humanity" (*hostis generis humani*). In Schmitt's account, the worst recriminations happen when ethical, economic, and perhaps religious motivations are indiscriminately merged in the pursuit of global supremacy. In this context, a war initially waged to "protect and expand economic power" will, with the aid of propaganda, "turn into a 'crusade' and even into the 'last war' of humanity (or humankind)." Thus, ostensibly benign or moralistic agendas can yield immense disasters, and the proclaimed abolition of war can pave the way for Armageddon. As Schmitt soberly comments: "This allegedly non-political and apparently even antipolitical ideology serves existing or newly emerging friend-enemy groupings and cannot escape the logic of 'the political.'"[13]

To be sure, an appreciation of Schmittian sobriety cannot silence critical qualms or reservations. There are several such qualms, but all of them have to do with conceptual rigidity, with the tendency to "essentialize" categories and to transform plausible differences into rigid dichotomies. One such rigidity concerns the self-other relation and, by extension, the friend-enemy distinction. Readers familiar with "postmodern" literature—especially writings by Derrida and Levinas

—extolling the value of "otherness" and the need to be "open" to others will be taken aback by Schmitt's stark antinomy. As he writes early in his text, the political enemy need not be "morally evil or aesthetically ugly," but "he is, nonetheless, the other, the stranger; and it is sufficient for his 'nature' that he is, in a specially intense way, existentially something different and alien, so that in the extreme case conflicts with him are possible." Somewhat later, in an extremely loose reference to Hegel, Schmitt adds: "The enemy is negated otherness. But this negation is mutual and this mutuality of negations has its own concrete existence, as a relation between enemies." The essentializing thrust of Schmitt's dichotomy becomes glaringly evident in a historical example he cites: Oliver Cromwell's speech to Parliament in September 1656. There, after first stipulating (in a Hobbesian vein) that "the first lesson of nature is being and preservation," Cromwell proclaimed: "Why, truly, your great enemy is the Spaniard. He is a natural enemy. He is naturally so; he is naturally so throughout—by reason of that enmity that is in him against whatsoever is of God." (Surely there is something odd about a "natural enmity" that is so entirely dependent on historical circumstances.)[14]

Another instance of Schmitt's essentializing bent surfaces in his anthropology or his conception of human nature. In this domain, by-passing subtle nuances and violating his own counsel against mixing political with theological ideas, Schmitt resolutely takes the side of those "detractors" of humanity who have always focused on the radical "fallenness" of human nature. As he writes, it is necessary to pay more attention to "anthropological presuppositions" and their implications. Thus, a theologian "ceases to be a theologian when he no longer considers man to be sinful or in need of redemption." Likewise, in the sphere of the political, the premise of "anthropological optimism" would "dissolve the possibility of enmity and, thereby, every specific political consequence." In Schmitt's view, all political thinkers with theological antennae—such as "Bossuet, Maistre, de Bonald, Donoso Cortés, and Friedrich Julius Stahl"—have understood this connection and hence emphasized the premise of "the evilness of the world and man." However, the connection has been understood even more fully by secular political thinkers who are not troubled by the vagaries of moral theology. At this point, Schmitt pays tribute to a number of political philosophers who have shaped his own thinking most decisively: "Political thinkers such as Machiavelli, Hobbes, and often Fichte presuppose with their pessimism only the reality or possibility of the distinction of friend and enemy. For Hobbes, truly a powerful and systematic political thinker, the pessimistic conception of man is the elementary presupposition of a specific system of political thought.... These political thinkers are always aware of the concrete possibility of an enemy."[15]

Final evidence of this essentialist bent is the privileging of the extreme option of war and armed conflict. Throughout his text, Schmitt frankly presents enmity and warfare as an extreme condition. As he writes: "What always matters [in politics] is the possibility of the extreme case taking place, the real war, and the decision whether this situation has or has not arrived." Although the extreme case "appears to be an exception," he adds, this "does not negate its decisive character but confirms it all the more." Somewhat later we read, that human grouping is "political" which "orients itself toward this most extreme possibility"; this grouping is "the decisive human grouping, the political entity." And somewhat later: "For as long as a people exists in the political sphere, this people must, even if only in the most extreme case ... determine by itself the distinction of friend and enemy. Therein resides the essence of its political existence." Now, it surely seems odd to define the "essence" of something by pointing to its extreme horizon or limit-case. This is like defining the essence of human life by referring to terminal illness or the nature of friendship by pointing to betrayal and the rupture of bonds. As indicated earlier, the extreme case for Schmitt—though "an exception"—does "not negate its decisive character but confirms it all the more." "One can say," he adds, "that the exceptional case has an especially decisive meaning which exposes the core of the matter. For in real combat is revealed the most extreme consequence of the political grouping of friend and enemy." But this argument is clearly circular, taking as its premise the "extreme" definition of "the political." Once this definition is accepted, little or nothing of political significance seems to be left over in nonextreme or nonexceptional situations.[16]

Leo Strauss's Comments

In the same year that Schmitt's text appeared (1932), Leo Strauss wrote a detailed critical review under the title "Notes on Carl Schmitt, *The*

Concept of the Political" (it now appears as an appendix to the English translation of Schmitt's work). In view of his wide recognition as an eminent political thinker, Strauss's comments deserve close attention. His review is subtle and raises a number of important issues; however, it does not in any way contest or depart from Schmitt's definition of "the political." Although renowned as a student of Plato and Aristotle, Strauss in this context does not allow classical teachings to impinge on Schmitt's focus on the "extreme" antinomy of friend and enemy. This convergence of views on the political may seem surprising, but what renders it at least partially intelligible is a shared overall agenda: the animus toward modern liberalism and progressivism. This issue is clearly addressed in the opening pages of Strauss's "Notes." What renders Schmitt's analysis so crucial, he observes, is the fact that "the movement in which the modern spirit has gained its greatest efficacy, liberalism, is characterized precisely by the *negation* of the political." For Strauss, liberalism has erased not the political (which would be impossible) but our "understanding of the political." Hence, the primary task or challenge of political thought—bravely shouldered in Schmitt's "polemic against liberalism"—must be a turnabout: "the first word against liberalism must be: the *positing* [or reaffirmation] of the political." As becomes clear in the ensuing pages, Strauss's animus is even stronger than that of his German colleague. In a series of deft moves, Schmitt's definition is in fact further radicalized, to the point that liberalism itself becomes part of an ideological friend-enemy polarity opposed to a radically different (non- or antiliberal) system of thought.[17]

In endorsing Schmitt's concept of the political, Strauss also subscribes (explicitly or implicitly) to the former's essentialism and "naturalism." From the outset, he writes, Schmitt "understands the question of the *essence* of the political as the question of *what is specific* to the political." Differentiating it from other social and cultural domains, Schmitt locates the "specifically political distinction" in the opposition between friend and enemy, where the latter is always understood as "the public enemy." Paraphrasing Schmitt's arguments, the "Notes" finds "the essence of political relationships" in a stark and concrete "opposition," adding that human life gains political significance "from the potential for war" seen as "the most extreme possibility," since "war has and retains a relationship to the real possibility of *physical killing.*" In Strauss's reading, the essence of the political also reflects a kind of naturalism in the sense that it captures the core of the "state of nature" (*status naturalis*) in opposition to the "civil state." This core of the natural condition was seen earlier by Hobbes, who described the natural state as a "state of war" (*status belli*). This insight was picked up and sharpened by Schmitt, who identifies the *status belli* with the essence of the political. In Strauss's words: "In Schmitt's terminology this [Hobbesian] statement means that the *status naturalis* is the genuinely *political* status. . . . It follows that the political that Schmitt brings to bear as fundamental is the 'state of nature' that underlies every culture. Schmitt restores the Hobbesian concept of the state of nature to a place of honor. . . . The political is a *status* of man; indeed, the political is *the* status as the 'natural,' the fundamental and extreme, status of man."[18]

Actually, for Strauss, the naturalism (or natural essentialism) of Schmitt is even more thorough than that of Hobbes, since the latter charted an escape route from nature through such devices as the social contract and the civil commonwealth. For Hobbes, Strauss comments, the fact that the state of nature is a state of war "is supposed to motivate the abandonment of the state of nature." In sharp contrast to this "negation of the state of nature or of the political," Schmitt affirms "the position of the political."[19] In addition to supporting this affirmation, Strauss follows Schmitt in his discussion of anthropology or basic human nature. If the political captures the core of the natural human condition, then human nature must incline toward enmity and violence. "The political," Strauss writes, "is not only possible but real, and not only real but also necessary. It is necessary because it is given in human nature." The issue, then, turns on the question of "whether man is by nature good or evil," where "evil" must be understood in the sense of violent or dangerous (prone to violence). On this issue, Strauss resolutely sides with Schmittian pessimism: "The thesis of man's dangerousness is the ultimate presupposition of the conception of the political." Dangerousness and evil, however, are not merely theoretical suppositions but are natural and essential: "The necessity of the political is as certain as man's dangerousness." At this point, Strauss begins to modify or correct Schmitt's account by infusing it with a distinctly moral or ideological flavor. He asks, why does Schmitt not merely analyze but "*affirm* the political?" And he answers that such affirmation, beyond its conceptual significance, carries "a 'normative,' *moral* meaning." Seen in this light, the assumption of human violence and dangerousness does not involve merely the "innocent" evil of animals or beasts but refers to "human evil as moral baseness." Accordingly, Strauss concludes, "the affirmation of the political [by Schmitt] is ultimately nothing other than the affirmation of the moral."[20]

From this point forward, Strauss's "Notes" betrays an increasingly moralizing bent. Departing from Schmitt's conceptual sobriety, Strauss's comments tend to burden the friend-enemy distinction with deeper moral and even theological agendas—something Schmitt carefully avoided in his text. Favoring a partially "esoteric" reading, the "Notes" finds Schmitt's text deceptively smooth and "neutral," but only to the untrained eye: "That Schmitt does not display his views in a moralizing fashion but endeavors to conceal them only makes his polemic more effective"; in reality, or in Schmitt's "actual opinion," the concept of the political can and must be "traced back to the position of the moral" (though not to liberal moralism). On closer inspection, the friend-enemy distinction in fact shelters or disguises a more basic distinction: that between right and wrong. "If one seriously asks the question of what is right," Strauss states, "the quarrel will be ignited, the life-and-death quarrel: the political—the grouping of humanity into friends and enemies—owes its legitimation to the seriousness of the question of what is right." The fact that Schmitt's text tends to muffle and even "conceal his moral judgment" only shows a lingering liberal bias; his conception of the political still leaves open the content of the polarity, the question of "*what* is being fought *for.*" But this can only be a preliminary strategy. In Strauss's words: "The affirmation of the political as such can only be Schmitt's first word against liberalism; that affirmation can only *prepare* the ground for the radical critique of liberalism." At this point, the "Notes" refers to Schmitt's comments (in another context) on Donoso Cortés, to the effect that "he despises the liberals, whereas he respects atheistic-anarchistic socialism as his mortal enemy." Strauss adds: "Each looks intently at his enemy; in order to gain a free line of fire, with a sweep of the hand they wave aside—without looking at—the neutral [liberal] who lingers in the middle, interrupting the view of the enemy."[21]

Recent French Political Thought

As previously indicated, Strauss's basically sympathetic reading of Schmitt can be explained, in large measure, by their shared disaffection with liberalism and their shared attachment to forms of (conceptual and anthropological) essentialism. That sympathy is much more difficult to explain in the case of more recent French thinkers—especially left-leaning intellectuals—who explicitly or implicitly follow Schmitt's conceptual strategy. In this case, several factors militate against an easy symbiosis. One such factor is the resolute opposition of most recent writers to all kinds of essentialism or (what is often called) metaphysical "foundationalism." The same stance puts pressure on all modes of essentializing bifurcations, such as the dichotomies between self and other, inside and outside, private and public, immanence and transcendence. On this score, Schmitt's designation of the "other" or "stranger" as the enemy runs counter to the central objective of engagement with otherness and alterity. A related factor has to do with the postmodern questioning of stable identity, especially the privileging of national, ethnic, and religious identities over proliferating forms of multiculturalism and pluralism. What renders affinities possible, despite these obstacles, is the rejection of bourgeois liberalism, particularly its naive trust in the possibility of achieving rational consensus without conflict. Rigorously pursued, this rejection can usher in a radical reversal of priorities, a replacement of harmony by dissensus, of rational order by fragmentation, thereby reinstating in a new guise the very polarities that postmodernism meant to contest.[22]

In a particularly surprising fashion, Schmittian affinities surface in the work of a thinker whose literary preoccupations often imply a distance from concrete politics: Jacques Derrida. Especially during the strongly Nietzschean phase of his development,[23] Derrida's writings betray a fondness for stark polarities with quasi-essentialist overtones, such as the polarities between reason and nonreason, continuity and rupture, calculating management and "exceptional" decision (reminiscent of Schmittian "extremism"). The parallels are particularly striking in Derrida's 1989 essay "Force of Law: The 'Mystical Foundation of Authority.'" In this essay, Derrida juxtaposes—without completely denying their relation—the domains of normal "law" (*droit*) and the "force" instituting the law that can come only from outside (but inevitably pervades) the law itself. What his text seeks to launch is a "deconstructive interrogation" that starts "by destabilizing or complicating the opposition between *nomos* and *physis,* between *thesis* and *physis* [nature] . . . between positive law and natural law." In the course of this interrogation, the force undergirding normal law is increasingly shown to be an incalculable "event," an exceptional intervention or sovereign decision (in Schmitt's sense) and hence not far removed from violence and enmity. "The very emergence of law," Derrida writes, "the founding and justifying moment that institutes law implies a performative force, which is always an interpretative force . . . in the sense of law (*droit*) that maintains a more internal, more complex relation with what one calls force, power or violence." He adds: "Its very moment of foundation or institution . . . , the operation that amounts to founding, inaugurating, justifying law (*droit*), would consist of a *coup de force,* of a performative and therefore interpretative violence that in itself is neither just nor unjust."[24]

In subsequent parts of the essay, this disruptive or interrupting force is increasingly identified with a kind of incalculable "justice," and the latter with the operation of "deconstruction" itself. For Derrida, deconstruction operates "in the interval that separates the undeconstructibility of justice from the deconstructibility of law (*droit*)." In the ensuing discussion, this separating interval increasingly acquires the character of a polarity akin to Schmittian "decisionism." "Law," Derrida states, "is the element of calculation, and it is just that there be law (*droit*); but justice is incalculable, it requires us to calculate with the incalculable." Calculating with the incalculable, however, implies the intervention of a decision that itself is not calculable and does away with the preceding indecision: "Justice is never exercised without a decision that *cuts,* that divides. . . . For if calculation is calculated, the *decision* to calculate is not of the order of the calculable and must not be." Clearly, a decision that "cuts and divides" necessarily entails a radical polarity and "dyssymmetry"; it relies, in fact, on what the essay calls an "irruptive violence" (not far removed from Schmittan enmity). At this point, Derrida—like Strauss before him—infuses conceptual polarity with metaphysical and quasi-theological overtones. Invoking an "infinite idea of justice," and borrowing a leaf from Kierkegaard, the text states that "we can recognize in [this idea] and indeed identify it as a madness, and perhaps another sort of mystique." And "deconstruction is mad about this kind of justice."[25]

Affinities with Schmitt can also be found among other recent French thinkers with more explicitly political leanings. A prominent case in point is philosopher Alain Badiou. Although more rationalist in outlook and strongly critical of postmodern deconstructionism, Badiou shares with Derrida the emphasis on interruption, disruption, and radical decision. As he argues in one of his major works, *Infinite Thought: Truth and the Return to Philosophy*, philosophical thinking should ascend beyond the flux of contingencies and reaffirm something radically noncontingent: namely, "truth" (in a quasi-Platonic, Cartesian sense) seen as a "principle of interruption" of ordinary beliefs. Emerging from the morass of bourgeois normalcy, he adds, philosophy should open itself "to the irreducible singularity of what happens" and allow itself to be "fed and nourished by the surprise of the unexpected" (what he also calls "the event").[26] Transferred to the political domain, this delight in surprise takes the form of a celebration of revolutionary (quasi-Jacobin) political activism, of the privileging of discontinuity over continuity, or, in Schmittian language, of exceptional decisions over normal routines. In the language of *Infinite Thought*, "political thinking always ruptures with the dominant state of things," a formula echoed in Badiou's *Primer on Metapolitics:* "Political truth always begins in trial and trouble . . . in rupture and disorder." As in the case of Derrida and Schmitt, the distinction between normalcy and exception has the character of a stark polarity. In fact, Badiou reserves the terms "politics" and "political" exclusively for events rupturing the status quo, while he treats normal public affairs as purely "managerial" (and hence nonpolitical).[27]

Similar arguments can be found in the work of Jacques Rancière, a thinker strongly influenced by the teachings of Badiou. In the words of Nick Hewlett: "Rancière's conception of politics relies on a notion of the 'gap' [or polarity] between the established order, on the one hand, and on the other, political interventions on the part of marginalized individuals or groups who disrupt the injustice of the status quo." Endorsing this reading, Badiou himself comments that, for Rancière, politics is not just an ordinary exercise of power but involves "a specific rupture in the logic of the *arkhé*," such that politics is rare, subjective, and exceptional.[28] Reinforcing and even further radicalizing the dichotomy of his compatriot, Rancière in effect distinguishes between routine public management, termed "police," and real or genuine politics, seen as abnormal or anomalous. As he states in "Ten Theses on Politics," politics exists only "as a deviation from the normal order of things," with the consequence that the "essence of politics" is "dissensus" rather than rational or calculable agreement. The dichotomy carries over into Rancière's theory of democracy, where he sharply distinguishes between calculable "liberal democracy" and genuine or real democracy. As we read in his text on dissensus (*La Mésentente*), "Democracy is the name of a singular interruption of this order of the distribution of bodies in a community that I have conceptualized as *police*. It is the name of that which interrupts the smooth functioning of this order through a singular process of subjectivization." This point is carried further in his more recent study titled *The Hatred of Democracy*, where democracy is presented as the opposite of any established regime or government: "Democracy means firstly *that*: an anarchic 'government' founded on nothing but the absence of any entitlement to govern."[29]

Claude Lefort and the Political

Examples of Schmittian affinities could be multiplied in recent political literature—an exercise I forgo. As it happens, recent political thought, including the perspective of postmodernism (so called), is by no means uniform and discloses important differences of accent. Actually, taken literally, "postmodernism" means or inaugurates an effort to overcome some of the dilemmas and polarities of modern, post-Cartesian thought, such as the dualisms of self and other, inside and outside, cogito and nature. Above all, the perspective seeks to move beyond the so-called philosophy of the subject, that is, the focus on the decontextualized and isolated ego deriving from Descartes. Leading philosophers have formulated this transgressive move differently: Ludwig Wittgenstein speaks of the constitutive role of "language games," while Heidegger depicts human beings explicitly as "beings-in-the-world" (as well as beings-in-language). Looked at from this angle, Schmitt's perspective—and that of his successors—is still thoroughly modernist in character, being rooted in a unilateral and subjectivized kind of agency, or what one might call a "transcendental" decisionism. As previously indicated, for Schmitt, the modern European state is the primary "subject of politics" (a role increasingly shared by substate entities or combative units). The same subject focus can be found in many contemporary writers, together with an essentialized dualism between ordinary life and external intervention. Thus, Derrida's later (Levinasian) celebration of "exteriority" implicitly returns to the division between inside and outside, self and other, immanence and transcendence.[30]

Clearly, there is an alternative way of dealing with modern predicaments, an alternative that emphasizes the "worldliness" or contextual situation of agents. Viewed from this angle, individual or collective agents are not eliminated, but they are inserted as participants in a worldly matrix, where they may (or may not) emerge as mutual enemies or opponents, but *not* by virtue of their "nature." In terms of political thought, such an approach has been pursued especially by Claude Lefort, the associate and close friend of Merleau-Ponty. Instead of focusing on "ontic" agents and their (friendly or unfriendly) dispositions, Lefort puts the accent on the "place" or space where political agency happens—a space that does not causally determine behavior but serves as a reservoir of possibilities or potentialities (including the potentiality of conflict). Consistent with this outlook, he radically reformulates Schmitt's concept of "the political," identifying it not with intensified hostility but rather with a shared arena of public action. The major locus of this reformulation is Lefort's 1986 book *Essais sur le politique,* translated into English as *Democracy and Political Theory.* As he states at the beginning, the purpose of his text is "to contribute to a revival of political philosophy" by rescuing it from the stranglehold of a narrow positivism or realism, and to do so by following "the thought of Merleau-Ponty." In the pursuit of this goal, it becomes clear that the crux of politics—the political—cannot be reduced to a description of empirical agents or even the description of intense rivalry. What is required instead, for Lefort, is a remembrance of the transempirical underpinnings of empirical actions, that is, attention to the (ontic-ontological) difference between possibility and actualization or between form and content.[31]

The difference from Schmitt's account (whose name is not mentioned) is manifest. Picking up the twin terms "the political" and "politics," Lefort locates their distinction not in the gap between exception and normalcy, nor in that between interruption and management, but in the relation of stage and play, of (ontological) space and performance. For Lefort, all social and political actions require or presuppose a stage, an inaugural matrix that "stages" them (*mise en scène*) and assigns "meaning" to them (*mise en sense*). Basically, inaugural staging opens up a "space of intelligibility" or frame of reference; seen from this angle, the political as such is not directly disclosed in politics or political activity but refers to the "double movement whereby the inaugural institution of social life appears and is obscured" (that is, in the revealing concealment of origins). The upshot of this argument is that concrete polarities, such as the conflict between enemies or adversaries, are embedded in a relational field that shapes and prefigures possible relationships. Following Merleau-Ponty, Lefort considers this ontological move as the only effective antidote to positivism. "If we fail to grasp," he writes, "this primordial reference to the inaugural institution of the social, to generative principles or an overall schema governing both temporal and spatial configurations, we lapse into a positivist fiction." In that case, "we inevitably adopt the notion of a pre-social society [the state of nature as a state of war], and posit as constitutive features what can only be grasped on the basis of an already social experience." This holds true of assumptions of social-political conflict, including the Marxist class struggle. What we tend to forget here is that *"social division* can only be defined insofar as it represents an internal division, insofar as it represents a division within a single matrix or milieu, within one 'flesh' (to use Merleau-Ponty's expression)—insofar as its terms are determined by *relations* and these relations are themselves determined by their common inscription within a shared space and testify to a shared awareness of this inscription."[32]

For Lefort, the connection between politics and the political is not static or invariant but subject to historical variations. In early historical periods, the dominant construal was that of conflation, whereby the political was directly "incorporated" or embodied in politics or a given political regime; this was the system of monarchical sovereignty, of the king's supreme representation of the public space of significance. Turning to the example of the ancien régime in France, he writes: "It is in effect within the framework of the monarchy . . . which, originally developed in a theological-political matrix, gave the prince sovereign power within the boundaries of a territory and made him both a secular agent and a representative of God, that the features of state and society were first inaugurated." In the traditional monarchical regime, "power was embodied in the power of the prince" who acted as "mediator between mortals and gods—or, once political activity became secularized, between mortals and the transcendental agencies represented by sovereign Justice and a sovereign Reason." Being anchored directly in a theological-political space-time matrix, the prince's power "pointed toward an unconditional, other-worldly pole, while at the same time he was, in his own person, the guarantor and representative of the unity of the kingdom." Testifying to the mixture of levels of reality, the traditional kingdom was "represented as a body, as a substantial unity," while the king was seen as the carrier of "two bodies": the worldly and the transcendent body. Under the auspices of this conflation, the entire "hierarchy" of members of society, together with "the distinction between ranks and orders," appeared to rest on "an unconditional basis."[33]

The situation changed radically with the revolutionary upheavals of the eighteenth and nineteenth centuries and the arrival of modern democracy. At this juncture, the old conflation or metaphysical essentialism was cast aside and the political as such was "disincorporated"; differently phrased, the ontic-ontological difference came to be seen not as an essential unity (or dichotomy) but as a "difference." In Lefort's words: "The birth of democracy signals a mutation of the symbolic order," something most clearly evident in "the new position of power." In a democracy, the political is no longer directly embodied in a prince who is the symbol of social unity; hence, the political space-time matrix is in a sense vacated and thus becomes *"an empty place,"* while power is dispersed throughout society (on the level of politics). As Lefort adds, in a striking formulation: "Of all the regimes of which we know, [democracy] is the only one to have represented [sovereign] power in such a way as to show that such power is an *empty place,* and to have thereby maintained the difference between the symbolic [or ontological] and the real." It does so by virtue of a discourse that reveals "that [ultimate] power belongs to no one; that those who wield it do not possess it; that they do not, indeed, embody it." Another mode of expressing this thought is to say that democracy is inaugurated and sustained by "the *dissolution of the* [traditional] *markers of certainty,"* that is, the dissolution of the identity of politics and the political. To be sure, efforts are constantly afoot to restore the earlier unity or conflation—efforts that are harbingers of chauvinism and totalitarianism culminating in the "fantasy of the People-as-One."[34]

As can readily be seen, Lefort's argument is highly innovative and suggestive. Nevertheless, he stops short—in my view—of developing fully the implications of his analysis. At this point, by way of conclusion, I want to point out two possible consequences of his thought in the domain of ethics and for the prospects of war and peace. Lefort's analysis is basically descriptive, confining itself to the level of a narrative phenomenology. However, it is not difficult to draw some possible ethical connotations. If it is true that, in a democracy, the political stage or matrix is an "empty place" and that, on the level of politics, no one can claim to "embody" ultimate power, it follows that all political agents are, in a sense, chastised or disempowered. Differently phrased, to function in a democracy, all political agents have to "empty" themselves of the pretension to ultimate power. However, this effort of emptying oneself, of curbing or restraining one's lust for power, is at the very heart of ethics seen as self-transcendence and self-transformation. Thus, to remain viable, the core of democracy cannot be captured on the level of positivist description alone but requires an ethical motivation or enabling spirit. This aspect was at the heart of Montesquieu's portrayal of democracy as anchored in the "love of equality," that is, a love militating against reckless self-aggrandizement and conducive to the cultivation of mutual respect and friendship. The same aspect also militates against an essentalizing anthropology, especially the denigration of human nature as evil or corrupt. If the space-time matrix is an empty place, this means that it cannot be reduced to a fixed substance but has to be seen as an arena of open possibilities, especially the possibilities for good and evil. Which of these possibilities is allowed to prevail depends precisely on proper nurturing and cultivation, that is, on ethical habituation in both the private and public domains.

Such cultivation, in turn, is of crucial significance for the prospect of war and peace. In Schmitt's portrayal of the political, the accent rests squarely on warfare and armed conflict; although acknowledged to be "extreme" and "exceptional," armed conflict captures the essence of his definition (thereby "normalizing" the exception). Lefort's treatment of the political dramatically changes the Schmittian portrayal: construed as an open arena and essentially empty space, the political emerges as a reservoir of possibilities, as an enabling potency for both warfare and peaceful relations. Again, which of these possibilities prevails depends on ethical cultivation and habituation. Seen from this angle, warfare and enmity are indeed extreme and exceptional, but without monopolizing the definition of the political. As in many traditional teachings, warfare is an option of "last resort," an option available only for defensive purposes and permissible only after all other alternatives have been exhausted.[35] Once warfare is properly relegated to the exceptional margin of political life, the central point of the political comes clearly into view again: in Aristotle's formulation, it is the promotion of the "good life" and the "flourishing" of all members of society, which today has to be extended to members of the global community. To see this, however, one does not have to rely on ancient writers; one can turn to a prominent American philosopher of recent times: John Dewey. As Dewey once remarked, in an Aristotelian as well as Gandhian spirit: "To take as far as possible every conflict which arises . . . out of the atmosphere and medium of force, of violence as a means of settlement, into that of discussion and of intelligence is to treat those who disagree—even profoundly—with us as those from whom we may learn and, in so far, as friends."[36]

3. The Secular and the Sacred
Whither Political Theology?

Rejoice greatly, O daughter of Zion.
Lo, your king comes to you,
humble and riding on a donkey.
                                        —Zechariah 9:9

"Sovereign is the one who decides on the case of exception."[1] With this sentence Carl Schmitt opens a treatise titled *Political Theology: Four Chapters on the Concept of Sovereignty*. The sentence appears forthright and crisp, but one is bound to wonder what it has to do with political theology. Schmitt's first chapter offers an overview of the historical development of the concept of sovereignty but is silent on political theology. Nor does the second chapter—dealing with the legal connotations of sovereignty—address that issue. It is not until the third chapter that the topic is finally taken up, and again with a lapidary opening statement: "All significant concepts of the modern theory of the state are secularized theological concepts." What is happening here? Clearly, the suggestion is that political sovereignty is somehow intimately, perhaps "essentially," linked with theology—or at least with a kind of theology involving faith in an omnipotent deity. The suggestion is fleshed out in the opening paragraph of the third chapter, which notes that, in their historical development, theological concepts were simply "transferred from theology to political theory" (or the theory of the state, *Staatslehre*) by "translating the idea of the omnipotent God into that of an omnipotent lawgiver." The transfer also relates to the case of exception, because "in jurisprudence, the exception is analogous to the miracle in theology."[2]

Can one leave matters there? Perhaps the relation between politics and theology is more complex than Schmitt's statements intimate. Perhaps there is the possibility of another kind of political theory and another kind of theology—a religious faith predicated not on the idea of an omnipotent God but on the image of a "humble God riding on a donkey." In the following I want to explore that possibility. The issue is all the more urgent as, in recent times, the notion of "political theology" has been taken up again by numerous intellectuals, frequently without an effort to differentiate their viewpoints from Schmitt's earlier conception.[3] From the latter's perspective, any denial of the close linkage of sovereignty and theology amounts to a denial or rejection of political theology as such. For me, this is precisely the claim that needs to be examined and contested. My presentation proceeds in three steps. First I review the Schmittian conception of political theology as it is developed both in the text mentioned above and in a sequel called *Political Theology II*. Next I turn to a very different version articulated by a theorist who, though rejecting the idea of sovereignty or political omnipotence, still clings to a mode of political theology: the notion of the theologico-political underpinning of politics formulated by Claude Lefort. By way of conclusion, I discuss a postsecular thinker who is able, in a novel way, to link the secular and the sacred beyond the poles of fusion and segregation: Spanish-Indian philosopher Raimon Panikkar. As I will show, Panikkar's notion of a *consecratio mundi* restores a kind of religious integrity to politics, while completely casting aside any form of political-theological triumphalism.

Schmitt's Political Theology

As indicated, Schmitt's text turns to the issue of political theology with some delay, after first discussing the historical development and the legal ramifications of sovereignty—a discussion that inevitably shapes and orients subsequent arguments. For Schmitt, the close linkage between theology and political rule was still acknowledged in early modernity, that is, in philosophy and political theory from Hobbes to Leibniz. He cites at this point a statement by Leibniz in his *Nova Methodus:* "We have with good reason transferred the model of our analysis from theology to public jurisprudence, because the similarity of these two disciplines is astonishing." The ensuing process of the European Enlightenment, however, increasingly obscured this similarity or analogy and finally consigned it to oblivion. From this point forward, Schmitt's text relates a story of steady decline leading away from belief in a sovereign deity. Wedded to invariant "laws of nature" and the strict rule of causality, modern science was bent on expunging all traces of mysterious happenings. In the same way, the "deistic" outlook shared by most Enlightenment philosophers reduced the deity to a distant "clock maker" no longer concerned with the actual working of his instrument. In Schmitt's words: "The idea of the modern constitutional state triumphed together with deism, a theology and metaphysics that banished the miracle from the world." Enlightened theology and metaphysics rejected "not only the transgression of the laws of nature through an exception brought about by direct divine intervention (as is found in the idea of a miracle), but also the sovereign's direct intervention in an established legal order." Hence, the rationalism of the Enlightenment "jettisoned the exception in every form," and thereby the concept of sovereignty as well as divine omnipotence.[4]

In due course, enlightened rationalism gave way to positivism and the more and more exclusive sway of natural-scientific methodology, expunging the last ethical-religious remnants of the earlier period. At this point, "the general validity of legal norms becomes identified with the lawfulness of nature which functions without exception." In the same manner, "the sovereign—who in the deistic worldview, though extra-worldly, had remained the engineer of the great machine—is radically pushed aside. The machine now runs by itself." In Schmitt's account, the bracketing of sovereign decision and intervention surfaces even in the work of Rousseau, despite his invocation of sovereignty: "In the case of Rousseau, the will of the sovereign was identified with the 'general will'; thereby, the concept of generality received a quantitative determination, which means that the people became sovereign." With this move, "the decisionistic and personalistic quality of the traditional conception of sovereignty was lost." From here, it is not far to the later idea of the "law state" (*Rechtsstaat*) and the legalistic formulation of democracy as articulated in the work of Hans Kelsen. In Kelsen's "pure theory" of law, democracy is entirely a legal system without any remnant of extralegal decision or sovereign intervention. Kelsen's conception of the "law state," Schmitt observes, "rests on an identification of state and legal order which, in turn, rests on a metaphysics which identifies the lawfulness of nature with normative lawfulness." In particular, Kelsen's commitment to modern democracy reveals the "basically mathematical and natural-scientific character" of his thought: democracy here becomes "the expression of a political relativism and scientism that, based on human reason and critical doubt, claims to be liberated from miracles and dogmas."[5]

To be sure, Kelsen's notion of the law state and a legalistic democracy was only a halfway house on the path to a complete rejection of sovereignty, coupled with a complete erasure of any higher authority and divine intervention. In Schmitt's portrayal, nineteenth-century positivism was a crucial stepping-stone on the road toward the dissolution of political order and ultimately toward secular atheism and forms of anarchism. "In the nineteenth century," he writes, "all thought was increasingly governed by conceptions of immanence." All the basic political ideas that dominate this century are "governed by conceptions of immanence: the democratic identity of ruler and ruled; the 'organic' theory of the state with its identity of state and society; . . . and finally Kelsen's theory of the identity of state and legal order." In due course, these antisovereign or antiauthoritarian tendencies were radicalized and intensified: "Among the radical opponents of all existing order, the ideological battle was directed, with growing awareness, against belief in God altogether, a belief seen as the most extreme and fundamental expression of a belief in authority and political unity." To give some historical examples: "Under the clear influence of August Comte, [Pierre-Joseph] Proudhon took up the battle against God; and Bakunin continued this battle with Scythian fury." At this point, Schmitt's text offers a broad overview that traces in dramatic strokes the development of both politics and religion in the modern West. "The main line of development," he writes, "moves undoubtedly in this direction: for the majority of educated people, all notions of 'transcendence' disappear or fall by the wayside, being replaced by a more or less resolute immanence-pantheism or else a positivist indifference toward metaphysics as such." Among the "most radical intellectuals," a "consistent atheism" becomes dominant—a tendency clearly illustrated by German left Hegelians, with their insistence that "humanity needed to replace God." As Marx and Engels never failed to recognize, "this ideal of an unfolding self-conscious humanity of necessity leads to anarchistic freedom."[6]

In this—for Schmitt—basically unappealing trajectory, his text lifts up an inspirational countermovement willing to challenge both political and religious decay: the work of Catholic counterrevolutionary thinkers Joseph de Maistre, Louis de Bonald, and Juan Donoso Cortés. In contrast to modern liberal-democratic and anarchistic tendencies, these thinkers are credited with upholding the core of political theology: the close correlation of political sovereignty and divine omnipotence. The final chapter of *Political Theology* is explicitly devoted to the "counter-revolutionary political philosophy" (*Staatsphilosophie*) of these three Catholic thinkers. What chiefly distinguishes them from liberal and liberal-democratic theorists is their awareness that politics requires an ultimately binding decision—a decision that must come from above or from a higher authority and cannot result from popular discussion, negotiation, or compromise. As Schmitt writes derisively, some German Romantics adhered to the "peculiar conception" of an "unending conversation or dialogue"; the counterrevolutionaries would have none of that. Although frequently described as "Romantics" because they were conservative or reactionary and idealized medieval conditions, the three Catholic thinkers would have considered the idea of an "unending conversation" rather like the product of a "gruesomely comic fantasy," for what characterized their political philosophy above all was "the recognition that the times needed a decision." Accordingly, with an energy that rose to "an extreme pitch" between the revolutions of 1789 and 1848, "they thrust the notion of the decision into the center of their thought." For them, as for Cardinal Newman, there could be "no mediation between Catholicism and atheism." Hence, they all articulated "the great Either/Or," whose rigor "sounded more like dictatorship than unending conversation."[7]

Ultimately, for the Catholic thinkers, the basic issue was not just a choice between partisan ideologies but a choice between good and evil, God and Satan, life and death—polarities that do not make room for synthesis or a middle ground. Among the three thinkers, the demand for sovereign decision in both politics and religion was articulated most consistently by de Maistre. For the French Catholic, Schmitt writes, "the value of the state lies in its ability to render a binding decision, just as the value of the Church resides in deciding matters of faith with finality." Hence, for de Maistre, "infallibility" constituted the essence of a binding decision, and in this respect, "the infallibility of the spiritual order was of the same nature as state sovereignty." From this angle, every sovereign institution acts "as if it were infallible," and every government has the aura of absoluteness. What matters most in this context is sovereign decision making as such, rather than the content of actual decisions. In this respect, de Maistre—like the other counterrevolutionaries—fudged the great either-or, that is, the struggle of goodness against evil. For him, the central issue was the sheer existence of a sovereign institution, irrespective of the quality of decisions. In Schmitt's words, in the teeth of radical liberals and anarchists, "de Maistre asserts the very opposite, to wit, that governmental authority is good once it exists." The reasoning behind this attitude is that "decision is inherent in the mere existence of governmental authority," and with regard to essential issues, "it is more important *that* a decision is rendered than *what* the decision decrees."[8]

What lies behind the counterrevolutionary strategy, in Schmitt's account, is not only a certain theology (oriented toward church authority) but also a distinct conception of human nature or anthropology. In stark opposition to an idea of original human goodness—often espoused by democratic and anarchistic thinkers—the Catholic counterrevolutionaries insisted on the "reality" of human corruption, fallenness, and original sinfulness. "Every political perspective," Schmitt comments, "in one way or another takes a position on the 'nature' of human beings and presupposes that they are either 'by nature good' or 'by nature evil.'" For the rationalism of the Enlightenment era, humans were "by nature ignorant and raw, but educatable"; hence, one was able to justify the notion of "legal despotism" on pedagogical grounds. The situation changed later: "For committed atheists and anarchists, human nature is decisively good and all evil is the result of theological domination and its derivatives, including all conceptions of authority, state, and government." In their rejection of this premise, the Catholic thinkers differed in terms of radical intensity, with Schmitt noting an increasing crescendo leading from de Maistre and Bonald to Donoso Cortés. For Cortés, human nature was irremediably corrupt and sinful, exceeding even the church dogma of "original sin." Yet, Schmitt comments, for the Spaniard, at issue was not a dogma but "a religious and political decision of enormous actuality": when he spoke of the natural wickedness of humans, "he polemicized against atheistic anarchism and its axiom of human goodness." In carrying forward this polemic, his zeal knew no bounds. In his rhetorical outbursts, his "contempt for humans" was total: "Man's blind reason, his weak will, and the ridiculous élan of his carnal longings appeared to him so pitiable that all words of human language did not suffice to capture the utter depravity of this creature."[9]

Profiled against this religious radicalism, the stance of modern bourgeois liberalism appears lame and halfhearted. In the view of the Catholic counterrevolutionaries, it was precisely the nature of modern liberalism "not to bring the battle [between good and evil] to a decision" but rather "to initiate a discussion," perhaps an "unending conversation." For Cortés, the liberal bourgeoisie was in fact synonymous with "a discussing class, *una clasa discutidora*." Thereby this class stands condemned because it "evades" the required decision. "A class," Schmitt comments, "that shifts all political activity onto the plane of conversation in the press and in parliament is no match in the looming social conflict." For the Catholic counterrevolutionaries, endless discussion without decision was incomprehensible, especially when religious or metaphysical issues were involved. In their eyes, the habit of suspending decision making by denying that there was anything to be decided was a "strange pantheistic confusion." On this point, Cortés was again most radical. Liberalism with its contradictions and compromises existed for him "only in that short interval in which it was possible to answer the question 'Christ or Barabbas?' with a proposal to adjourn or appoint a commission of inquiry." As Schmitt comments: "It belongs to the decisionism of someone like Donoso Cortés to assume always the extreme case, to anticipate the Last Judgment." This outlook explains "why he was contemptuous of liberals, while he respected atheistic-anarchistic socialism as his deadly foe and endowed it with a diabolical stature." In this manner, he expressed the epitome of "political theology" in the proper sense.[10]

Some four decades elapsed between the reviewed text and its sequel, known as *Political Theology II*. The later text is in many respects surprising, but also anticlimactic. *Political Theology II* does not present a new perspective, nor does it elaborate or flesh out the conception articulated in the earlier book. In large measure, the second book seeks to vindicate or defend the idea of a politicized theology or theologized politics that forms the heart of the first one. Two main critical rejoinders are considered. One criticism is the argument of those who contest the relevance and viability of political theology in the modern secular age, which is dominated by nontheological reason and natural science. A prominent spokesman of this view is Hans Blumenberg, whose famous book *The Legitimacy of the Modern Age* challenged the central maxim of Schmitt's early work—namely, that all the significant concepts of modern political philosophy are "secularized theological concepts."[11] Somewhat disappointingly, *Political Theology II* does not respond extensively to Blumenberg's argument but confines some remarks to a postscript (*Nachwort*).[12] The main focus of the new text is on a different criticism formulated not by a secularist nor an atheistic anarchist but by a theologian—in fact, a Catholic theologian with Augustinian leanings. In 1935, theologian Erik Peterson published a treatise titled "Monotheism as a Political Problem," which dealt basically with the relation between monotheism and monarchy during the early period of Christianity. Although seemingly remote, the treatise contained a serious challenge that was perhaps more serious than the one issued by Blumenburg: namely, a *theological* challenge to the viability and even the possibility of "political theology" in Schmitt's sense.[13]

Despite this challenge, the choice of focus is surprising. For one thing, Peterson's treatise did not explicitly engage Schmitt's work (consigning a brief reference to a footnote). For another thing, some four decades had passed, and many things had happened during that time. One can only surmise that Schmitt considered the challenge more salient than others and had mulled over the issue at considerable length. What was this salience? In his treatise, Peterson confined the possibility of political theology to two cases: strict monotheism and paganism. In monotheism, the idea of an omnipotent transcendent deity could serve as a metaphor for worldly theocracy; in paganism, worldly rulers could (and often did) assume the status of sovereign deities. These options were ruled out in Christianity: the idea of divine incarnation threw a wrench into theocratic ambitions; theologically, St. Augustine's distinction between two realms—the worldly city and the heavenly city—rendered impossible the conflation of these realms in a political theology (or a politicized *civitas Dei*). In Peterson's view, this conflation, however, was at the very heart of Schmitt's early conception. To add insult to injury, Peterson's treatise juxtaposed two important figures of the early church: Bishop Eusebius of Caesarea and Bishop Augustine of Hippo. On the one hand, grateful for the end of the persecution of Christians, Bishop Eusebius had praised Emperor Constantine as a religious and divinely inspired ruler standing in the tradition of "divine monarchy." On the other hand, Bishop Augustine (with his differentiation of realms) had liberated Christian faith "from the entanglement with the Imperium Romanum" and thereby put an end to both theocratic and pagan forms of political theology. The parallel between Eusebius and Catholic monarchists and counterrevolutionaries could hardly be missed.[14]

Despite the considerable lapse of time, Schmitt was clearly stung by Peterson's argument, especially by insinuations of religious triumphalism and "caesaropapism," but not sufficiently so to modify his earlier conception. On only one point does he make a partial concession—regarding his own theological competence. "As a nontheologian," he writes, "I would not dare to enter into a dispute with theologians on questions of the trinity." Thus, at least on theological grounds, his earlier conception could not claim dogmatic certainty or infallibility. Consistent with this point, *Political Theology II* shifts the accent from theology resolutely to legal and political theory—a field in which Schmitt could claim some expertise. Countering Peterson's retreat into "pure" theology, based on a radical Augustinian dualism, Schmitt insists that politics and the political are inescapable, and so is the need for final political decisions. In his words: "The question remains 'Who decides'? (*Quis judicabit*)," both in politics in general and in distinguishing "what is worldly and what spiritual"?[15] By emphasizing this question, Schmitt scores an important point, but not necessarily one that vindicates his political theology. Although a renowned legal and political theorist, his conception of politics and the political, like his theology, obviously could not claim indisputable certainty (it was in fact contested by many of his colleagues, including Hans Kelsen). Thus, in the domain of legal and political theory, as in that of the trinity, the issue of decision making could not be resolved through appeal to a higher authority or an arbitrary fiat, but only through careful deliberation and discussion. Contrary to the claim of Cortés, one might add, discussion does not necessarily involve a shallow relativism or an unwillingness to search for truth, but rather a process in which no one can claim absolute knowledge and decisions remain revisable in the light of better insight.

Claude Lefort and the Theologico-political Question

As indicated, Peterson as theologian had challenged the very possibility of a political theology (whether on theocratic or pagan premises). By retreating into a purely spiritual realm, however, his argument remained vulnerable to Schmitt's rejoinder of a neglect or evasion of politics (an evasion not ultimately feasible). As it happens, efforts have been afoot in recent decades to develop a political theology that would bypass both the Schmittian amalgamation and the radical Augustinian segregation of realms. Prominent examples of these efforts are the "new political theology" formulated by such Catholic and Protestant thinkers as Johann Baptist Metz and Jürgen Moltmann and the Latin American "theology of liberation" associated with Gustavo Gutierrez, Juan Luis Segundo, Leonardo Boff, and others.[16] What one notices in all these initiatives is the determination not to cloak power politics with a religious halo but to infuse a genuine religious spirit—the spirit of the gospels—into established and often oppressive political regimes. To this extent, the initiatives pay a certain tribute to St. Augustine—but to an Augustine who recognized the differentiated and tensional interrelation between worldly and spiritual realms. Thus, relying strongly on the Reformed Augustinian tradition, especially the tradition of the covenant, Jürgen Moltmann criticizes Schmitt's "Eusebian" leanings, stating that the bar against "religious politics" (or the simple fusion of politics and religion) is "remembrance of the Christ crucified in the name of the Roman Leviathan. . . . Ultimately, it is always the cross of Christ which stands between the church and the political unity of religion and politics, and tears that unity apart." By the same token, the remedy against Leviathan cannot be found in the simple internalization or "privatization" of faith, since this move provides "no point of departure for resistance" to unlimited power. Hence, the "new political theology" advanced by Moltmann (and Metz) presupposes "the public testimony of faith, and freedom for the political discipleship of Christ." Whereas the aim of Schmitt's political theology was "to fit religion into the confines of [power] politics," the intent of the new approach is "to strip the magic from political and civil religion, and to subject to criticism the state ideologies which are supposed to create unity at the cost of liberty."[17]

The initiatives formulated above have been advanced by professional theologians, which accounts for the subtlety of their theological arguments. Yet, seeing that Schmitt was primarily a political and legal thinker (rather than a theologian), it may be appropriate in this context to seek an alternative vision from a distinguished political philosopher: Claude Lefort. In my view, Lefort deserves attention here because of his unique combination of qualities: his sensitivity for religious or theological issues coupled with his firm grounding in modern political thought and especially the theory of democracy. His studies on Machiavelli and the "political forms of modern society" have been acclaimed as benchmarks of sound scholarship and good judgment.[18] For present purposes, I limit my discussion to his book *Democracy and Political Theory*, and mainly to the chapter "The Permanence of the Theological-Political?" In his text, Lefort treats modern democracy not as a slight variation of earlier forms of government but as a genuinely innovative type of regime in which the ultimate ground of unity is dispersed, "disembodied," and held in abeyance. In contrast to earlier political forms, sovereignty or the ultimate decision-making authority is no longer anchored in a king or prince or aristocratic body but is "vacated" in such a manner that the locus of ultimate power is an "empty place" that can be intimated only distantly but remains the target of political struggle and contestation. In earlier regimes, he writes, "power was embodied in the prince, and it thus gave society a [unified] body." This background reveals "the unprecedented feature of democracy," where ultimate power becomes "an empty place," something that cannot be "occupied" or represented with finality. What remains visible or tangible in democracy are only "the mechanisms of the exercise of power," only "the men, the mere mortals who hold political authority" in a contestable manner. This change does not mean that there is absolutely no social unity, no shared frame of reference or intelligibility. Turning to the *"form* of society," the "essence of what once was termed the 'city,'" Lefort adds: "The core of the political is thus revealed, not in what we call [overt] political activity, but in the double movement whereby the mode of institution of society appears and is obscured."[19]

As a French thinker, Lefort finds the distinctive character of democracy most compelling in a comparison with the ancien régime. "It is within the framework of the old monarchy," he writes, "or that particular type of monarchy which, arising originally in a theologico-political matrix, gave the prince sovereign power in a territory and made him both a secular agent and a representative of God—that the categories of state and society were first outlined and that the separation of state and society first occurred." In portraying in detail the features of the ancien régime, Lefort does not rely on de Maistre (or other counterrevolutionary writers) but on historian Jules Michelet, author of *History of France* and *Historical View of the French Revolution*. In his erudite historical studies, he notes, Michelet uncovered the theologico-political matrix of the old monarchy: the unity of France was "based upon the idea of a religious and political incarnation" whereby a "God made flesh" was invoked to unite church and state. The same studies helped Michelet discover "something that de Tocqueville failed to see"— namely, "the mystery of the monarchical incarnation," the fact that "beyond the conscious representation of a divine-right king whose power restores something of the presence of Christ" there lies an "unconscious representation of a society embodied in a king, a society whose political institutions are not simply ordered in accordance with a 'carnal principle,' but whose members are so captivated by the image of a body that they project onto it their own union or unity." In this manner, Michelet anticipated the idea of "the king's two bodies" formulated later by Ernst Kantorowicz: "one being the natural king, a mortal man subject to time and common laws, . . . and the other being the supernatural king, immortal, infallible and omnipotent within the time and space of the kingdom."[20]

Although appreciating Michelet's historical and theoretical insights, Lefort is not willing to follow the historian in every respect. Where he does find the latter inspiring is in his emphasis on the role of the theological-political ground and its possible operation even under changed circumstances. Together with many other thinkers of the nineteenth century, Lefort notes, Michelet was trying to find an antidote to social fragmentation after the French Revolution; there was a general tendency to look to "the religious" as a means "to reconstitute a pole of unity" that could prevent "the break-up of the social ensuing from the defeat of the Ancien Regime." Where Lefort parts company with these thinkers is in their habit of deriving human monarchy from divine monarchy and political institutions directly from religious institutions—a derivation he finds overly simplified and in need of more nuanced elaboration. This caveat, however, leaves untouched the status of the theologico-political matrix as such. Rather than deriving the political from the religious or subordinating the former to the latter, he writes, it might be more appropriate to assume that "a theologico-political *formation* is, logically and historically, a primary datum." In that case, one might want to examine "certain schemata of organization and representation" that survive over time "thanks to the displacement onto new entities of the image of the body and of its double nature, of the idea of the 'One,' and of a mediation between the visible and the invisible, between the eternal and the temporal." Proceeding in this manner, one would be in a better position to ask "whether democracy is the theater of a new mode of transference, or whether the only thing that survives in it is the phantom of the theologico-political."[21]

As a democratic theorist, or a theorist of modern democracy, Lefort is deeply concerned about a phantom-like survival, and especially about the usurpation of the religious matrix by spurious surrogates such as "the nation," "the party," or "the people." These surrogates, in his view, disregard democracy's evacuation of sovereignty into an "empty place" and its dissolution of the traditional "markers of certainty." In his words: "When society can no longer be represented as a body or embodied in the figure of a prince, it is true that people, state, and nation acquire a new force and become major poles through which social identity and social communality can be signified." Yet the limits of this acquisition are evident: to assert under these changed conditions "that a new religious [or quasi-religious] matrix takes hold is to forget that this identity and this community are indefinable" and cannot offer "markers of certainty." This is not the end of the story for Lefort, however, for the radical denial of the theologico-political matrix conjures up problems of a different sort. To treat this matrix as "a sign of pure illusion, as liberal thought encourages us to do, is to deny the very formation of society, to erase both the question of sovereignty and that of the meaning of the political institution—which are always bound up with the ultimate [and inescapable] question of the legitimacy of what exits." Under liberal auspices in particular, the simple erasure of the matrix can lead to dismal consequences. It can lead to "reducing ultimate power . . . to an instrumental function, and the people to a mere fiction . . . ; it finally implies regarding only individuals and coalitions of interests and opinions as real." By adopting this view, "we replace the fiction of unity-in-itself with that of diversity-in-itself"; we also "deny ourselves the means" of understanding many important aspects of modern democracy.[22]

What Lefort's reflections lead to is a tensional position where the theologico-political cannot be positively instantiated or where it can only be simultaneously affirmed and denied (in the tradition of apophatic theology). In our age of democracy, he states, it would be "quite illegitimate to leap to the conclusion that religion as such must disappear or, to be more accurate, that it must be confined to the realm of private opinion." How, in fact, could one argue this "without losing all sense of its symbolic dimension, of the dimension constituting the relations of human beings with the world?" Seen from this angle, the relation of philosophy—including political philosophy—to religion is bound to be "ambivalent." As long as it is not reduced to a crude positivism, Lefort observes in a remarkable passage,

> what philosophic thought strives to preserve is the experience of a *difference* which goes beyond differences of opinion; the experience of a difference which is not at the disposal of human beings, whose advent does not take place *within* human history and which cannot be abolished therein; the experience of a difference which relates human beings to their humanity and which means that their humanity cannot be self-contained, that it cannot set its own limits and that it cannot absorb its origins and ends into those limits. Every religion *states* in its own way that human society can only open onto itself by being held in an opening it did not create. Philosophy says the same thing, but religion said it first, albeit in terms which philosophy cannot accept.

As he adds in a statement full of Heideggerian and Merleau-Pontyan resonance: "Once we recognize that humanity opens onto itself by being held in an opening it does not create, we have to accept that a change in religion is not simply a sign that the divine is a human invention, but a sign of the deciphering of the divine or, beneath the appearance of the divine, of the excess of *being* over *appearance*."[23]

Raimon Panikkar on Sacred Secularity

Lefort's observations on the theologico-political and its permanence are written from the angle of philosophy and, more particularly, that of democratic political theory. His comments are an important supplement or corrective to a purely theological approach that would try to escape from politics by absconding into a realm of pure (privatized) faith. The notion of a tensional or differential relation between politics and religion is eloquently expressed in Lefort's text but is not solely confined to it. Here, I want to bring attention to the work of the Spanish-Indian thinker Raimon Panikkar, who recently turned ninety and whose writings point in a similar direction to Lefort's. The difference between the two authors, to be sure, is not negligible. Lefort's argument proceeds mainly on the level of philosophy and political theory —but a theory that is not closed to religious belief. Panikkar's work is more strongly imbued with religious faith—but a faith accompanied and corroborated by philosophical learning and political insight. While Lefort's frame of reference is basically Western philosophy and the Western Christian tradition, Panikkar is widely renowned for his cross-cultural leanings and his involvement in interreligious dialogue or conversation.

Even a cursory acquaintance with Panikkar's writings leaves the reader stunned: his work is sprawling and multifaceted, ranging from hermeneutics and philosophy of religion to Indology, anthropology, and even political theory. In the present context I limit myself to the topic of political theology and, more particularly, to the theme of the relation between the "sacred" and the "secular"—a theme to which Panikkar has made a crucial (though not fully recognized) contribution. In his writings on the topic, Panikkar does not amalgamate the two terms; nor does he counterpose sacredness and secularity to each other in polar fashion. Rather, he elucidates their mutual embroilment and differentiated correlation. Seen from this angle, modern secularism or secularization appears not so much as the denial or antithesis of religious faith but rather as a new window for glimpsing the divine "through a glass darkly." Just as Lefort views democracy as a new access route to the theologico-political, Panikkar perceives modern secularity as a gateway to the recessed quality of the sacred—a quality that can never be directly instantiated or appropriated for extrinsic purposes. The contours of this perspective emerge clearly in several of his publications, dating from both his early years and later periods.

In the field of political theology, Panikkar's 1973 book *Worship and Secular Man* is particularly noteworthy because of its poignant and crisp formulations. At the beginning of this text, he briskly states his approach: "To put forward my thesis straightaway: only worship can prevent secularization from becoming inhuman, and only secularization can save worship from being meaningless."[24] With this statement, Panikkar boldly aligns himself with one of the crucial philosophical and theological developments of the twentieth century: the removal of the sacred from a transtemporal or extraworldly sphere—endowed with absolute power or sovereignty—and the recognition of mundane temporality as a possible site of worship. Differently phrased, Panikkar puts himself at odds both with a purely otherworldly and perennial conception of the divine and with a secular worldliness oblivious to or destructive of religious faith. In the encounter of worship and the world, he notes, a mutual "total risk" emerges: namely, worship may wish to "eliminate or anathematize secularization, as being the main evil confronting man," while secularism may try to "get rid of worship as being a remnant of an age dead and gone." To make headway in this confrontation, Panikkar first of all elucidates some of the key terms employed. As he states, on the one hand, "worship" in this context means a "human action symbolizing a belief" or, more precisely, a "symbolic act arising from a particular belief" (where "symbolic" carries a transcendental or ontological significance). "Secularism," on the other hand, can be traced to the Latin *saeculum*, denoting a particular world age (in the sense of *aion* or *kairos*). To this extent, the term "secular" designates the "temporal world" or the "temporal aspect of reality," and its status varies with the evaluative assessment of temporality.[25]

If time and temporality are viewed negatively (as in much of traditional philosophy), then *saeculum* means the "merely" secular and transient world as distinct from the sacred and eternal world; in that case, secularization is seen as a process "invading the realm of the sacred, the mystical, the religious." By contrast, if temporality is positively valued, then *saeculum* may stand as a symbol for "regaining or conquering the realm of the real, monopolized previously by the sacred and the religious"; accordingly, secularization tends to denote "the liberation of mankind from the grip of obscurantism," with "secular man" emerging as "the full human being" shouldering, without higher help, responsibility in and for the world. This opposition appears clear-cut and has played itself out in numerous variations in modern history (as part of culture wars). However, things are not that simple and cannot be grasped in a straightforward, antinomial account. As Panikkar writes, with characteristic verve: "Now, what is emerging in our days, and what may be a 'hapax phenomenon,' a unique occurrence in the history of mankind, is—paradoxically—not secularism, but the sacred quality of secularism. In other words, what seems to be unique in the human constellation of the present *kairos* is the disruption of the equation sacred-nontemporal with the positive value so far attached to it. The temporal is seen today as positive and, in a way, sacred."[26]

The revaluation of temporality, in Panikkar's view, is linked with a reinterpretation of human existence: a shift from the traditional conception of the "animal with reason" (*animal rationale*) to that of a symbolic or symbolizing being (*homo symbolicus*) designating a distinctive mode of being-in-the-world open to, or standing out into, the meaning of reality (or Being). In a phrase deliberately patterned on Heidegger's key notion of ontological difference, Panikkar speaks of a "symbolic difference," indicating the differential entwinement between symbol and reality—an entwinement that allows him to say that reality "discloses itself only as a symbol," with the result that "what reality *is*, is its symbol." With regard to human experience, symbolic difference means that human secular worldliness is genuine only in an "ek-static" mode that reaches out to "the other pole, the other shore." This aspect inevitably puts pressure on secularization, revealing it as a "constitutively ambivalent" process implying a change—for good or ill—in fundamental human and religious symbols: on the one hand, it can erode or destroy traditional forms of worship; on the other, it can purify and renew them. The fruitful or promising dimension of secularization emerges only against the background of an "integral anthropology" that sees human personhood as ultimately symbolical or liturgical. The basic aim of his book, Panikkar observes, is to affirm "the liturgical nature of man, thus considering worship to be an essential human dimension, while, at the same time, recognizing secularization to be a major phenomenon of our age, a phenomenon which, from now on, is assuredly destined to assist the growth of man's consciousness. Today, anyone who is not exposed to secularization cannot hope to realize his humanity to the full, at least not in terms of the twentieth [or twenty-first] century. On the other hand, man without worship cannot even subsist."[27]

In addition to stressing the symbolic quality of experience, *Worship and Secular Man* offers broader reflections on secularization silhouetted against the history of Western metaphysics. According to Panikkar, this history can be conveniently grouped and expounded under three headings—"heteronomy, autonomy, and ontonomy"—where "heteronomy" designates a worldview relying on a hierarchical structure of reality regulating behavior from above, "autonomy" insists on radical human self-reliance and self-determination, and "ontonomy" refers to a perspective shunning both internal and external constitution and accentuating instead a web of (ontological) relationships. Ontonomy, he writes, means "the realization of the *nomos* of being" at that profound level "where unity does not impinge upon diversity"; it rests on the "*specular* character of reality," where each part "mirrors the whole" in a refracted way. Sharply deviating from recent celebrations of heteronomous "exteriority," Panikkar criticizes an approach that denudes or desacralizes the world in favor of religious (often clerical) authority and authoritarianism (sometimes culminating in theocracy or caesaropapism). In Western history, the Renaissance and Reformation ushered in the age of "profane autonomy," which privileges the state over the church, science over philosophy, and the profane over the sacred. As Panikkar astutely perceives, autonomy is, in the last analysis, always "a reaction against heteronomy," that is, a rebellion "against the abuses of the heteronomic structure." In the Enlightenment and its aftermath, there is still a limited place for God, but "for a God who respects the rules of the game, for a God, as it were, whose nature and whose attributes I discover and in a sense I postulate." Above all, the divine here is radically privatized and reduced to a target of subjective choice or preference.[28]

In Panikkar's account, what is coming into view in our late modern age—partly as a result of secularization—is the perspective of a "theandric" or "cosmotheandric" ontonomy that stresses the integral though differentiated connection among the divine, the human, and nature (or the cosmos). What this outlook opposes above all are traditional metaphysical dualisms or dichotomies: "The field of the sacred is no longer defined in opposition to that of the secular, nor is a development of worship made at the cost of work, politics or any other human activity." Human beings in this view are considered neither as sovereign agents nor as passive victims of authority but rather as participants in the ongoing disclosure or epiphany of "being," in the effort of a *consecratio mundi* pervading the deepest strands of reality. Whereas heteronomy typically views secularization as a "blasphemous" undertaking soiling the garment of hierarchical authority, and whereas autonomy greets secularization as the "grand achievement" of modernity and the "greatest victory for the liberation of man," ontonomy construes the same process in a different light: namely, as the tapping of the hidden potential or promise of the world. In doing so, Panikkar comments, ontonomy seeks to "enlighten our vision" to make us realize "that the worship that matters is the worship *of* the secular world," and he interprets this genitive all the while as a subjective genitive: "it is the worship *of* (possessed by, coming from, corresponding and fitting to) this secular world."[29]

About a decade after *Worship and Secular Man*, Panikkar returned to the topic of secularization and the meaning of secularity, focusing more specifically on the relation between religion and politics. In the new text, titled "Religion or Politics: The Western Dilemma," the earlier notion of "symbolic difference" is modified or amplified by a further difference or differential entwinement. According to Panikkar, the history of Western civilization has been dominated by two contrasting models: either religion and politics have been fused, leading to forms of theocracy or caesaropapism, or they have been separated and pitted against each other "as if religion and politics were mutually incompatible and antagonistic forces." The first model gives rise to such dangers as religious opportunism, fundamentalism, and even variants of totalitarianism; in the second model, favored by agnostics and "all types of liberalisms," separation readily leads to degeneracy in politics by reducing it to a "mere application of techniques." Adopting again a secularization perspective (focusing on our *saeculum*), Panikkar sees our age as capable of moving beyond the "Western dilemma" of monism-dualism or immanence-transcendence. As he notes, various developments in our time warrant the conclusion that "we are approaching the close of the modern Western dichotomy between religion and politics, and we are coming nearer to a nondualistic relation between the two." This rapprochement is liable to be beneficial to both sides, rescuing each from an endemic mode of pointlessness or aporia: "Religion without politics becomes uninteresting, just as politics without religion turns irrelevant."[30]

As in his earlier text, Panikkar attends to the clarification of terms. In his view—distantly echoing Aristotle—"politics" denotes the "sum total of principles, symbols, means, and actions" whereby humans endeavor to attain "the *common good* of the *polis*"; "religion" refers to the "sum total of principles, symbols, means, and actions" whereby humans expect to reach "the *summum bonum* of life." Differently phrased, politics is concerned with the "realization of a human order," while religion aims at "the realization of the ultimate order"—with the two concerns highlighting the tensional difference (though not segregation) between politics and religion. In the history of Western culture, the latter distinction has often been captured in institutional terms, for example, by opposing papacy and empire, church and state; on a different level, the opposition has been between professional clergy and laity, or between private faith and public neutrality (vis-à-vis all faiths). Panikkar's aim is to challenge these and related dichotomies. Employing vocabulary introduced earlier, he opposes the perspective of ontonomy to intrinsic fusion and extrinsic cleavage. As he states: "The relationship can also be *ontonomous;* that is to say, it can be one of constitutive interdependence regulated by the very nature of both religion and politics as being two elements of one and the same human reality." This outlook rescues both terms from a mutual isolation that undermines their meaning. All too often, he notes, it is taken for granted that religion is "only concerned with the divine, the supernatural, the eternal, the sacred," while politics is consigned to "the earthly, the natural, the profane." The task today is to move beyond these dualisms without lapsing into monistic coincidence: "God and the world are not two realities, nor are they one and the same. Moreover, to return to our subject, politics and religion are not two independent activities, nor are they one indiscriminate thing. There is no politics separate from religion. There is no religious factor that is not at the same time a political factor. . . . The divine tabernacle is to be found among men; the earthly city is a divine happening."[31]

By way of conclusion, let me turn to a more recent writing by Panikkar that touches on the same topic from a more distinctly religious or faith-based angle. First published in Italian in 1999, the text was translated in 2004 as *Christophany: The Fullness of Man*. One of the book's epigraphs reads: "*Ad lucem hoc in saeculo peregrinantibus / qui sperant se ambulatores esse in luce.*" This means: "Dedicated to those traveling toward the light in this our *saeculum*, in the hope that they may be walking in the light." Here again, the image of a link between sacredness and secularity comes to the fore, illuminated from above. In this book, Panikkar asks the question: is Christian faith founded on a doctrine, on a historical book, or on personal experience? His answer leans toward personal experience, but with a twist, whereby personal experience is precisely ek-static or more than itself. Father Francis d'Sa, who introduces the English version, writes: "For Panikkar, Jesus came to give life, not to hand down doctrines. It is this life [*hoc in saeculo*] that has to be lived and realized. Its lifeblood is the experience of the ultimate reality." Elsewhere Panikkar states: "Yes, I do have a 'me' but I am not identical with that me. My 'I' seems to be found beyond that 'me.'"[32]

One of the biblical texts Panikkar ponders is John 16:7: "Nevertheless, I tell you the truth: it is to your advantage that I go away because, unless I do, the Paraclete will not come to you. But if I go, I will send him to you." Here is a going away, a sheltering or retreat of the sacred or divine, which is at the same time the essence of giving, of life as a gift. It is an absence that allows the revealment of the plentitude of presence, a revealment that excludes any possibility of triumphalism or a theocratic imperialism (in the sense of *Pantocrator*). In Panikkar's words: "Let us not forget that it is good that he has gone, and good that we realize it was not necessary for him to remain—just as it was not necessary for an omnipotent God . . . to prevent us from abusing our freedom. It is good for the church to be in human [secular] hands, that humanity forge its own destiny, and that we become co-responsible for the world's dynamism."[33] Here it becomes clear that "Christophany" as revealing the "fullness of man" coincides with emptiness, with the self-emptying or *kenosis* mentioned by St. Paul (in his Letter to the Philippians 2:7).

Panikkar treats Christ's statement as a *mahavakya* (great saying), observing: "It seems no exaggeration to assert that this *mahavakya* represents the acme of the experience of Jesus the Christ, more or less conscious of being 'the splendor of God's glory and the imprint of God's being' (Hebrews 1:3). In fact, 'leaving' on the part of Jesus is a symbol of the trinitarian *perichoresis*, the revelation of the divine life in the whole of that reality that I have called 'theanthropocosmic' or 'cosmotheandric,' in order to join the Christian tradition which extends the expression of the divine glory to the whole cosmos."[34] Let me end with these words of Panikkar (remembering his ninetieth birthday): "Although we all know that we shall leave, a certain wisdom is required to learn that it is good that it be so. Eternity is neither a long nor a definite time. Eternal life is no continuation of living in the future; it is, rather, the infinite life lived in the experience (and also hope) of the 'tempiternity'" or fullness of time.[35]

4. Postsecular Faith
Toward a Religion of Service

> But I am among you as one who serves.
> —Luke 22:27

Somewhere in the middle of his life, John Dewey penned a short tract titled "A Common Faith" in which he distinguished between organized "religion" and religiosity or a "religious" disposition. Whereas the former denotes a formal institution wedded to official doctrines and rituals, the latter involves practical conduct, an ethically and perhaps spiritually informed manner of leading one's life.[1] Dewey does not reject religion per se but rather its tendency to sideline lived experience or to privilege orthodoxy over "orthopraxis." Despite changed circumstances, his tract on the whole has stood the test of time. Recent decades have seen the renewed upsurge of religion (in Dewey's sense), most often in the form of a reaffirmation of traditional doctrines or dogmas. Disturbingly, this kind of religion has also made a comeback in the political arena, a return that has been described as the "revenge of God." After having been exiled (at least in Western societies) from the public domain and confined to the field of private taste, religion in its various guises is suddenly back in the public limelight, with often unsettling consequences.

The return has elicited conflicting responses. For some observers—especially devotees of the modern liberal state—the upsurge of religion constitutes an assault on the basic acquisitions of modernity: principally the neutrality of the state, enlightened rationality, and the principle of religious freedom, that is, the freedom of individuals both to practice and to refrain from religion. For others—chiefly religious traditionalists—the upsurge signals a welcome renewal of the past, coupled with the defeat of modern Enlightenment and secular liberalism. In many contemporary debates, and especially in the ongoing culture wars, these two positions tend to monopolize the stage. However, there is the possibility—and this is the assumption that guides the following pages—that religion is returning in a new or (what may be called) "postsecular" form, whereby religion, having traversed modern secularism, is freed from the hierarchical dross of the past.[2] This possibility—akin to Deweyan religiosity—heralds a new meaning of religious freedom and also the prospect of what I call a religion of service.

This prospect can be assessed in numerous ways, including in terms of Max Weber's notion of "legitimacy." As is well known, Weber presents legitimacy as an "inner justification" that renders a given social and political order meaningful and acceptable in a durable sense. As a historical sociologist, he differentiates several types of justification, among which I select only two. Premodern or traditional societies, in his view, were held together by "traditional legitimacy" anchored in "the authority of the 'eternal yesterday,'" that is, the mores and religious beliefs sanctified by their age and presumably sacred origin. A dramatic change occurred with the onset of modernity (in the West), sidelining mores and religious beliefs in favor of the pure "legality" of a given regime. At this point, a public order is seen as legitimated—we might say "thinly" legitimated—by virtue of the "validity of legal statutes," a validity deriving from the assumption that rules are "rationally established by enactment, contract, or imposition."[3] Broadly speaking, this "legal" kind of justification forms the bedrock of the modern secular "law state" (*Rechtsstaat*), where older mores and beliefs retreat into the privacy of psychic tastes. The question that arises here, which Weber did not consider, is whether the bifurcation of public and private spheres is viable in the long run. This leads to the question of whether a postsecular religiosity or a new "common faith" is emerging, making room for a novel form of legitimacy.

To explore these questions, I proceed in three steps. First, I examine lectures presented by Dewey's fellow pragmatist William James on the topic of "religious experience," together with a recent discussion of these lectures by Charles Taylor. As will be seen, Taylor transposes the difference between premodern and modern forms of justification into a Durkheimian vocabulary. In the second step, I introduce a distinction between modes of religious faith that, though indebted to James, moves beyond Jamesian individualistic psychology: the distinction between a religion of authority or mastery and a religion or religiosity of service. By way of conclusion, I reflect on the implications of this distinction for contemporary domestic and global politics.

Varieties of Religious Experience

William James presented his Gifford Lectures on *The Varieties of Religious Experience* in Edinburgh in 1901–1902. At that time, psychology had just established itself as a new mode of inquiry and was attracting broad attention among both European and American intellectuals. This background is important for an understanding of the lectures. As a psychologist, albeit a very philosophical psychologist, James regarded religion basically as a mode of psychic experience—or as the name for a variety of psychic experiences—rather than a theological doctrine or official creed. As he confesses in his preface, one possible title of his lectures, which he later abandoned, was "man's religious appetites."

The opening lecture is even more explicit in this respect. Disclaiming any expertise as a theologian or "a scholar learned in the history of religions," James presents psychology as "the only branch of learning in which I am particularly versed," suggesting that the proper theme of his lectures is a "descriptive survey of religious propensities." The second lecture goes a step further by spelling out the meaning of such phrases as "religious propensities" or "religious sentiments" and identifying the latter as particular "states of mind." "As concrete states of mind, made up of a feeling *plus* a specific sort of object," we read, "religious emotions, of course, are psychic entities distinguishable from other concrete emotions"—although there is no ground to assume a uniform sense of "religious emotion."[4] With these statements and elaborations, James clearly showed himself to be a "modernist" concerned mainly with the inwardness of religious feeling rather than its broader social role, although the lectures' overall thrust was to rescue religious sentiment from neglect and to vindicate its general relevance.

The "inward" orientation is underscored and corroborated in subsequent passages of the lectures. Basically, James divides religion, or the phenomena characterizing the "religious field," into two broad branches: "On the one side . . . lies institutional, on the other personal religion"; the former branch keeps "the divinity" uppermost in view, while the latter focuses on "man." In the first branch, James lumps together a host of practices, customs, and formal settings: "worship and sacrifice, procedures for working on the dispositions of the deity, theology and ceremony and ecclesiastical organization"—all features that, in his view, define religion as "an external art, the art of winning the favor of the gods." What James's comments seem to anticipate, in an uncanny way, is Weber's notion of "traditional legitimacy" predicated on established beliefs and habitual forms of doing things, although his own concerns are far removed from questions of legitimacy. What matters to the psychologist is not the external dross but the domain of private inward feeling—a domain set free by modernity and the consequences of the Reformation. Despite the persistence of some "outward" or traditional features on a subsidiary level, the accent in modern times has dramatically shifted. "The acts to which this sort of religion prompts," we read, "are personal not ritual acts; the individual transacts the business by himself alone, and the ecclesiastical organization, with its priests and sacraments and other go-betweens, sinks to an altogether secondary place," making room for a religious feelings moving directly "from heart to heart, from soul to soul." Stressing the inward outlook—and sidelining questions of public legitimacy—James defines the core of personal religion as involving "the feelings, acts, and experiences of individual men in their solitude, so far as they apprehend themselves to stand in relation to whatever they may consider the divine."[5]

About a hundred years after James's lectures, Canadian philosopher Charles Taylor took up the leads contained in the former's arguments in an effort to pinpoint their relevance or significance in our own secular or postsecular age. Curiously, the initial impulse was another set of Gifford Lectures presented by Taylor in 1999, in the course of which he encountered anew the work of his predecessor and decided to offer some of his own reflections or afterthoughts. (A brief version of these reflections—to which I limit myself here—was published in 2002 and titled *Varieties of Religion Today: William James Revisited*.) Taylor's comments are not a pliant *explication de texte*. Although he is genuinely appreciative of James's work, the point of the revisitation is critical and reconstructive. As the first page tells us, James had "certain blind spots in his view of religion," which are "widespread in the modern world." The main blind spot troubling Taylor is the narrow accent on individual feeling and personal or private inwardness. "James," Taylor writes, "sees religion primarily as something that individuals experience." Hence he makes a sharp divide "between living religious experience, which is that of the individual, and religious life, which is derivative because it is taken over from a community or church." Particularly troubling in this context is the core definition of personal religion (cited earlier), with its accent on "the feelings, acts, and experiences of individual men in their solitude." What is completely blended out in this definition is the role of churches and religious communities. Thus, a central facet of the Jamesian approach, Taylor observes, is the role of experience or feeling set "against the formulations by which people define, justify, rationalize their feelings" (operations frequently undertaken by churches).[6]

To some readers, Taylor's critical qualms might suggest a nostalgic traditionalism, but this would be far off the mark. Although respectful of churches, Taylor is fully aware of the danger of "corporate" or "dogmatic dominion" and strongly in sympathy with the historical trend (in the West) toward individual religious freedom. His text offers a captivating overview of the main manifestations of this trend (an overview differing sharply from the story of religious decline depicted by Carl Schmitt in his *Political Theology*). As he notes, at least since the late Middle Ages, we can see in Western societies "a steadily increasing emphasis on a religion of personal commitment and devotion over forms centered on collective ritual." Evident initially in devotional movements and associations closely linked with the church, the trend reached a new stage with the Reformation, which, by insisting on salvation through faith alone (*sola fide*), had the effect of radically devaluing "ritual and external practices in favor of inward adherence to Christ as Savior." Subsequently, the same tendency was picked up by the Counter-Reformation, which spawned devotional movements of its own and proceeded to regulate the lives of believers along higher levels of inward commitment. Viewed against this background, James's "take on religion" appears to be quite "in line with our modern understanding," which stipulates that to take religion seriously means "to take it personally, more devotionally, inwardly, more committedly."[7]

In an effort to provide sociological scaffolding to the sketched historical trend, Taylor turns mainly to Émile Durkheim, especially *The Elementary Forms of Religious Life*.[8] As he notes, religion for Durkheim was basically a collective undertaking, a "life-form" in which religion furnishes society with ultimate meaning by correlating mundane arrangements and sacred significance. In its traditional meaning, religion supported something like an "enchanted world" where God was seen as present in society, specifically, "in the loci of the sacred." This view carried distinct political connotations. As Ernst Kantorowicz has shown, in earlier societies, kingdoms existed "not only in ordinary, secular time" but also "in higher times," thus endowing the king with "two bodies." Later periods brought a growing "disenchantment" (in Weber's sense). Metaphysically speaking, Taylor observes, "there was a shift from the enchanted world [of the past] to a cosmos conceived in conformity with post-Newtonian science," a cosmos regulated and held together by natural laws. To the extent it persisted, religious belief—rather than finding the sacred in the world—now construed it as a transcendent principle, relegating God to the role of a distant "designer" or architect of the world. In social and political terms, this change translated into a society of individual designers or entrepreneurs, fashioning social life contractually in accordance with general laws (or the designs of "nature's God"). In large measure, this vision inspired the modern nation-state seen as a "law state" (*Rechtsstaat*), coupling higher norms with individual rights. In more recent times, this precarious "synthesis" gave way to what Taylor calls the "new individualism" of late modernity.[9]

Simplifying his historical account somewhat, Taylor introduces a number of variations on the Durkheimian conception of "religious life." Basically, three such variations are juxtaposed in the manner of ideal types: a "paleo-Durkheimian," "neo-Durkheimian," and "post-Durkheimian" dispensation or arrangement. The first type corresponds, in essence, to the traditionalist understanding of religion as the warrant of an "enchanted" world and emblem of a divinely sanctioned authority structure. "Under the paleo-Durkheimian dispensation," we read, "my connection to the sacred entailed my belonging to a church, in principle coextensive with society"—a church representative of "higher times" or a divine order. The second or neo-Durkheimian dispensation refers to the coexistence of religion and society in the modern state, where a "neutral" or procedural framework makes room for a variety of churches, denominations, and sects. In this neo-Durkheimian mode, Taylor states, we find "an important step toward the individual and the right of choice. One joins a denomination because it seems right to one," although there is still a pervasive sense that all choices are somehow held together by a broader, divinely designed architecture. This assumption erodes or vanishes in the non- or post-Durkheimian setting inaugurated or unleashed by the "new individualism." At this point, the last traces of social "holism" and a unified church structure give way to a radical celebration of private inwardness. Differently phrased: belief of any kind is privatized and detached from social-political contexts. "In our post-Durkheimian dispensation, the 'sacred,' either religious or 'laïque,' is uncoupled from our political allegiance."[10]

Returning to the lectures of his famous predecessor, Taylor places William James (perhaps too quickly) in the context of an emerging post-Durkheimian world. Although separated from us by a century, he notes, James is "very close to the spirit of contemporary society," in that he was "already living in his own post-Durkheimian dispensation." The basic question animating Taylor's text can be stated as follows: has the new individualism really succeeded in erasing all modes of religious or spiritual holism? Differently phrased: does the accent on "personal religion"—though valuable as a crucial harbinger of religious freedom—really preclude the possibility of shared religious practices in a social and political community? Properly pursued, this question brings into view the contours of a "postsecular" (rather than post-Durkheimian) society and, with it, the prospect of a postsecular mode of public legitimacy. Without using the latter terminology, Taylor at least gestures in that direction. As a philosopher, he is supported in this postindividualist move by the so-called linguistic turn—the emphasis on shared languages inaugurated by Wittgenstein, Heidegger, and others—and by the so-called decentering of the subject promoted by poststructuralist writings. If these initiatives are well grounded, Taylor asks, would they not necessarily affect religious life as well? Differently put: although the modern intellectual trajectory has a strongly inward or "individualist component," does this necessarily mean or entail that the content of belief will be "individuating"?[11]

At another point in his text, Taylor ventures a bit further into the terrain of a postsecular religiosity. Suppose, he argues (I freely paraphrase), we do not wish to return to the constraints of a paleo-Durkheimian collectivism. Suppose we wish to have no truck with the bigotries of the "corporate" or "dogmatic dominion" of the past and prefer to celebrate (with James) the modern trend toward inwardness as a gateway to religious freedom: Does this attitude really confine us to "experiences of individual men in their solitude"? Does not an inwardly cultivated religious commitment stimulate the desire to share our lives with other people and participate in their joys and agonies? In the Hegelian terminology familiar to James, is there not ample room for transitions, linkages, and mediations? Let us imagine, Taylor writes, that a religious calling—or the demand laid upon us by God—is not so much a call to solitude as a call to service. Let us further imagine that what we are asked to do is "to live together in brotherly love, and to radiate outward such love as a community." If we accept this supposition, then the locus of religious life, or our "relation with God," has to be "through the community, and not simply in the individual."[12] But if this is so, the isolating post-Durkheimian setting gives way to a postsecular social setting in which religious belief can again be a resource of social responsibility and ethical legitimacy.

Toward a Religion of Service

Apart from discussing James's work, Taylor's text points in the direction of a new social religiosity, perhaps a common faith, although his comments remain sketchy and brief. As it happens, he has fleshed out his views a bit more on other occasions, such as his 1996 Marianist Award Lecture on the possibility of a "Catholic modernity." The central issue addressed in the lecture is whether a mode of religious commitment can be preserved in the modern and contemporary context without succumbing to the "new individualism" or being confined to a privatized inwardness. As in his *Varieties of Religion Today*, the answer for Taylor cannot be found in a simple return to the past, especially not the paleo-Durkheimian dispensation of traditional Christendom wedded to corporate or dogmatic dominion over people. Such a return would cancel the entire modern trajectory toward personal belief and religious freedom, a trajectory that (in his view) has put an end to the "continual and often bloody forcing of conscience" that was the blight of so-called Christian centuries. The question remains, however, whether personal religion is necessarily limited to the feelings of "individual men in their solitude" (according to the early James), or whether it can radiate out into social and public life in noncoercive ways, thereby regaining a "holistic" quality. Taylor clearly opts for the second alternative. A new Christian spirituality is emerging, he notes. It can be described "either as a love or compassion that is unconditional . . . or as one based on what you are most profoundly: a being in the image of God." In either case, the love is not predicated on "the worth realized in you just as an individual" or an isolated creature: "Our being in the image of God is also our standing among others in the stream of love," which demands service to others.[13]

In many ways, Taylor's turn to a religiosity of service was anticipated by French philosopher Paul Ricoeur in writings penned several decades ago. The starting point of Ricoeur's reflections was precisely the modern move toward privatization and religious inwardness—a move that he both welcomed as a gateway to religious freedom and criticized as a possible retreat or exodus of faith from the world and social concerns. As he wrote hopefully in an essay from 1958: "After several centuries during which Christians have been preoccupied with the inner life and personal salvation, we are discovering afresh what is meant by 'you are the salt of the earth' (Matthew 5:13). We are discovering that the salt is made for salting, the light for illuminating, and that the church exists for the sake of those outside itself." Like Taylor later, Ricoeur was not enamored with the paleo-Durkheimian arrangement whereby church and faith exert a dominant (quasi-sovereign) political control in society. Despite the long historical trajectory toward freedom, he noted, the old dispensation tends to assert or reassert itself in many guises. There is still a widespread illusion that religion can play "a direct political role as an independent political power"—an illusion (often coupled with hypocrisy) that manifests itself in the pretense of so-called Christian governments, Christian parties, or Christian policies. But another alternative is possible: "When it emerges from this illusion, the church will be able to give light once more to all men—no longer as a power, but as a prophetic message."

Giving light to all men also means to serve, guard, and rescue. "Christian love," Ricoeur adds, "consists in seeking out the fresh forms of poverty which occur at any period" (where poverty includes all forms of deprivation, oppression, and injustice). Today, in our globalizing age, it must "direct its attention toward the great world problems."[14]

In the meantime, the critique of religious mastery in the paleo-Durkheimian mode has spread from isolated remonstrations to broader intellectual endeavors, including theology, philosophy of religion, and (even) political philosophy. In the theological domain, the critique finds resonance in a current of thought aiming to shift the emphasis from a sovereign (possibly imperial) creator God to the legacy of the "suffering servant" extolled by deutero-Isaiah, a legacy sometimes linked with the notion of God's "co-suffering" with the world.[15] In some respects, this shift joins hands with another perspective called "liberation theology," characterized by an accent on "exodus" from unjust power structures and a "preferential" engagement for the poor.[16] Similar tendencies are present in contemporary philosophy of religion, a field strongly marked by the intellectual upheavals associated with Nietzsche and his postmodern followers. Thus, distancing himself from the notion of divine omnipotence, John Caputo speaks provocatively of the "weakness of God," where "weakness" does not denote impotence but rather the recessed quality of divine calling. "I treat God," Caputo writes, "not as an eminent omnipotent power capable of leveling tall buildings and reducing his enemies to ashes, but as the weak force of a call." This weak force of God, he adds, "is to lay *claim* upon us . . . but not the way a sovereign power . . . invades and then lays claim to a territory, overpowers its native population and plants a foreign flag, but in the way of a summons that calls and provokes, an appeal that incites or invites us, a promise that awakens our love."[17] In a similar way, Richard Kearney speaks of the "powerlessness" of divine empowerment, stating: "By choosing to be a player rather than an emperor of creation, God chooses powerlessness," a choice that "expresses itself as self-emptying, *kenosis,* letting go." God, he adds, thus "empowers our human powerlessness by giving away his power, by possibilizing us and our good actions—so that we may supplement and co-accomplish creation."[18]

Somewhat surprisingly—because of the usual association of politics with power—the critique of the religion of mastery also surfaces today in versions of political theory or philosophy. For purposes of illustration, I choose the theorist William Connolly because his writings fully resonate with this critique and also reconnect us with the work of William James. In his book titled *Pluralism,* Connolly pays tribute to James as the author not only of *The Varieties of Religious Experience* but also of *A Pluralistic Universe,* a text penned a few years after his Gifford Lectures. For Connolly, James was a pioneering thinker who, ahead of many others, was able to articulate modern (and perhaps postmodern) sensibilities not by relying on abstract categories but by turning to concretely lived experience. In pursuing this path, he was a partner of Henri Bergson and Dewey and a precursor of such later thinkers as Wittgenstein, Heidegger, and Merleau-Ponty. His turn to concrete experience prompted James to reject the notion of a fully mapped, totally transparent, and rationally intelligible cosmos. As he wrote in *A Pluralistic Universe:* "The substance of reality may never get totally collected, . . . some of it may remain outside of the largest combination of it ever made."[19] The inference Connolly draws from this statement is that "there is no omnipotent, omniscient God outside or above the world who gathers all of the universe together into one system of intelligible relations—though there may be a limited God who participates as one important actor among others in the world." The pluralistic view sponsored by James, one should note, does not entail an endorsement of radical chaos, fragmentation, or chance, which would be another abstract and totalizing maxim. Rather, fragmentary elements and sensations are already linked, though in unmappable and often surprising ways: "The Jamesian idea is that sensations, set in the protracted pulse of time in which they occur, arrive already equipped with a set of preliminary connections."[20]

In the domain of religious faith, Connolly together with James opposes the idea of a sovereign, imperial deity—a stance that leads him to critique recent attempts to restore paleo-Durkheimian arrangements in the West. Addressing some fellow theorists who are overly nostalgic for the past, he chides their hankering for a religion of mastery manifest in an "exclusionary, imperious sensibility" favoring the imposition of a uniform creed. In challenging dogmatic uniformity, Connolly does not mean to lend aid and comfort to the simple privatization of faith, to the neo-Durkheimian separation of the neutral state and the private inwardness of belief. As he observes in a striking formulation, defenders of liberal neutrality pretend to identify "a forum entirely above faith through which to regulate diverse faiths," while ignoring "faith practices themselves." Hence, he adds, "if the nobility of secularism resides in its quest to enable multiple faiths to exist on the same public space, its shallowness resides in the hubris of its distinction between private faith and public reason." By taking religious practices seriously, Connolly's book also departs from *The Varieties of Religious Experience* by transgressing the feelings of "solitary men" in the direction of shared religious engagements, a shared postsecular sensibility conducive to public legitimacy. "Deep pluralism," he writes, "reinstates the link between practice and belief that had been artificially severed by secularism; and it overturns the impossible counsel to bracket your faith when you participate in politics." In the best-case scenario, faith-imbued practices of devotion are joined with civic practices that instill "forbearance and presumptive generosity [toward others]" in social life. In this preferred situation, each faith is able to embed "the religious virtue of hospitality and the civic virtue of presumptive generosity into its relational practices."[21]

Multiple Faiths in a Shared World

Connolly's text is important here not only for its Jamesian sensibilities but also for its attention to multiple faith traditions and the desirability of fostering "generous" relations among them. His notion of a "deep" or "expansive" pluralism gains acute significance precisely in the context of our globalizing and multicultural world. "The most urgent need today," he writes, "is to mix presumptively generous sensibilities into a variety of theistic and nontheistic creeds, sensibilities attuned to the contemporary need to transfigure relations of antagonism between faiths into relations of agonistic respect." The point here is not to obliterate differences between faiths in a bland ecumenicism but to forge "a positive ethos of public engagement between alternative faiths."[22] The question often asked with regard to interfaith relations—especially relations animated by generosity—is whether mutual recognition is not purchased at too high a price: that is, the shallowness or lukewarmness of one's own faith commitment. Does navigating in the "pluriverse" of different faith traditions not necessarily erode the firmness of one's convictions and possibly lead to alienation from traditional faith practices? This question (it seems to me) is predicated on a basic antinomy between "vertical" and "horizontal" human relationships. In terms of this antinomy, only the vertical relation between humans and God is considered properly religious, while interhuman relations are devalued as secular, worldly, and possibly harmful to religious faith. The governing assumption is that of a zero-sum game, where the winnings of one side are the losses of the other side.

If interfaith relations really want to get off the ground, this assumption has to be defeated not just in theory but in practical life. A prominent exemplar of such lived practice is Jonathan Sacks, widely renowned as a religious leader, intellectual, writer, and peacemaker. Although intensely involved in interfaith relations, Sacks is not a shallow believer; he is an Orthodox Jew and, in fact, the chief rabbi of the United Hebrew Congregations of Britain and the Commonwealth. Among his numerous writings, particularly relevant in the present context is his 2002 book *The Dignity of Difference: How to Avoid the Clash of Civilizations*. The book seeks to make a contribution to interfaith harmony and, through it, to global peace. As Sacks writes in the opening pages: "One of the unexpected delights of becoming a religious leader has been the friendships I have made with leaders of other faiths, nationally and internationally," bonds that demonstrate that "the world's great faiths have a significant potential role in conflict resolution and not merely . . . in conflict creation." To advance and foster this role, something more is required than bland coexistence or even shallow tolerance among faiths: "Something stronger will be needed if different nations, faiths and cultures are to live together in a world with no global governance, in an age of [sometimes] extreme and counter-modern religiosity." As the text makes clear, the author is speaking as a believing Jew, placing himself in the Jewish faith tradition. He is able to do this and still celebrate "difference" because Judaism, in his account, has always been located at the cusp between particularism and globalism: "The book of Genesis was the first to see all humankind as bound by a universal covenant, and yet to acknowledge the legitimacy of profound religious and cultural differences." Hence, for Sacks, vertical and horizontal (or lateral) relations are not in conflict; they supplement each other: "My primary aim has been to suggest a new paradigm for our complex, interconnected world, in such a way that, the more passionately we feel our religious commitment, the more space we make for those who are not like us."²³

It is important to note that passionately held religious commitment here does not suggest a hankering for political power. Together with Taylor and Connolly, Sacks is not a devotee of paleo-Durkheimian dispositions or a religion of mastery; nor does he favor a retreat into privacy. As he writes: "Religious leaders should never seek power, but neither may they abdicate their task of being a counter-voice [or a voice resisting oppression and injustice] in the conversation of mankind." Together with Connolly, *The Dignity of Difference* celebrates a deep or expansive kind of pluralism; in several respects, however, it moves beyond the level of simple recognition or an "agonistic respect" (perhaps grudgingly granted). In a stunning formulation, Sacks articulates an idea that belongs to the core of a religion of service. A faith community, he writes, "should encourage its members to do an act of service or kindness to someone or some group of another faith or ethnicity—to extend a hand of help, in other words, *across* the boundaries of difference and thus turn communities outward instead of inward." As a Jew, Sacks invites members of other faith communities to join him in prayer, but prayer needs to be linked with action and practical engagement on behalf of the marginalized and the persecuted. In this respect, his text is again exemplary by counseling not mindless activism (in the service of possibly self-aggrandizing agendas) but rather engagement in response to a summons or call. Sacks at this point invokes the great biblical exhortation *Shema Israel*, where *shema* means "to hear, to understand and to respond, to listen in the fullest range of senses," especially to the agonies of the suffering and oppressed. "I believe," he adds, "that God is summoning us to a new act of listening" that involves, above all, a caring attentiveness to some of the side effects of globalization: "its inequities, its consumerism and exploitation, its failure to address widespread poverty and disease, its juggernaut insensitivity to local traditions and cultures, and the spiritual poverty that can go hand in hand with material wealth."²⁴

Religiously speaking, Sacks's account of what needs to happen is surely on solid ground. As we know, the central message of the biblical *Shema Israel* was the dual plea addressed to Jews: first, to love God or the divine with all their being, and second, to love their fellow beings in an equal manner (Deuteronomy 6:5; Leviticus 19:18). This dual plea was taken over almost verbatim in the Christian gospels (Matthew 22:37–40; Luke 10:27–28; Mark 12:29–31). Thus, in pleading for a religion of loving service, Sacks speaks from the heart of at least two great faith traditions. But the biblical *Shema* is by no means alien to the Islamic tradition either. First of all, Islam does not cancel but builds on the older foundations of Hebrew faith (including the passages in Deuteronomy and Leviticus). Second and more important, the Qur'an itself resonates fully with the older biblical exhortations. Thus, Sura 3 speaks of the human love for God—a love reciprocated and even anticipated by God's love for humans—and Sura 90 speaks of interhuman love that yields the demand or duty "to free a neck (from the burden of debt and slavery), or to feed in times of famine the orphan near in relationship or the poor in distress."[25] In the Hindu faith tradition, the Bhagavad Gita eloquently portrays the vertical relation between humans and the divine as a mode of mutual bonding, stating: "In whatever way humans love me, in that same way they find my love." This bonding, however, is instantly joined with another, more lateral connection that takes the form of "consecrated" action or interhuman service: "Let your aim be the good of all (*lokasamgraha*), and thus carry on your task in life." The central role of compassion and ethical-spiritual service in Buddhism is well known, a tradition that exhorts its followers to strive for the awakening and "liberation" of all sentient creatures "however innumerable they may be."[26]

Sacred scriptures and holy texts, however, are dead letters unless they are taken up by real-life people and translated into appropriate action in a concrete time and place. In our own time, the concrete context is marked by globalization, including global militarism and worldwide terror wars. Given the dominant view in politics—especially international politics—that power and security always trump ethics and religion, faith-based traditions face an uphill struggle in trying to have their voices heard. Fortunately, even today there are courageous people able and willing to "speak truth (especially religious truth) to power." Among them is Richard Falk, well known for his work on international politics.

In a recent essay on religious resurgence in the era of globalization, Falk soberly but hopefully assesses the prospect of a faith-based transformation of prevailing political practices in the world. As an expert in this field, he is fully aware of the obstacles facing this prospect. As he writes: "The religious dimension of human experience has been generally excluded from the serious study and practice of governance for several centuries, especially in the West." Experiences of the last two centuries, however—world wars, the Holocaust, and genocide—have revealed the limitations or dark downsides of modern "disenchantment," thus triggering a return to recessed and previously sidelined religious resources. As Falk makes abundantly clear, he does not place his trust in revivalist triumphalism or any paleo-Durkheimian arrangements. "In many occasions," he acknowledges, "the religious establishment of the day defends the status quo, and is itself part of the oppressive social and political order." Too often, established religious institutions find the visions of reformers unsettling and disruptive and hence "tend to marginalize their impact." Against this Durkheimian model, Falk joins James and Taylor in embracing a more inward and personal mode of religiosity practiced in everyday life: "Religion is understood here as encompassing not only the teachings, beliefs, and practices of organized religions but all spiritual outlooks that interpret the meaning of life by reference to faith"; in this sense, religion includes "belief in God and gods, but does not depend on theistic convictions, or for that matter, theological dogma of any kind."[27]

As in the case of Taylor and Ricoeur, cultivation of personal religiosity for Falk does not signal retreat into solitude but means to radiate out into the world. In an eloquent formulation that captures the gist of what I call a religion of service, Falk writes: "A belief in the transformative capacities of an idea that is sustained by spiritual energy lends itself to nonviolent forms of struggle and sacrifice, thereby challenging most secular views of human history as shaped primarily by governing elites, warfare, and a command over innovative military technology." Despite certain differences of emphasis, Falk's outlook in this respect resonates fully with Sacks's construal of religion as a response to a divine *Shema* or exhortation: the call to justice. "The religious framing of reality," Falk notes, "is rooted in the present, but is also hopeful about deliverance from suffering and privation. Indeed, the central founding narratives of the world's great religions are preoccupied with liberation from oppressive social and political arrangements, promising that by adhering to faith, emancipation will be attained." The greatest present-day stumbling block for transformation, he adds, resides in a renewed imperialist agenda, the attempt to erect a uniform super-Leviathan governing the world. "Only the great world religions," he concludes (and I fully concur), "have the credibility and legitimacy to identify and reject the idolatry that seems to lie at the core of this project of planetary domination."[28] Eloquently formulated, we find here the prospect of a postsecular global legitimacy.

5. Religion and the World
The Quest for Justice and Peace

> I want you to set your eyes and your hearts on these
> people who are suffering so much—some from poverty
> and hunger, others from oppression and repression. . . .
> Ask yourselves: what have I done to crucify them? What
> do I do to uncrucify them?
>
> —Ignazio Ellacuría

According to a biblical passage (cited earlier), religious faith is meant to be "the salt of the earth" (Matthew 5:13). This suggests that religion is meant to be neither separated or divorced from the world nor collapsed into it, but to serve as a ferment or challenge in the midst of human affairs. The same idea is captured in the well-known phrase that religious or spiritual people are *in* but not *of* this world. By *religion* here I do not mean a set of doctrines or dogmas but rather a kind of bonding, relatedness, or attentiveness: a relatedness to a realm of goodness that lies beyond human appropriation, manipulation, or control. Given its peculiar in-between status—its location at the interstices of immanence and transcendence—religious faith appears ideally suited to contribute to the promotion of peace and justice in the world. A similar contribution, to be sure, can also be made by ethical-philosophical teachings referring to the "golden rule" and the need for interhuman or intersocietal justice and fairness. However, while ethical-philosophical teachings often appeal mainly to the mind or intellect, religious or spiritual legacies have the unique capacity to enlist the human heart, that is, the precognitive layers of human motivations and dispositions. For this reason, well-meaning secularists are ill advised (in my view) to dismiss the resources of religious faith and ignore their relevance to human and social well-being.

To be sure, this contribution of faith is mostly potential and rarely actual. There are numerous factors that impede the fruition of its role, and many of these factors are strictly "worldly" and thus extrareligious. Among such factors are the lust for untrammeled political power, the striving for unlimited wealth, and the ravages caused by chauvinism, xenophobia, and genocidal mayhem. More than ever before, our world today seems to be brimming over with these ills and destructive urges. Yet, at least in some of its guises, religion cannot be entirely absolved of complicity. More often than one would wish, religious faith stokes the flames of enmity and destruction while failing to hold up the torch of justice and peace. In the following, I explore some of the intrareligious factors obstructing religion's fruitful potential. As I will show, three main factors have acted as barriers in the past and continue to do so in the present. The first is the recruitment of religion for strictly "worldly" purposes, that is, its enlistment in the pursuit of power, wealth, and social domination. I call this the "politicization" of religion. The second feature reflects an opposite move: the retreat of faith into a purely inward or "private" disposition, shunning all involvement in social and intersocietal affairs. This can be called the "privatization" of religion. The third aspect—relevant especially in international politics—results from a certain Manichean or quasi-Manichean construal of human nature and the in-between status of religious faith. In this version, human nature is seen as basically corrupt and—except in a narrowly private domain—as entirely incapable of struggling effectively against the injustices in the world. Let us call this the "Manichean" derailment. By way of conclusion, I return to the issue of justice and peace and indicate a more hopeful path, avoiding the pitfalls of both utopian optimism and Manichean pessimism.

Politicized Religion

One of the oldest and most persistent temptations of religious faith is the desire to wield political power. In large measure, this desire or ambition is fueled by the image of divine sovereignty or God's rule over the world—an image that presumably grants religious leaders a share in this power. And since God's rule is assumed to be comprehensive and all-pervasive, religious leaders in the past have often claimed extensive and nearly totalitarian authority over society. As history teaches, this claim to power comes at a steep price, both for religion and for society. For people in society, the price is tutelage and, in Kant's memorable phrase, a condition of sustained "immaturity." But the religious cost is equally high, and here the parallel with divine rule is instructive. If seen as omnipotent or all-powerful, God is necessarily the source of not only all good things or blessings but also all the ills and miseries of this world; since, in light of God's omnipotence, these ills and miseries are preventable, their nonprevention amounts to gross negligence or else culpability. The same charge of negligence or culpability carries over to religious institutions and their leaders, seen as stand-ins for or vice-regents of God's omnipotence. The perceived negligence or culpability of religious institutions regarding worldly miseries leads sooner or later to their indictment: the charge that religion is ultimately nothing but an instrument of domination and exploitation.

Given the good intentions of many religious leaders, the charge appears overwrought—but only to a degree. Wittingly or unwittingly, religious institutions have tended to invite the accusation by carelessly flirting with the lure of worldly power. There is hardly a religion or religious institution that has not flirted with or directly succumbed to this temptation. The history of Western Christianity is replete with dubious collusions and complicities. The medieval doctrine of the "two swords," wielded in tandem by pope and emperor, and the later formula of "throne and altar" are prominent examples of dubious alliances or misalliances—not to mention the more glaring political derailments of the Inquisition, the Crusades, and religious wars. Another kind of alliance can be found in Eastern Christianity, especially in the idea of "caesaropapism," with its near-amalgamation of power in "one sword." In this instance, Jesus's comment on the coin owed to Caesar seems to be entirely forgotten or else twisted beyond recognition.[1] Worldly collusions, however, have not been confined to the history of Christianity. To some extent, and in different periods, all the so-called Abrahamic religions have entered dubious alliances, either by supporting forms of theocracy (administered by priests as vice-regents) or by granting a religious group or denomination exclusive control of government. In the Indian tradition, the idea of *ramarajya* has sometimes been construed—or, rather, grossly misinterpreted—as sanctioning the exclusive rule of the country by Hindu religionists under the label of "Hindutva."[2]

As the latter example suggests, the yearning for power is not limited to the historical past. In the contemporary period the striving for religious-political power is most prominently associated with (what is often called) "political Islam," that is, a strand in Muslim thought and practice aiming at the establishment of a near-theocratic Islamic state. Proponents of this strand often invoke the idea of God's absolute sovereignty over the world—an absoluteness that is transferred to the Islamic state and its rulers, eliding the obvious difference between God and a self-appointed clerical establishment. Foremost among advocates of this idea are Pakistani thinker Abul-'Ala Mawdudi and Egyptian activist Sayyid Qutb. Mawdudi, in particular, propounded the idea of *al-hakimiyyah*—meaning God's exclusive sovereignty over His creation—combining it with the notion of *khilafa* or vice-regency and suggesting that Muslim vice-regents are divinely legitimated and entitled to implement all the different facets of divine law (or *sharia*). Carried to its logical extreme, the implications of this conception are totalitarian and, according to some scholars, at variance with genuine Islamic tradition. In the words of Islamic scholar Asma Afsaruddin: "Like the totalitarian communist utopia, Mawdudi promises that his Islamic State will obliterate all class, social, and racial distinctions." What is problematic here is not the idea of divine rule as such (as a corollary of the belief in a Supreme Being) but rather its politicization and conflation with religious autocracy. Even more problematic is the slim scriptural basis of the idea. As Afsaruddin adds: "Mawdudi's grand notion of *al-hakimiyyah* with a fabricated Qur'anic lineage is meant to compensate for the lack of explicit scriptural provisions for a so-called Islamic State or government."[3]

Although frequently singled out for its theocratic tendencies, Islam by no means stands alone in the hankering for religious power. In the United States, recent decades have witnessed the rise of the so-called Christian Right (or Religious Right), a movement notorious for its indiscriminate welding of faith and power politics. What is distinctive about this movement—and what also sets it off from political Islam—is the simultaneous endorsement of corporate capitalism, consumer culture, religious fervor, and political ambition. Given their closeness to corporate and military elites, leaders of the movement often exhibit a triumphalist spirit, rendering them receptive to crusading ventures and especially to the doctrine of preemptive warfare. As it happens, there has been no lack of voices challenging this bellicose kind of triumphalism (or what Taylor calls "paleo-Durkheimian" dispensation). A few years ago, a group of evangelical Christians issued a statement strongly indicting the power-political abuse of faith. "Evangelical churches today," they stated, "are increasingly dominated by the spirit of this age rather than by the spirit of Christ." Hence, instead of preaching "good news" to the world and especially to the poor, Christians are in danger of worshipping the present-day "idols of the market" and proclaiming a "health and wealth gospel" for the privileged few.[4] This indictment had been preceded several decades earlier by theologian Richard Niebuhr's book *The Church against the World*. In this text, Niebuhr warned Christians against immersing themselves entirely in the "fleshpots of Egypt," that is, contemporary market culture. As he wrote, when the church enters into an alliance "with converted emperors and governors, merchants and entrepreneurs, and begins to live at peace in the culture, faith loses its force . . . , repentence grows formal, corruption enters with idolatry, and the church, tied to the culture which it sponsored, suffers corruption with it."[5]

Niebuhr's indictment, in turn, has the backing of a long religious tradition and especially of the gospels themselves. With regard to power-political ambitions, an event recorded in both Luke's and Mark's gospels is particularly memorable. According to this story, a dispute arose among some disciples regarding who was preeminent and most likely to share in divine glory—a dispute to which Jesus responded: "You know that the rulers of the Gentiles lord it over them, and their great men exercise authority over them. But it shall not be so among you; but whoever would be great among you must be your servant" (Mark 10:42–43; see also Luke 22:25–26). In this statement the notion of lordship or supremacy is clearly inverted or twisted beyond recognition, as is also the case in the story of Golgatha. Christians are fond of saying that "Christ rules from the cross," but this rule is clearly a peculiar kind of nonrule, this power a peculiar kind of nonpower and subtle empowerment. In recent times, Christian theology and philosophy have wrestled with this sort of nonpower, coming up with the conception of a "death of God" theology, where death means the demise of the omnipotent or sovereign God and His replacement by the image of a "suffering servant," burdened with the afflictions of the world (and, to this extent, emerging as a "becoming God").[6] A leading Western philosopher wrote not long ago about "God without sovereignty" and even about the "weakness of God," while another contemporary thinker, reflecting on the divine "kingdom" or the "promised land," states that this land "can never be fully possessed in the here and now," and "we can only ever find the kingdom by losing it, by renouncing the illusion that we possess it here and now."[7]

Privatized Religion

Historically, the ambition to appropriate and dominate the world has not been the only obstacle preventing religion from performing its role of contributing to peace and justice. Less frequently and with less grievous consequences, religious faith has also chosen the near-opposite path: the path of exodus or world denial by sequestering itself either in small communities or in the private space of individual solitude. To be sure, the problem does not reside in temporary or even periodic withdrawal from the busy affairs of the world; on the contrary, as experience teaches, such retreat is desirable and perhaps even necessary for maintaining and regenerating the resources of faith. It is only in the case of permanent seclusion that faith is in danger of losing its seasoning and transformative strength. This danger may have been courted occasionally by monastic orders in both the Christian and the Buddhist traditions that cultivated an esoteric aloofness while being neglectful and even disdainful of social problems. The danger of exclusiveness or withdrawal clearly does not apply to preaching or teaching orders, given their close interaction with laypeople in their ordinary lives.

In modern Western societies, retreat from worldly affairs is no longer associated mainly with monasticism but with the rise of individualism and, more specifically, with the retreat of faith into the primacy of individual conscience. In part, this development is the outgrowth of the Protestant Reformation, especially its emphasis on "faith alone" in opposition to all external rites and worldly activities. In the aftermath of Protestant denominationalism, the core of individualism remained in place, serving as the anchor of all religious and nonreligious beliefs. In the European context, a primary spokesman of individualistic Christian faith was Søren Kierkegaard, a staunch opponent of official Lutheranism and all forms of religious establishment. In the American context (as mentioned before), the individualizing tendency was carried even further by the pragmatist, or pragmatic psychologist, William James. As he noted in his famous Gifford Lectures on *The Varieties of Religious Experience*: "In the more personal branch of religion, it is on the contrary the inner dispositions of man which form the center of interest: his conscience, his deserts, his helplessness, his incompleteness."[8]

Although not anticipated and perhaps not even condoned by either Kierkegaard or James, the stress on inward feeling has often turned religious believers away from worldly engagement or social participation. In the view of many evangelical or strictly pietistic Christians, the only point of religion in our time is to promote personal salvation—a salvation accomplished through faith and divine grace alone, without any need for social work or activity. To a considerable extent, this outlook is the standard doctrine of (what is often called) Christian conservatism today, especially in America. For supporters of this outlook, concern with social ills such as injustice, violence, and exploitation is simply extraneous and not part of the religious "agenda." As in the case of monastic retreat, the issue is not the striving for salvation or the reliance on divine grace but rather the lopsided emphasis that, wittingly or unwittingly, contributes to social injustice. In Christian terminology, what happens here is a truncation and even perversion of the gospel: instead of proclaiming "good news" to the poor and persecuted, the gospel is in danger of sanctioning all the miseries of the world and, to this extent, announcing "bad news" for the poor and "good news" only for the oppressors and exploiters.[9]

The lopsidedness of this outlook stands in opposition to a more genuine Christian tradition. The narrow focus on inner belief, barring outward activity, is challenged in several passages of the New Testament itself. Thus, in denouncing the rantings of "false prophets," Jesus states that the only way to discern their real nature is "by their fruits" or their actions, adding that "a sound tree cannot bear evil fruit nor can a bad tree bear good fruit. . . . Hence you will know them by their fruits" (Matthew 7:16, 18–20). In the same vein, in critiquing the behavior of scribes and Pharisees, Jesus admonishes his followers to "practice and observe whatever they tell you, but not what they do; for they preach but do not practice" (Matthew 23:2–3). The strongest indictment of inner belief without outward conduct, however, is found in the Letter of James. There, the recipients of the letter are exhorted to "be doers of the word and not hearers only, deceiving yourselves." Elaborating on this admonition, James adds: "What does it benefit, my brethren, if a man says he has faith but has not works?" For example: "If a brother or sister is ill-clad and in lack of daily food, and one of you says to them 'Go in peace, be warmed and filled' without giving them the things needed for the body, what does it benefit? So faith by itself, if it has no works, is dead." To dispel misunderstanding, James makes it clear that his admonition is not a novelty but rather in accord with older biblical teachings. "Was not Abraham our father justified by works, when he offered his son Isaac upon the altar?" (James 1:22, 14–17, 23).

To be sure—and as James leaves no doubt—Abraham's action occurred under extreme circumstances and cannot serve as a general model for everyone. In the same letter he actually offers a yardstick of genuine or "pure" religiosity that is simple and compelling: "to visit orphans and widows in their affliction, and to keep oneself unstained from the world" (James 1:27). With this formulation, James touches the core of every genuine religion, including but also going beyond the specifically Christian tradition. In this respect I can rely on insights articulated by Chandra Muzaffer in his pioneering book *Rights, Religion and Reform*. There Muzaffer states quite persuasively that "nearly every prophet and sage known to mankind reflected upon the human condition, the state of society, in order to discover the answers to the vital questions of life and death" and to find remedies for individual and social afflictions. Thus, Gautama Buddha "was deeply moved by human suffering—the suffering caused by disease, old age and death. It was the agony of suffering that took him on one of humanity's noble quests for truth [the Noble Eightfold Path] that culminated in the attainment of *nirvana*." In a similar vein, Muzaffer adds, Confucius's code of ethics "covering a wide range of subjects was spawned in a troubled and turbulent era, characterized by moral chaos"—a chaos he sought to overcome through "goodness" (*ren*) and "propriety" (*li*).

Likewise, though in a more prophetic register, the long line of Hebrew prophets "struggled against tyranny and oppression and sought to give their people an alternative vision of life." Finally, the prophet Muhammad too "fought relentlessly against the corruption and decadence, the hatred and bigotry that had become too pervasive in his day." As a remedy, they advocated "righteous conduct expressed by a commitment to freedom and equality, integrity and compassion, as well as unity and justice."[10]

I am sure Muzaffer would also include in this account the great sages of the Hindu tradition and the long line of Indian sacred sculptures culminating in the Bhagavad Gita. As we know, the Bhagavad Gita outlines a number of pathways or *yogas* guiding to salvation—the paths of knowing, loving, and doing—but assigns a special preeminence to the action path (*karma yoga*), stating: "Great is the human being who, free from worldly attachments and with a mind ruling its powers in harmony, works on the path of *karma yoga*, the path of consecrated action" (Gita 3:7). As we also know, one of the greatest devotees of the teachings of the Gita in recent times was the Mahatma Gandhi, who described himself as a *karma yogin*. For Gandhi, pursuing the path of action meant involving himself in political life, but in such a manner as to shun the temptation of power and domination and thus remain "free from worldly attachments." A corollary of shunning the lure of worldly power is avoiding violence, or at least reducing it to a minimum (*ahimsa*), and enlisting goodness and divine grace in the struggle against injustice and oppression (*satyagraha*). In Gandhi's own words: in the context of struggle and "in the application of *satyagraha*, I discovered in the earliest stages that pursuit of truth did not admit of violence being inflicted on one's opponent, but that he must be weaned from error by patience and sympathy." Such sympathy, in turn, must be generated not through violence but only through self-restraint and self-suffering and through identification with the victims of oppression.[11]

Manicheism and International Politics

To practice *karma yoga* properly is not an easy matter. To be actively engaged in the world and yet remain free from worldly attachments requires a kind of transformative self-restraint that is difficult to achieve. This difficulty is plainly acknowledged by the texts previously cited. Thus, James exhorts his fellow believers not to present themselves too quickly as models, for "we all make many mistakes, and if perchance anyone makes no mistakes in what he says or does, he is a perfect person able to bridle the whole person also" (James 3:2). Somewhat later in his letter, James points to the consequences of the lack of self-restraint. "What causes wars, and what causes fightings among you?" he asks. "Is it not your passions that are at war in your members? You desire something and do not have it; so you kill. You covet and cannot obtain; so you fight and wage war" (James 4:1–2). Likewise, in the Bhagavad Gita, Lord Krishna—responding to Arjuna's inquiry about the causes of strife—states: "It is greedy desire and wrath, born of passion, the great evil, the sum of destruction: this is the enemy of the soul. All is clouded by base desire: as fire is by smoke, as a mirror by dust, as an unborn baby by the womb." And he adds: the fire of base desire is all-consuming, takes "innumerable forms," and can never find satisfaction (Gita 3:37–39).

These words are stirring and certainly need to be weighed carefully, though not as inducements to despair. In some religious quarters, the evidence of sinfulness or sinful desire is taken as evidence of humanity's brokenness or fallenness, as a stain marking human life and canceling any hope for improvement. A certain extreme version of Augustinianism has led some theologians to affirm the sinful character of all political orders or regimes, an affirmation often coupled with a strange bifurcation of public and private domains. According to this version, even though individuals may achieve a degree of moral decency in their private lives, the public realm is entirely in the grip of power or the lust for power. A prominent proponent of this view was Protestant theologian Reinhold Niebuhr (brother of Richard Niebuhr, previously mentioned). In several of his writings, but especially in his book *Moral Man and Immoral Society,* Niebuhr insists that a "sharp distinction" must be drawn between "the moral and social behavior of individuals," on the one hand, and the behavior of "social groups, national, racial and economic," on the other. Although "individual men may be moral in the sense that they are able to consider interests other than their own in determining problems of conduct," such achievements "are more difficult, if not impossible, for human societies and social groups," where there is "less reason to guide and to check impulse, less capacity for self-transcendence." As Niebuhr acknowledges, the polemical edge of his book is directed mainly against those "moralists, both religious and secular," who imagine that the egotism of individuals is being "progressively checked by the development of rationality or the growth of religiously inspired good will" and that "nothing but the continuance of this process is needed to establish harmony between all societies and collectives."[12]

What moralists—whether religious or secular—ignore, in Niebuhr's view, are "those elements in man's collective behavior which belong to the 'order of nature' and which can never be brought completely under the dominion of reason or conscience." Differently put, what they fail to recognize is the role of power and the imperative of political struggle: the fact that "when collective power, whether in the form of imperialism or class domination, exploits weakness, it can never be dislodged unless power is raised against it." In making this claim, the theologian was not unaware of the prevalence of social injustices resulting from domination and exploitation; however, the remedy for these injustices (in his view) could not reside in well-meaning exhortations or ethical appeals. "Social injustice," he asserts bluntly, "cannot be resolved by moral and rational persuasion alone. . . . Conflict is inevitable, and in this conflict power must be challenged by power." For Niebuhr, as for Schmitt, what is sidestepped by pious moralists and intellectuals is an understanding of "the brutal character of the behavior of all human collectives, and the power of self-interest and collective egotism in all inter-group [and international] relations." Hence, the "romantic" belief in a "growing brotherliness" between peoples and nations must be unmasked as an illusion not only by hard-nosed empiricists but also by religious "realists." Returning to the basic theme announced in the book's title, Niebuhr confines the possibility of justice narrowly to the interpersonal level, while basically dismissing it on the intersocietal and international level. "The relations between groups," we read, "must therefore always be predominantly political rather than ethical, that is, they will be determined by the proportion of power which each group possesses." The upshot of his argument is the primacy of power over ethics, of force over persuasion. "The sentiments of benevolence and social good will," he concludes, "will never be so pure or powerful . . . as to create the possibility for the 'anarchistic' millennium which is the social utopia, either explicit or implicit, of all intellectual or religious moralists."[13]

Niebuhr's arguments might be dismissed as the ruminations of a pessimistic theologian, which would be a mistake. For all practical purposes, his views on justice and intersocietal relations have become standard doctrine in contemporary international politics, especially in the school of international "realism" inaugurated by Hans Morgenthau. In one of his early writings, Morgenthau pits "scientific man" against "power politics." By "scientific man," Morgenthau means pretty much what Niebuhr targeted as the "liberal intellectual" and enlightened "moralist" (now amplified by trust in modern science). Under the influence of Enlightenment rationalism, modern Western society has tended to assume that social life is susceptible to rational moral guidance—an assumption flatly contradicted by "the experiences, domestic and international, of the age." As a result of this assumption, politics and political power have been sidelined or denounced as an evil to be overcome. Particularly grievous, for Morgenthau, is the fact that international politics has been made the "object of condemnation"—a condemnation that "not only [ignores] the moral value of political power" but also "denies, if not the very existence of power politics as a matter of fact, at least its organic and inevitable connection with the life of man in society." What is needed in his view is a stark reversal of accents leading to the recognition that "the aspiration for power over men" is the "essence of politics" and that, in the reality of international affairs, "power is pitted against power for survival and supremacy." Although not completely denying the role of ethics or morality, Morgenthau, like Niebuhr, confines it to a narrow private sphere, stating that "the selfishness of [individual] man has limits," while the "will to [political] power has none"—a conclusion adding up to a "tragic conflict" or "unresolvable discord" between private morality and politics.[14]

A few years after the cited text, Morgenthau published his most famous book, *Politics among Nations,* which eloquently defends a "realist" approach to international politics. Differentiating it from a strictly normative perspective, Morgenthau defines "realism" as an approach governed by the "objective laws" or objective facts rooted in "human nature." Foremost among these objective facts is the inevitability of the struggle for political power, where "power" means "man's control over the minds and actions of other men." This feature is said to be particularly prominent in international politics, which "like all politics, is a struggle for power." Whatever the ulterior aims of international politics may be, Morgenthau points out, "power is always the immediate aim." Thus, statesmen may claim to pursue various aims such as freedom, prosperity, and even the spreading of democracy, but whenever they seek to realize their goals on the international scene, "they do so by striving for power." A crucial corollary of international politics thus defined is "armed strength," seen as "the most important material factor making for the political power of a nation." As in the earlier text, a major polemical target in *Politics among Nations* is the sidelining or "deprecation" of power politics, which can be traced to the moralizing tendencies of liberalism as well as the protective shield of "isolationism" that seemingly exempts (or exempted) America from world politics. In Morgenthau's words: "From the shores of the North American continent, the inhabitants of the New World watched the strange spectacle of the international struggle for power unfolding on the distant shores of Europe, Africa, and Asia"—observing it with both bemusement and disdain. Thus, the general conception formed in the nineteenth century of the nature of foreign affairs, combined with specific elements in the American experience, managed to produce the belief "that involvement in power politics is not inevitable, but only a historic accident, and that nations have a choice between power politics and other kinds of foreign policy not tainted by the desire for power."[15]

It cannot be my task here to discuss in detail the arguments of political realists (nor the still bolder claims of so-called neorealists). I limit myself to a few basic points, without dwelling on general philosophical or metaphysical questions, such as the meaning of "reality" presupposed by political realists or the conception of human "nature" presumably undergirding the claimed incorrigibility of the human lust for power. Confining myself to religious and ethical issues, I simply note the following: Outside of an extreme (Manichean) Augustinianism, sacred scriptures and religious teachings of the world's major faiths do not provide a warrant for the stark opposition between "moral man" and "immoral society" nor for the claimed primacy of political power over ethical or moral considerations. Nor, in my view, can one find such a warrant in the major ethical teachings contained in diverse cultural traditions. To sharpen the point further: the separation of ethics from politics or the struggle for power is not just a neutral analytical procedure but implies a tacit endorsement of current global political practices that have in fact emancipated themselves from, and often stand in flagrant contradiction to, ethical norms. In my view, it cannot be the business of religious and ethical persons—and certainly not the business of a Christian theologian—to give aid and comfort to rampant acts of global aggression perpetrated today by large and small nation-states. In this respect I can rely on the words of Martin Luther King Jr. when, in his struggle for racial justice, he affirmed: "He who passively accepts [or endorses] evil is as much involved in it as he who helps to perpetrate it."[16]

Quite obviously, King in his own struggle did not ignore political reality or the presence of a dominant power structure in the country. However, he and his followers engaged in political struggle not to gain dominant power for themselves but to bring more justice into, and improve the ethical fiber of, existing society. The same can be said of the Mahatma Gandhi. In struggling against the British Empire, Gandhi did not aim to promote a selfish nationalism or an India for Hindus only. As he wrote in his famous 1909 book *Hind Swaraj* (Indian Home Rule), the point of the struggle was not to perpetuate the English type of political rule "without the Englishman." This was like wanting "the tiger's nature, but not the tiger." Moreover, in pursuing the goal of independence, Gandhi insisted that the means had to be congruent with the end: that is, a just and more equitable social order could be furthered only though just and nonviolent means (*ahimsa*), even if this entailed hardship and painful consequences for oneself. As he stated in another context: "Suffering is the law of human beings; war [or violence] is the law of the jungle."[17]

In his stress on the congruence between means and ends, Gandhi was in full accord with American philosopher John Dewey and the latter's emphasis on the need for peaceful though occasionally "radical" social change. As Dewey wrote in 1937, at a time when democratic self-rule (or *swaraj*) was threatened by fascist waves in Europe and elsewhere: "Democracy means not only the ends pursued . . . [but] also a primary emphasis on the *means* by which these ends are to be fulfilled." These means have to be "voluntary activities" in opposition to coercion, "assent and consent" in opposition to violence. As he concluded: "The fundamental principle of democracy is that the ends of freedom and individuality for all can be attained only by means that accord with those ends"—and certainly not by military force or imperialistic conquest.[18]

Toward Peace and Justice

As the examples of Gandhi, King, and Dewey indicate, striving for peace does not mean just preserving the status quo, adjusting complacently to the prevailing state of affairs—a state that may be rampant with injustice and exploitation. In case of such pliant adjustment, peace would be nothing more than a shallow tranquility purchased at the price of oppression. As one can see, peace is not only accidentally but essentially or constitutively linked with justice. This is in accord with the words of the prophet Isaiah: "Peace is the work (or the fruit) of justice" (Isaiah 32:17). It is also in agreement with the emphasis of all religious traditions as well as ethical teachings on the centrality of justice and equity in social life. As we read in Deuteronomy: "Justice, and only justice, you shall follow, so that you may live" (Deuteronomy 16:20). And the psalmist proclaims: "For the Lord loves justice, he will not forsake his saints" (Psalms 37:28). Again, in the Qur'an we read, "O ye believe! Stand out firmly for justice as witnesses to God" (Sura 4:135) and "Be just: for that is next to piety" (Sura 5:8). In a somewhat longer passage, the Qur'an states: " We sent aforetime our apostles with clear signs, and sent down with them the book and the balance of right and wrong, that men may stand forth in justice" (Sura 57:25). As Muzaffer correctly comments: "Justice is the real goal of religion. It was the mission of every prophet and is the message of every scripture."[19]

These comments might readily be supported by glances at non-Abrahamic religious and ethical teachings (such as Buddhism and Confucianism). The question that emerges in all these contexts, however, concerns the meaning of "justice" or equity. What are we expected to do when we are exhorted to "stand for justice"? As is well known, philosophy since its beginning has wrestled with this question and provided a number of answers. For some, justice is a set of abstract principles; for others, it is the outcome of a "felicitous calculus" of interests; for still others, it is a mode of proportional allotment of benefits. In recent times, some Western philosophers have reached dubious (and even extravagant) conclusions. Impressed or overwhelmed by the rampant injustices prevailing in the world, they have concluded that justice can only be a transcendent intrusion or interruption of the world, a kind of radical, apocalyptic dismantling of existing social arrangements and conventions. To give an example: one recent French philosopher claimed that justice has the character of a "decision" that "always marks the interruption of juridical, ethical or political cognitive deliberation," adding that "the instance of just decision must rend time and defy dialectics."[20] What is correct in this construal is that justice always involves a certain turning around and transformation of self-centered dispositions. What is wrong is the neglect or dismissal of concrete ethical practices, of the labor and "heart-churn" (to use Gandhi's expression) involved in the struggle against injustice and oppression.

Regarding justice, I believe it is always good to return to the classical teachings of Plato and Aristotle, amplified by the teachings of classical Islamic philosophers as well as Asian ethical thinkers. As one may recall, Plato's *Republic* revolves entirely around the issue of justice and emphatically rebukes the notion that justice is simply the decision or command of the powerful. Briefly stated, justice for Plato maintains a proper balance between different human virtues and, at the same time, represents the apex or culmination of ethical virtue as such. Aristotle goes a step further by linking justice with concrete ethical practices and by insisting on the need to cultivate these practices through habituation. As he writes in *Nicomachean Ethics:* "Virtues we acquire just as we acquire crafts, by having trained and activated them. . . . Hence, we become just by doing just actions, temperate by doing temperate actions, brave by doing brave actions." He adds: "It is not unimportant to acquire a [virtuous] sort of habit, right from your youth. Actually, it is very important, in fact all-important." Regarding justice as a virtue, the *Nicomachean Ethics* offers this formulation: "What we call just is whatever produces and maintains happiness or blessedness [*eudaimonia*—not chaos, destruction, or madness] for the whole of a political community and its parts."[21]

It would not require much effort to show the congruence of these Platonic and Aristotelian teachings with the works of classical Islamic philosophers, especially Alfarabi and Avicenna. Alfarabi's *Virtuous*

City, in particular, is closely patterned on Plato's *Republic* and Aristotle's *Ethics*. Nor would it be difficult to extend the parallels further. The virtuous action or *karma yoga* recommended in the Gita is oriented toward individual and collective happiness or blessedness, that is, toward the individual and communal practice of justice. In turn, in stipulating the Noble Eightfold Path, the Buddhist tradition insists on the assiduous cultivation of virtuous and just habits in the domains of thought, speech, and outward conduct. Likewise, in center-staging "humaneness" (*ren*) and "propriety" (*li*), the texts of Confucius and Mencius offer clear guideposts for ethical conduct in the family, in society, and in the world. There is one additional feature in all these teachings, though one that is particularly highlighted by Aristotle: namely, that justice and virtue are ends in themselves and not pursued for some ulterior motives or for the sake of something else. As we read in the *Nicomachean Ethics:* happiness or blessedness is "choiceworthy in itself, never because of something other"; hence, it is "self-sufficient" and "lacking nothing."[22] Thus, justice is not a means or an instrument for the attainment of power, wealth, or political control but a synonym for the attainment of happiness or blessedness.

This teaching—which I consider persuasive and correct—throws light on an issue mentioned earlier: the issue of pessimism and optimism. In pursuing justice, and peace through justice, we are required to bracket questions of outcome, that is, considerations of success or failure, of good or bad fortune. Differently phrased: in the pursuit of just peace, possible failure cannot be a deterrent; nor can success be the guiding motive. In the words of the Gita, *karma yoga* has to be practiced "without attachment to the fruits of action." The tragic example of prominent *karma yogins* is worth remembering: Gandhi was assassinated; so were Martin Luther King Jr. and Bishop Romero of El Salvador. Their conduct clearly escaped the opposition between optimism and pessimism; they did what needed to be done, without expectation of reward. Simply put: blessedness is not a success story but a matter of faithfulness. As a young Indian once told me, in a phrase that beautifully captures the spirit of self-giving faithfulness: "We are only flowers thrown into a temple."

6. Hermeneutics and Cross-Cultural Encounters

Integral Pluralism in Action

> The future survival of humankind may depend on our readiness . . . to pause in front of the other's otherness—the otherness of nature as well as that of historically grown cultures of peoples and countries.
> —Hans-Georg Gadamer

As customarily defined, *hermeneutics* means the theory, or rather the practice or art, of interpretation. In its primary and traditional sense, *interpretation* means textual interpretation, that is, the encounter between a reader and a text. In this encounter, something has to happen, some work has to be done: the reader needs to discover the meaning of the text, which is usually far from self-evident. The difficulty of the work is increased in the case of temporal or spatial distance: when the reader wishes to understand a text from another age or in a different language. Yet to some extent, the difficulty prevails even in the absence of such distance—for example, in reading the letter of a friend. Basically, the problem derives from the peculiarly ambivalent character of interpretation: the reader cannot remain entirely passive, nor must he or she be overly active. The interpreter cannot find the meaning by passively copying or transliterating the text; nor should he or she willfully foist a meaning on the text, thereby manipulating or coercing it. Hence, the labor is transformative: the reader must bring himself or herself to the text, but in an open manner so as to allow a new learning experience to happen. This is why we say (or why leading hermeneuticists say) that interpretation is necessarily interactive or dialogical. This is also why we might say that hermeneutics is an illustration of integral pluralism, since difference is both acknowledged and bridged.

In the present context, the question I want to raise is whether this meaning of hermeneutics can be transferred from the reading of texts to interhuman relations and especially to the relations between cultures or civilizations. Obviously, cultures are different from written texts. Cultures are complex semantic clusters; following Wittgenstein, we might say that they are complex language games and, even more, they are "forms of life" comprising, in addition to written texts, social customs, religious beliefs, rituals, and practices. Moreover, cultures are internally diversified and unfinished, that is, always evolving and on the move. Given this character, some people consider cross-cultural or intercultural hermeneutics impossible or futile. The main reasons they cite for this impossibility are the internal complexity and the incommensurability of semantic clusters or forms of life. This is a weighty objection; carried to the extreme, it lends credence to the thesis of a looming "clash" of cultures or civilizations (famously formulated by Samuel Huntington). However, this seems to be an overly pessimistic and debilitating outlook. As in the case of textual interpretation, we might agree that the difficulties are considerable and proceed nonetheless. My own preference, in any case, is to adopt the experimental approach of hermeneutical inquiry and see how far it leads us.

This is basically the approach I follow here, and I proceed in three main steps. First, I discuss the historical development and basic meaning of hermeneutics as expounded by the leading proponent of modern and contemporary hermeneutics, Hans-Georg Gadamer. At this point, I also review some possible practical applications of the hermeneutical perspective in the social and cultural domains, highlighting certain parallels between hermeneutics and practical philosophy. Next, drawing on the insights of both Gadamer and more overtly political thinkers, I elaborate on the specific relevance of hermeneutics for cross-cultural or intercultural understanding and dialogue. Finally, I turn to some writings by Maurice Merleau-Ponty to underscore the necessary linkage between interactive dialogue and concrete embodied engagement. Undercutting purely mentalist or "idealist" misconstruals of dialogue, this linkage shows the mutual compatibility between Gadamerian hermeneutics and existential phenomenology.

Hermeneutics: Its Meaning and Development

Regarding the meaning and development of hermeneutics, Gadamer's magisterial *Truth and Method* is an indispensable resource. As Gadamer points out, hermeneutics has followed a complex trajectory and has undergone profound transformations in its history: from limited, closely circumscribed beginnings, it evolved over time until it came to coincide with human life experience as such. In its infancy, hermeneutics was basically a specialized art or method employed in the fields of theology, classical philology, and jurisprudence. While theologians needed to decipher the meaning of scriptures that were removed in time and place, philologists faced the task of capturing the meaning of classical texts in modern idioms, and jurists needed to detect the significance of classical law books in postclassical (say, Germanic) societies. At the onset of the modern age, these endeavors were continued and refined by Renaissance humanism and Protestant theology, with scholars in both fields seeking to distill a more original meaning from later corruptions or deformations. A major innovation or change of focus occurred in the Romantic era, and especially in the work of Friedrich Schleiermacher. Departing from the earlier use, Schleiermacher extended the role of hermeneutics to all literary expressions while also "psychologizing" the methodology. The task of interpretation, in his view, is to discern the "author's mind" (*mens auctoris*) or the inner spirit or inspiration animating a given work.

This approach was broadened and given a more robust academic anchorage by the Historical School of the nineteenth century, whose chief spokesman was Wilhelm Dilthey. For Dilthey, all of human history had to be approached hermeneutically, which meant that a scholarly, disciplined effort had to be made to decipher the meaning of historical events or activities by examining the motivating intentions of historical actors. In Gadamer's words, it was "Dilthey who consciously took up Romantic hermeneutics and expanded it into a historical method—indeed into an epistemology of the human sciences." For Dilthey, the point was not just that historical sources are encountered as texts but that "historical reality as such is a text in need of understanding." In this manner, the enterprise of hermeneutics was "transposed to the study of history"; differently put, "hermeneutics emerged as the basis of the study of history," which is a field of vast dimensions.[1] Although broadening and transforming the role of interpretation, Dilthey and the Historical School still remained hostage to certain premises that restricted its scope. The main premises obstructing a full flowering were epistemological: the aspiration of historical study to be recognized as a "science" on a par with the natural sciences. In trying to grasp history scientifically, the historian had to adopt a superior or neutral standpoint, extricating himself or herself from the flow of historical experience. Critiquing this approach, Gadamer observes that historical experience cannot be reduced to a "procedure" or have the "anonymity of a method." Despite Dilthey's best intentions, the "epistemological pull of Cartesianism" proved too strong, preventing him from "integrating into his thought the historicity of historical experience itself."[2]

For Gadamer, the most important event in recent times—the event that basically reshaped the role of hermeneutics—was the shift from epistemology to ontology, a shift associated with Martin Heidegger. Involved in this shift was the transformation of interpretive understanding from a methodology tailored for academic disciplines into a mode of human existence, of human being-in-the-world. "Under the rubric of a 'hermeneutics of facticity,'" Gadamer states, Heidegger opposed not only the ambitions of historical science but also the restrictive "eidetic phenomenology of Husserl, with its distinction between fact and essence." In contrast to Husserl, "the contingent and underivable 'facticity' of existence or *Dasein*—and not the epistemic *cogito* as warrant of essential universality—came to represent the ontological yardstick of phenomenological questioning." For Heidegger, interpretive or hermeneutical understanding was not the province of specialized human disciplines (nor of a transcendentally construed phenomenology) but rather a constitutive feature of every human being inserted both in the world and in the movement of temporality. According to Gadamer, with his thesis that "being itself is time," Heidegger called into question the "basic subjectivism of modern philosophy" as well as the entire "frame of reference of modern metaphysics which tended to define being as what is present." At the same time, by focusing on the "understanding character" of human *Dasein*, Heideggerian ontology departed from and overcame the "historicist" dilemmas of the Historical School. In contrast to Dilthey, understanding is no longer a mere "methodological concept"; rather, it pinpoints the "original mode of being of human life itself." Through his "analytic of *Dasein*," in particular, Heidegger revealed "the projective [not merely present-ist] character of all understanding and conceived the act of understanding itself as a movement of transcendence, of moving beyond the existent [state of affairs]."[3]

From Heidegger's perspective, interpretive understanding is not so much a methodology as a happening or temporal event—a happening with possibly transformative consequences for the interpreter. In the case of textual exegesis, for instance, the text may (and usually does) prove recalcitrant to immediate access. In the attempt to gain leverage, the reader does not approach the text with a "blank slate" (*tabula rasa*), which would permit passive appropriation; rather, to gain entry, the reader has to apply to the text a tentative frame of reference—what Heidegger calls a "pre-understanding" (*Vorurteil*) or a "projected meaning" (*Vorentwurf*). As Gadamer describes the process: "Whoever is trying to understand a text, always engages in projecting (*Entwerfen*): he/she projects a meaning for the text as soon as some initial meaning comes to the fore. That initial meaning, however, emerges only because the text is read with certain expectations regarding its meaning." Yet, when approached with this "fore-meaning" or "pre-understanding," the text may refuse to yield and prove resistant. This resistance, in turn, may force the reader to revise his or her initial assumptions or presumptions, which may prove wrenching or painful. In revising initial assumptions, the reader is not required to abandon all critical reservations or queries; rather, what is demanded is a certain openness to the issues raised in the text and to the possibility that prior assumptions may have been wrong or lopsided. In Gadamer's words again: when reading a text, "we are not expected to jettison all our 'fore-meanings' concerning its content. All that is asked is that we remain open to the intrinsic lesson of the text (or of another person)." Hence, he adds, "a person trying to understand a text must be prepared to be told something by the text. That is why a hermeneutically trained person must be, from the start, sensitive and receptive to the text's alterity or difference (*Andersheit*)."[4]

These comments bring into view a crucial aspect of hermeneutics as conceived by Heidegger and Gadamer: the dialogical and circular character of understanding. Gadamer, in particular, is famous for his insistence on the close linkage and even convergence of dialogue and hermeneutical understanding. As we read in *Truth and Method:* "That a historical text is made the object of exegesis means that it puts a question to the interpreter. Hence, interpretation always relates essentially to the question that is posed to the reader." But every question solicits a response and thus leads into the thick of dialogue. A genuine dialogue, Gadamer observes, necessarily has the "structure of question and response." To conduct such a dialogue requires that the participants be "attentive to each other" and not "talk past each other." Above all, dialogue demands a certain modesty and nonaggressiveness, a willingness to listen and a refusal to try to "overpower the other partner." By placing at the center the "weight" of the respective opinions, dialogue is a mode of "experimental testing" (*Erproben*) or inquiry; its fruit is not the triumph of one opinion over another but rather a mutual learning process during which the partners gain a better understanding of both the subject matter and themselves. This feature leads Gadamer to a poignant formulation of the relation between dialogue and hermeneutics, a formulation that is quintessential of his entire approach: "What characterizes a dialogue . . . is precisely this: that—in the process of question and answer, in giving and taking, talking at cross purposes and coming to an agreement—dialogical discourse performs that communication of meaning which, with respect to the written tradition, is the task of hermeneutics. Hence, it is more than a metaphor: it is a recollection of what is originally at stake when hermeneutical inquiry is seen as entering into dialogue with a text."[5]

Dialoguing with a text, just as dialoguing with a human partner, is a difficult process fraught with many pitfalls and possible derailments. Occasionally, Gadamerian hermeneutics is accused of, or identified with, a facile consensualism, with a happy blending of views devoid of conflict. To some extent, his *Truth and Method* has encouraged this construal, especially through its notion of a "fusion of horizons." As we read at one point: understanding does not recognize limits but is always "the fusion of these horizons supposedly existing by themselves."[6] Yet, at a closer (and more sympathetic) look, what is involved here is not so much a fusion in the sense of convergence but rather an unlimited openness to horizons, in such a manner that interpretive understanding can never be fully stabilized or completed. This aspect is admirably highlighted by Gadamer at another place when he speaks of the tensional character of all understanding—a tension derived from the distance or difference between reader and text, between self and other, between present and past. "Hermeneutics," he writes, "must start from the position that a person seeking to understand has a bond with whatever a transmitted text tries to say and thus is connected with the tradition from which the text speaks." At the same time, however, hermeneutical inquiry is aware "that this connection does not have the character of an unquestioned, self-evident consensus (as would be the case in an unbroken stream of tradition)"—hence the tensional nature of all understanding. "Hermeneutical work," Gadamer adds pointedly, "is based on a polarity between familiarity and strangeness (*Fremdheit*)," although this polarity should be construed not psychologically (with Schleiermacher) but ontologically. "Here is the tension: the play between strangeness and familiarity encountered in tradition is the mid-point between a distantiated object of history and membership in a living tradition. The true locus of hermeneutics is this in-between."[7]

This tensional character also affects the circular quality of interpretation—what is called the "hermeneutical circle." This circle is not a closed sphere, permitting only an empty turning "round and round," but an open circle fostering a learning process or a steady amelioration and transformation of understanding. This, in any event, is the construal favored by Heidegger. In approaching a text, the reader projects a "fore-meaning" of the whole, which runs aground because portions of the text refuse to be integrated. Hence, a new holistic projection is needed, triggering an ongoing adjustment of parts and whole. In Gadamer's description, it was Heidegger who gave the circle an existential-ontological significance deriving from the constitutive role of understanding for human *Dasein*. Given this constitutive role, the circle for Heidegger cannot achieve closure, although it points toward an infinite completion. In Gadamer's words: "The circle of whole and part is not dissolved [or terminated] in genuine understanding but, on the contrary, is most fully realized." Seen in this light, the circle is not "formal in nature" but ontological; it is "neither subjective nor objective" but rather pinpoints understanding as "the interplay of the movement of tradition and the movement of the interpreter." The anticipation of meaning that governs the interpreter's understanding of a text is "not an act of subjectivity" but proceeds from "the commonality linking us with the tradition." But this commonality, Gadamer adds, is never finished but in "a constant process of formation (*Bildung*)."[8]

Hermeneutics and Practical Application

Hermeneutics is not, and has never been, a purely abstract theory, but is closely linked with lived experience and human conduct. This linkage has been intensified in recent times with the shift from methodology to ontology, when understanding comes to be seen as part and parcel of our living and being-in-the-world. Yet, even in earlier times, the linkage was never entirely lacking. As we read in *Truth and Method*, an integral part of traditional hermeneutics was the so-called *subtilitas applicandi,* the ability to bring the meaning of a text to bear on a given situation. Thus, it was commonly assumed that a proper understanding of textual meaning involved "something like applying the text" to the situation of the interpreter and reader, that is, relating that meaning to practical human conduct. Gadamer gives the prominent examples of scriptural and legal or judicial interpretation. Clearly, scriptural exegesis was not meant to merely increase theological knowledge but to provide a resource for pastoral preaching, which in turn was designed to mold the lives of the faithful. The same connection prevailed (and prevails) in judicial interpretation when a judge is asked to discern the relevance of a legal norm in the particular situation or context. "A law," Gadamer comments, "does not just exist as an historical object or entity, but needs to be concretized in its legal validity by being interpreted." Similarly, the gospel does not exist simply as an edifying historical document but needs to be approached "in such a way as to disclose its message of salvation." Hence, to be properly grasped, a given text—whether scriptural or legal—needs to be understood "at every moment, in every concrete situation, in a new and different way." As a consequence, "hermeneutical understanding always involves a mode of application."[9]

As indicated before, this linkage with application or practical conduct is greatly intensified in Heidegger's ontological approach. Construed as an interpretive creature, human *Dasein* is now seen to conduct life under hermeneutical auspices. From the angle of Heidegger's "hermeneutics of facticity," Gadamer writes, understanding is no longer a method through which an inquiring consciousness targets a given object; rather, it means being situated in a temporal happening, in an ongoing "process of tradition" (*Überlieferungsgeschehen*). In fact, "understanding proves to be itself a lived happening" and, as such, a mode of human conduct that is neither predetermined by fixed rules (presumably beyond interpretation) nor purely whimsical or arbitrary. In this context, to illustrate the sense of "happening," Gadamer invokes the tradition of Aristotle and especially the legacy of Aristotelian ethics, which is not an ethics of purely cognitive principles (like Kantian morality) nor of irrational will power (like "emotivism") but an ethics of concretely lived praxis. On the level of practical application, he writes, Aristotle's ethical analysis offers "a kind of model of the problems of hermeneutics." As in the case of the practice of virtues, hermeneutical application is not merely "an occasional feature or subsequent addition" to the process of understanding but permeates this process from beginning to end. As in ethical praxis, application does not consist in merely relating a predetermined general principle to a particular case; rather, the interpreter has to make sense of his or her situation in light of the broader "process of tradition" (comprising both that situation and the text). Hence, to understand a text and its general teaching, the interpreter "must not try to disregard his/her particular hermeneutical situation" but rather must "correlate that text with this situation if understanding is going to be possible at all."[10]

Moving beyond the strictly ethical dimension, *Truth and Method* also comments on some social and political implications of hermeneutical application or praxis. As Gadamer indicates, such application cannot really happen in a society or political regime where norms or rules of conduct are entirely static and exempt from further interpretation, that is, where there is a ban on creative exegesis and transformation. At the same time, hermeneutics cannot flourish in a society or regime dominated by arbitrary power or a Hobbesian sovereign. In Gadamer's words, hermeneutics presupposes a dialogical give-and-take occurring in a continuity of tradition: "Where this is not the case—for example, in an absolutist state where the will of the absolute ruler is above the law—hermeneutics cannot exist, since the ruler can abrogate the rules of interpretation." In such a situation, the arbitrary will of the ruler (who is *lege solutus,* or not bound by any law) can render decisions without regard for the law and hence without the effort of interpretation. Hermeneutics, for Gadamer, hence presupposes a constitutional regime (perhaps a democratic constitutional order) that does not rely on arbitrary decisions or willful domination and that makes room for the hermeneutical balancing of "whole and parts" and the dialogical inquiry into the conditions of social justice and fairness. "It is part of a properly constituted legal order," he writes, "that the decision of a judge [as well as the policy of rulers] does not proceed from an arbitrary and unpredictable fiat, but rather from a just weighing up of the whole" or the balancing of all elements involved in a situation. The possibly democratic connotations of this outlook are evident when Gadamer adds that "anyone [that is, any citizen] is capable of undertaking this just weighing up, provided she has immersed herself in the concrete particular situation" as seen in a broader social context.[11]

Gadamer's comments on application and practical conduct are not limited to *Truth and Method.* Some ten years later he published an essay specifically focused on the relation between hermeneutics and practical philosophy. As the essay emphasizes, hermeneutics should not be viewed simply as an abstract theory, for it always implies or implicates a reference to practical conduct. Since its beginnings, hermeneutical inquiry has always claimed "that its reflection on the possibilities, rules and means of interpretation is somehow directly useful or advantageous for lived *praxis.*" For this reason, Gadamer notes, interpretation has often been treated as an art form or artistic skill (*Kunstlehre*) rather than a routine technique. As in the earlier volume, the essay traces the development of hermeneutics from its roots in scriptural and juridical interpretation to the shifts occasioned by Renaissance humanism, Reformation, and postrevolutionary Romanticism and historicism. As before, the basic sea change in the meaning of hermeneutics is attributed to the work of Heidegger, to his break with the static (or presentist) metaphysics of the past and his inscription of understanding into the lived, temporal experience of *Dasein.* "It was Heidegger's great merit," we read, "to have broken through the aura of self-evidence of the Greek concept of 'being,'" as well as the presumed self-evidence of the modern concept of consciousness or "subjectivity"—thus paving the way for a new understanding of "being" as a mode of temporal experience and practical conduct. In this context, Gadamer stresses the significance of Heidegger's famous lecture "What Is Metaphysics?"—treating this lecture as an illustration of (what might be called) a hermeneutics of suspicion. By focusing on the elusive quality of the "being" (the "is") of metaphysics, he writes, the lecture queries "what metaphysics really denotes in contrast to what it claims to be." Understood in this manner, Heidegger's query "acquires the force of a provocation and reveals itself as example of a new conception of interpretation."[12]

By turning to "being" as lived occurrence, Heidegger's work forcefully discloses the intimate linkage between understanding and *praxis* (which had always been implicit in the hermeneutical tradition). As in *Truth and Method*, Heideggerian ontology is correlated with Aristotle's notion of "practical philosophy" (though minus the latter's metaphysics of "substances"). In Gadamer's account, praxis and practical philosophy in the Aristotelian tradition are not the antithesis to theory or theoretical thought but rather intimate a thoughtful conduct. "The semantic field in which the word and concept '*praxis*' have their proper place," he writes, "is not primarily defined by its opposition to theory or as the mere application of a (given) theory." Rather, praxis denotes "the mode of conduct of living beings in the broadest sense." Differently phrased: praxis means "the actuation of life (*energeia*) of anything alive—anything that displays in some fashion life, a mode or conduct of life (*bios*)." To be sure, in contrast to animal behavior, human conduct is distinguished by a certain measure of deliberation and the employment of language and symbols. The most important distinction, however, prevails between practical conduct and mere instrumental fabrication or technical production (*poiesis, technē*). In Gadamer's words: "Practical philosophy is determined by the line drawn between the practical insight of a freely choosing person, on the one hand, and the acquired skill of an expert (which Aristotle names *technē*), on the other." Hence, practical philosophy has to do "not with readily learnable crafts and skills" but rather "with what is fitting for an individual as citizen and what constitutes his/her civic virtue (*arête*)." At this point, the connection between praxis and hermeneutics emerges clearly into view. To quote a crucial passage of the essay:

The knowledge that guides action is essentially called for by the concrete situations in which we need to choose the fitting response (*das Tunliche*)—and no skillful technique can spare us the needed deliberation and decision. As a result, practical philosophy seeking to cultivate this practical ability is neither theoretical science (in the style of mathematics) nor expert know-how (in the sense of mastering technical processes), but a knowledge of a special kind. [As in the case of the hermeneutical circle] this knowledge must arise from *praxis* and, though moving through various generalizations, must relate itself back to *praxis*.[13]

Hermeneutics and Intercultural Dialogue

From Gadamer's perspective, hermeneutics is related not only to practical conduct in general but also to such conduct in a given time and place. In our time of globalization, when different societies and cultures are pushed closer and closer together, hermeneutical understanding is bound to transcend local contexts and to acquire a crosscultural or transnational significance. At this point, members of a given society or culture are called on to interpret not only the modalities of their own tradition but also the complex lineaments of quite alien texts and life-forms. To make headway in this endeavor, individuals and groups have to bring to the encounter their own "fore-meanings" or preunderstandings and then expose them to correction or revision in an interactive (or dialogical) process of give-and-take. Gadamer is keenly attentive to these cultural issues in some of his later writings, especially *Legacy of Europe*, a text responsive to the ongoing process of European unification. For Gadamer, Europe represents a model of "unity in diversity" that is characteristic of hermeneutical dialogue in which, coming from distinctly different backgrounds, each partner seeks to discern the other's meaning. The deeper philosophical and hermeneutical significance of Europe, he observes, resides not in its presumed "universality" but in its multicultural and multilingual composition, in its historical practice of "cohabitation with otherness in a narrow space." In our time, this cohabitation can provide a lesson for humanity at large, for an evolving ecumenical world culture. In his words: "To live with the other, as the other of the other—this basic human task applies to the micro- as well as to the macro-level. Just as each of us learns to live with the other in the process of individual maturation, a similar learning process holds true for larger communities, for nations and states."[14]

Just as in the case of hermeneutical dialogue, the point of intercultural encounter is not to reach a bland consensus or uniformity of beliefs but to foster a progressive learning process involving possible transformation. For this to happen, local or indigenous traditions must be neither jettisoned nor congealed (or essentialized). As Gadamer points out, the role of local or indigenous traditions is endemic to the "hermeneutical circle," with its emphasis on fore-meanings or prejudgments, which are seen as corrigible but *not* expendable starting points of understanding. In a similar fashion, participants in cross-cultural encounter are expected neither to erase themselves (in a vain attempt to "go native") nor to appropriate and subjugate the other's difference; rather, the point is to achieve a shared appreciation and recognition of differences (what Heidegger calls "letting-be"). In Gadamer's words: "Where the goal is not [unilateral] mastery or control, we are liable to experience the otherness of others precisely against the backdrop of our own pre-judgments. The highest and most elevated aim we can strive for in this context is to partake in the other, to share the other's alterity." The stakes in this encounter are high, both for individual societies and for humanity at large. In fact, "the future survival of humankind" (he says) may depend on the proper cultivation of cross-cultural understanding and dialogue and, more particularly, on "our readiness not to utilize the immense resources of power and technical efficiency [accumulated in some states] but to pause in front of the other's otherness—the otherness of nature as well as that of historically grown cultures of peoples and countries." If we are able to do the latter, a transformative and humanizing learning experience may result, for "we may then learn to experience otherness and human others as the 'other of ourselves' in order to partake in one another (*aneinander teilzugewinnen*)."[15]

As Gadamer leaves no doubt, his observations are not narrowly tailored to European integration but are relevant to broader global developments. Although initially triggered by Western colonialism, social and political ferment now engulfs countries around the world. "What we are witnessing," he writes, "is in truth a global process which has been unleashed by the end of colonialism and the emancipation of the former members" of European empires. The central issue today is no longer Europe but "the cultural changes produced by the global economy and the world-wide network of communications." In this situation, many societies are engaged in the difficult search for a mode of life capable of reconciling "their own traditions and the deeply rooted values of their life-world with Western-style economic [and technological] progress" or advancement; "large segments of humanity" are now facing this agonizing dilemma.[16] In an interview with an Indian political thinker conducted a few years before his death, Gadamer clearly pinpoints the global significance of hermeneutical understanding. "The human solidarity that I envisage," he states, "is not a global uniformity but unity in diversity [another name for integral pluralism]. We must learn to appreciate and tolerate pluralities, multiplicities, cultural differences." As he frankly concedes, such an appreciation is in short supply and is actually undermined by the rampant power politics pursued by military-industrial complexes: "The hegemony or unchallengeable power of any one single nation . . . is dangerous for humanity; it would go against human freedom." Hence, the unity in diversity that has been a European legacy must today become a global formula; it must be "extended to the whole world—to include China, India, and also Muslim cultures. Every culture, every people has something distinctive to offer for the solidarity and well-being of humanity."[17]

To flesh out and corroborate Gadamer's perspective, I invoke here the testimony of two thinkers friendly to his perspective—the first directly, the second indirectly so. The first is Canadian political philosopher Charles Taylor. Following in Gadamer's footsteps, Taylor has underscored the importance of hermeneutical interpretation both for philosophy as such and for the academic practice of the human and social sciences.[18] Moving beyond the confines of textual exegesis, Taylor has ventured into the domain of intercultural understanding and dialogue, concentrating in particular on the difference between the traditional Western conception of selfhood and the Buddhist notion of "no-self" or "emptiness" of self (*anatta, sunyata*), together with the contrasting social visions deriving from this difference.[19] Significantly, Taylor has also tackled one of the persistent charges leveled against hermeneutics: that "understanding everything means condoning everything," such that hermeneutics is left devoid of critical ethical standards. As he points out in any essay specifically dealing with intersubjective and intercultural "recognition," understanding others or other cultures does not always entail acceptance. What another culture has in its favor is only a "presumption of worth"—a presumption calling for attentive study but capable of being dislodged or defeated through contestation. To be sure, once hermeneutical understanding is seen not as a neutral occurrence but—with Gadamer and Aristotle—as an ethical praxis, understanding is already inhabited by an ethical criterion (and does not need to be supplemented by borrowings from "critical theory," as Paul Ricoeur has sometimes intimated).[20]

The other thinker more indirectly or distantly related to hermeneutics is John Dewey, who is sometimes called "America's philosopher of democracy." In large measure, Dewey's so-called pragmatism can actually be seen as a practical philosophy displaying distinct affinities with Gadamerian hermeneutics. A central parallel resides in the refusal to divorce thinking from doing, in the effort to link theory and praxis under the rubric of lived experience. Together with Gadamer (and Heidegger), Dewey rejected the legacy of Cartesian rationalism focused on the cogito, together with its corollary, the "spectator theory of knowledge," which exiles the observer from the context of human being-in-the-world. In opposing that theory, he did not opt for a crude empiricism or positivism but rather insisted that sense data or sensory phenomena are perceived in a semantic frame of significance—a frame provided by language and symbolization (and hence in need of interpretation). Together with Gadamer (and again Heidegger), Dewey did not subscribe to a static metaphysics of essences but preferred a dynamic ontology in which being and temporality converge in an ongoing process of the disclosure of possibilities. Most important, human life for Dewey was not a solitary venture but was basically formed in the crucible of interhuman "interactions" or "transactions"—a crucible closely connected with communication, dialogue, and contestation. As in the case of Gadamer's hermeneutics, social interactions for Dewey were a mode of praxis (in the Aristotelian sense) and as such were imbued with ethical connotations. This aspect is illustrated in his presentation of society as an ethical community and especially in his depiction of democracy as the "idea" or "ideal" of community life—an idea constantly in the process of improvement or perfection.[21]

Given my concern here with intercultural understanding, there is another parallel between the two thinkers that deserves to be highlighted. Dewey was at no point a fervent nationalist nor a supporter of rigid friend-enemy distinctions (as formulated by Carl Schmitt). This aspect is particularly evident in his essay "Nationalizing Education," written during a time of war. The essay sharply distinguishes between a benign and a destructive sense of nationalism or patriotism. Too often, he writes, the development of a sense of national unity has been "accompanied by dislike, by hostility, to all without." What happens is that "skillful politicians and other self-seekers" know how "to play cleverly upon patriotism and upon ignorance of other peoples, to identify nationalism with latent hatred of other nations." Especially during wartime, many influential people "attempt to foster the growth of an inclusive nationalism by appeal to our fears, our suspicions, our jealousies and our latent hatreds." Such people like to measure patriotism by "our readiness to meet other nations in destructive war rather than our fitness to cooperate with them in constructive tasks of peace."[22] In contrast to this outlook, Dewey upholds the prospect of a global ecumenism that does not erase local or national loyalties but uses them as a springboard for intercultural cooperation. "We are faced," he states, "by the difficulty of developing the good aspect of nationalism without its evil side: of developing a nationalism which is the friend and not the foe of internationalism," which is a matter "of ideas, of emotions, of intellectual and moral dispositions."[23] As it seems to me, this prospect is not far removed from, and even coincides with, Gadamer's vision of a global "unity in diversity"—a unity not imposed by "one single nation"—and his plea that "the future survival of humankind" may depend on our willingness to engage dialogically with others on both the personal level and the level of larger human communities and cultures.

Merleau-Ponty and Intercorporeal Engagement

To elaborate further, I now turn to another cross-cultural thinker roughly of Gadamer's generation: French philosopher Maurice Merleau-Ponty. What renders Merleau-Ponty's work particularly important in the present context is his opposition to an idealistic consensualism and his insistence on the linkage between dialogue and embodiment. As he continually emphasized, dialogue is not simply a cerebral process or an abstract "meeting of minds" but rather involves a concrete existential and bodily engagement among participants. This point is made particularly forcefully in his essay titled "Dialogue and the Perception of the Other" contained in *The Prose of the World* (assembled posthumously by his friend Claude Lefort). Distinguishing between a purely abstract, logical algorithm and a concrete encounter between human beings, Merleau-Ponty states boldly: "Alongside the analytic truth espoused by the algorithm and leaving aside the possibility of the algorithm's being detached from the thinking life in which it is born, we affirm a truth of transparency, recovery, and recollection in which we participate—not insofar as we think *the same thing* but insofar as we are, each in his own way, moved and touched by it." This being "moved and touched" in an encounter cannot and should not be understood as a simple intellectual convergence but rather as a kind of mutual embroilment and trespass: "the trespass of oneself upon the other and of the other upon me."[24]

In his essay, Merleau-Ponty first turns to the "silent relationship with the other" as a prologue to the understanding of interactive speech. In opposition to many writers on "intersubjectivity," he considers it "not sufficiently noted that the other is never directly present face to face." In effect, the interlocutor or adversary is "never quite localized: his voice, his gesticulations, his twitches, are only symptoms, a sort of stage effect, a ceremony." Their producer is "so well masked that I am quite surprised when my own responses carry over." What comes to the fore here is that the other's "self" is not preconstituted and exists neither before nor somehow behind the voice but rather emerges in the encounter itself, in the inchoate relationship being forged. "The other, in my eyes," Merleau-Ponty writes, "is always on the margin of what I see and hear, he is this side of me, he is beside or behind me, but he is not in that place which my look flattens and empties of any 'interior.'" This insight leads him to one of the stunning formulations that are a trademark of his existential phenomenology: "Myself and the other are like two *nearly* concentric circles which can be distinguished only by a slight and mysterious slippage. This alliance is perhaps what will enable us to understand the relation to the other that is inconceivable if I try to approach him directly, like a sheer cliff."[25]

In the encounter with another human being, the other is both my partner or accomplice and different from or nonabsorbable by me. "I give birth," Merleau-Ponty writes; "this other is made from my flesh and blood and yet is no longer me. How is that possible?" The solution to the riddle must be found in the realization that the difference I encounter is not only external but also internal, that somehow I myself am inhabited by difference. "There is," we read, "*a myself which is other*, which dwells elsewhere and deprives me of my central location." At this point, the roles of the seeing subject and what is seen are "exchanged and reversed." For Merleau-Ponty, the central issue is to understand "how I can make myself into two, how I can decenter myself" or become decentered—how the experience of the other is always at the same time "a response to myself." Like the other human being, the self is not a compact entity or thing; nor is it a self-transparent mind (or cogito). From this angle, there cannot be a fixed or stable human "nature" nor a self-contained "identity." In lieu of the atomistic units found in an imaginary "state of nature," all one finds is a fluid cohabitation in a dwelling place to which none of the partners has privileged access or the unfailing passkey: "It is in the very depths of myself that this strange articulation with the other is fashioned. The mystery of the other is nothing but the mystery of myself." What is intimated here is an identity constituted by noncoincidence, but unable to escape elsewhere (outside the world).[26]

Ultimately, the dwelling place of which Merleau-Ponty speaks is not an individual nor even a collective "project" but rather a shared experience where seeing and being seen, speaking and being heard, come together. It is the very bodily experience, he says, that marks "my hold on the world" and makes me capable of perceiving another imprinted with the same "hold" or bond. "As long as it adheres to my body like the tunic of Nessus," he continues in another vintage formulation, "the world exists not only for me but for everyone who makes gestures toward it. There is [perhaps not a universality of reason but] a universality of feeling or sensation—and it is upon this that our relationship rests, the generalization of my body, the perception of the other." Thus, the notion of an interpersonal (and intercultural) relation for Merleau-Ponty is incomplete or inadequate as long as it does not take into account our embodiment or "intercorporeality." This means that there would be no others for me "if I did not have a body, and if they had no body through which they could slip into my field [or world], multiplying it from within, and oriented to the same world as I." To be sure, the notion of a "same world" here does not mean a uniform or identical world but only a plural and loosely shared world, because everyone opens onto it in different ways: "A field tends of itself to multiply, because it is the opening through which, as a body, I am 'exposed' to the world."[27]

At this point, Merleau-Ponty turns (or returns) to language, and first of all to the "silent language" of sensations and bodily interactions. The problem of understanding words is no greater or lesser than the task of understanding "how the movements of a body patterned into gestures or actions can reach us" or "how we are able to find in these spectacles anything other than what we have put into them." The solution, for Merleau-Ponty (as for Heidegger), consists in the bracketing of a constituting ego, of a self-contained mind or subjectivity. What we have to grasp, he notes, is that "our sensibility to the world, our synchronized relationship to it—that is, our body, the thesis underlying all our experiences—removes from our existence the density of an absolute and singular act, making a transferable signification of our 'corporeality,' and creating a 'common situation.'" The same process operates in speech and especially in reciprocal speech or dialogue. With regard to "the particular gesture of speech," we read, "the solution lies in recognizing that, in the experience of dialogue, the other's speech manages to reach us in our significations, and that our words, as the replies attest, reach in him his significations." This mutual encroachment testifies to the power of language, which is in principle inexhaustible, and to our participation in a shared "cultural world"—or at least our effort to foster communication across and beyond sedimented cultural worlds. In this sense, the language we speak is something like a dispersed or "anonymous corporeality" that we share across boundaries.[28]

In this connection, Merleau-Ponty introduces a thought that points beyond neutral communication in the direction of ethical and political practice. The "expressive" operation, and speech in particular, establishes a "common situation" that is not merely a juxtaposition or a relationship of knowing but "a community of *doing*." At this point, the common world fostered by language involves not only a sharing of ideas or points of view but also a sharing of practices, which includes a willingness to learn about unfamiliar practices, rituals, rites, and customs. Willingness to learn about such practices, in turn, involves a form of existential participation or engagement—a participation in past memories, present agonies, and future hopes and aspirations. Clearly, such participation moves beyond the level of narrow self-interest and idle curiosity, proceeding in the direction of ethical well-being and a shared concern with the "good life." In this respect, Merleau-Ponty joins Gadamer, as well as Taylor and Dewey, in the endeavor to foster a "great community" without hegemony, exploitation, and oppression—a community that has to be dialogically and differentially cultivated on a global level. To recall the statement made by Gadamer in his interview with the Indian colleague: "The human solidarity that I envisage is not a global uniformity but unity in diversity. We must learn to appreciate and tolerate pluralities, multiplicities, cultural differences." To this one might add a statement by Merleau-Ponty about cross-cultural learning in an essay dealing with the emerging global space-time matrix in our era:

> Civilizations lacking our philosophical and economic equipment take on an instructive value. It is not a matter of going in search of truth or salvation in what falls short of [Western] science or philosophical awareness, nor of dragging chunks of mythology as such into our thinking, but of acquiring . . . a sense of the theoretical and practical problems *our* institutions are faced with, and of rediscovering the existential field they were born in and that their long success has led us to forget. The Orient's "childishness" has something to teach us, if it were nothing more than the narrowness of our "adult" ideas.[29]

7. A Man for All Seasons
Mahatma Gandhi's Integral Pluralism

> A high order of intelligence is not incompatible with religious belief.
>
> —Erasmus

As the saying goes: the center does not hold. If one were to highlight a central feature of the modern age, one could plausibly point to its centrifugal momentum, its tendency toward fragmentation. In the intellectual domain, the tendency is patently evident in the process of specialization, the relentless segregation of fields of knowledge. However, the trend exceeds the knowledge domain. Together with other thinkers of his time, the philosopher Hegel saw modernity marked by radical "diremptions" or divisions (*Entzweiungen*)—divisions between knowledge and action, thinking and feeling, private self-interest and the common good—with the prospects of reconciliation growing steadily dimmer. Since Hegel's time, things have fallen apart even more. Today, every kind of human pursuit has gained, and insists on, absolute autonomy. The market economy has unleashed a scramble for private wealth that pushes out of sight all ethical or religious considerations. As a corollary of globalization, politics—equated with the sheer struggle for power—pursues vast planetary (and even galactic) ambitions. In the meantime, ordinary people—sidelined by both politics and economics—are left to the comforts of private self-indulgence and the endless acquisition of consumer goods. Ethics and religious faith are similarly sequestered or privatized, unless they are released from their ghetto for the sake of a forced synthesis (sometimes labeled "fundamentalism").[1]

The diremptions of modernity have clear effects on personal life and (what is called) the "human condition." In the realm of personal life, the effects surface in the form of internal splits, psychic pathologies, or personality disorders. Rare are the individuals who are able to develop as well as harmonize their different faculties—people the Indian scriptures call stable or *sattva* because, by bringing "all their senses into harmony," they maintain stable balance.[2] In recent history, one prominent individual illustrates the *sattva* quality in exemplary fashion: the Mahatma Gandhi, a statesman, erudite intellectual, man of letters, and devotee of the arts, as well as an ethicist and person of faith. To profile more clearly, at least for Western readers, the Mahatma's *sattva* character, I compare him in the following pages with an earlier figure well known in European history, a figure who witnessed and endured the birth pangs of modern diremptions: Sir Thomas More. Like Gandhi, More was a capable statesman, an intellectual, and a prolific writer; he was a man of affairs, a patron of the arts, and also a deeply ethical and religious person. In a famous stage play, Robert Bolt celebrated Thomas More as "a man for all seasons." The same description also applies to his Indian counterpart. Not long ago, the distinguished political theorist Anthony Parel, well known for his earlier writings on Gandhi and Machiavelli, published a book that ascribes to the Mahatma a similarly balanced disposition: *Gandhi's Philosophy and the Quest for Harmony*.[3] Following some remarks on More, I reflect in some detail on this study of Gandhi's work. At this point, however, all I want to do is stress their common struggle and their common fate: both tried to preserve a certain balance between pursuits—especially the pursuits of politics and ethics—and both ultimately fell victim to the machinations of power released from ethics: More to the cabals of a ruthless king, and Gandhi to the zeal of a nationalist fanatic.

A Man for All Seasons

In his stage play, Bolt at one point has Thomas More speak these lines: "Some men think the earth is round, others think it flat; it is a matter capable of question. But if it is flat, will the king's command make it round? And if it is round, will the king's command flatten it?"[4] In these lines, More shows himself flexibly tolerant in matters where opinions might reasonably differ, but staunchly opposed to the idea of allowing truth and falsity, right and wrong, to be settled by arbitrary sovereign fiat. Thus, More maintained and insisted on the distinction between rightness and power, between truth and governmental authority, but not in the sense of disparaging politics and government altogether. What he rejected was the usurpation of all domains of life by political power, that is, the king's attempt to extend a totalizing monopoly over ethics, law, and religious faith. Throughout his play, Bolt shows More anxious to preserve his loyalty to his country and government and not to appear as a reckless rebel willing to violate social bonds. In the end, his act of defiance was meant to safeguard the country's deeper constitutional order against royal arrogance. As Bolt's More states shortly after being sentenced to death: "This indictment is grounded in an act of Parliament which is directly repugnant to the law of god. The king in Parliament cannot bestow [on the king] the supremacy of the church which is a spiritual supremacy," especially since the latter immunity is "promised both in Magna Carta and the king's own coronation oath!" This final apology is added: "I am the king's true subject and pray for him and all the realm . . . I do no harm, I say no harm, I think no harm."[5]

That More was not in principle opposed to politics and government is evident from his own illustrious career of public service. Born in 1478 and having studied law in London, More was admitted to the bar in 1501 and entered Parliament in 1504. His public career was briefly interrupted due to certain altercations with King Henry VII but regained momentum speedily during the reign of Henry VIII. In 1510 he was appointed undersheriff of London, and during the ensuing years he became one of the king's trusted friends and companions. In 1518 he was chosen a member of the Privy Council, and he was knighted in 1521. A few years later he was elevated to the position of Speaker of the House of Commons and Chancellor of the Duchy of Lancaster. The high point of his career came in 1529 when he was made Lord Chancellor, a position he held until his break with the king in 1532 (three years before his execution).[6] In all the positions he held, More showed himself capable, industrious, fair-minded, and never servile or obsequious. His dispute with Henry VII arose over his unwillingness to approve excessive expenditures for the king's military adventures. As undersheriff in London he gained a reputation for being fair and equitable and especially for being a caring protector of the poor. His concern for the underprivileged extended to foreigners, as was evident in his condemnation of antiforeign riots in London in 1517. As Speaker of the House of Commons, More helped establish the parliamentary privilege of free speech—a privilege that was subsequently subjected to severe tests. Shortly before his elevation to Lord Chancellor, he refused to sanction the king's divorce from Catherine of Aragon, just as a few years later he refused to endorse the king's marriage to Anne Boleyn. He also refused to swear the "oath of supremacy" and to accept the Act of Succession, proceedings that, in his view, violated both religious faith and common law.

Although enjoying enormous prestige for several decades, More was never dazzled by public acclaim or the glitter of the court. As he once remarked to a friend: "I may tell you I have no cause to be proud of; for if my head would win [the king] a castle in France, it should not fail to go off."[7] In large measure, More's resistance to being dazzled can be traced to his many other interests and endeavors—pursuits that helped him keep all things in perspective. In addition to his political activities, he was a learned intellectual and prominent writer who enjoyed the friendship of some of the leading "humanists" of his time. As a youth, he was educated at some of the best schools in London, where he avidly studied Greek and Latin literature. During that time he wrote some comedies in the revived classical style of the Renaissance. Tellingly, one of his first publications was an English translation of a biography of Italian humanist Pico della Mirandola. In later years, he became a close companion of the Dutch humanist Erasmus, who often visited him in England. Together the two friends delighted in classical studies and, among other things, wrote Latin translations of the works of the satirist Lucian. One of Erasmus's own major works, the satirical *Encomium Moriae* (Praise of Folly, 1509), was dedicated to More; in turn, More's most famous literary work, *Utopia* (1516), was published under Erasmus's guidance and supervision in Louvain. Despite increasingly heavy political burdens, More's literary endeavors never ceased. Even at the most difficult time, when imprisoned in the Tower of London awaiting execution, he composed a text reminiscent of the best classical spirit of Seneca: *A Dialogue of Comfort against Tribulation* (1534). The desperate circumstances did not dim More's literary flair or his serene wit, as demonstrated by the jocular multiculturalism of the text's subtitle: "Written by a Hungarian in Latin, and translated out of the Latin into French, and out of the French into English."[8]

Without doubt, *Utopia* is More's most well-known literary legacy; it is also intensely controverted and widely misunderstood. Following in the footsteps of Plato's *Republic* and later imitators, the book ostensibly seeks to offer a picture of an ideal political regime and a perfectly constituted society. This intent is confirmed by the book's original title: "Concerning the Best State of a Commonwealth and the New Island of Utopia." Yet on almost every page, the high seriousness of the intent is undermined or held in check by witticisms or satirical gestures, as manifest by this passage on the title page: "A Truly Golden Handbook, no less Beneficial than Entertaining." Interpreters of the text have tended to place the accent on either its uplifting or its entertaining quality. For some readers, *Utopia* presents a blueprint or panacea for a totally perfect (perhaps totalitarian) society; for others, the book is sheer satire with no serious purpose at all. What both sides ignore is a third possibility: the critical exposure of both totalizing management and total fragmentation and corruption. Following the collapse of communism and "real-life" socialism, it has become widely fashionable to disparage all attempts at social and political improvement as dangerous "utopian" schemes, or else as mere *jeux d'esprit*. However, does the collapse of false ideals justify by itself the status quo? Does the demise of an oppressive collectivism by itself sanction rampant individual greed and unrestrained lust for power? Seen in this light, *Utopia* can be read as neither a coercive blueprint nor a merely entertaining joke but as a text stimulating critical thought by pointing to "utopia" as an arena of untapped possibilities. Robert Adams, one of the book's editors, pinpoints the book's critical thrust in this manner. The book, he writes,

> propounds a set of riddles which every sincere man who enters public life is bound to ask himself, whether he is living in early-capitalist England, late-capitalist America, or any society dominated by the money-mad and the authority-intoxicated. He must think: What good can I do as an honorable man in a society of power-hungry individuals? What evil will I have to condone as the price of the good I accomplish?
>
> Surely these are questions for all times and all seasons.[9]

Another quality that allowed More to keep things in perspective was his deep religiosity. His religious faith, to be sure, was never that of the mindless zealot or fanatic, but it was profound nonetheless. Together with Erasmus he was able to combine erudition and piety (*eruditio et pietas*) in such a manner that they mutually nurtured and deepened each other. As a young man, at a time when he was intensely involved in classical studies, he underwent (what has been called) a "spiritual crisis." Although interested in, and drawn to, many pursuits, he felt at the time that his true calling might be in the priesthood or a monastery. Accordingly, he went into retreat and, without taking vows, spent some four years in seclusion, seeking (as one author says) "through prayer and penance to learn his true vocation." In the end, he was persuaded by his confessor and other mentors that his proper course of action was in public life and as a married man. Nevertheless, during his years at the court and in the company of courtiers, he retained his yearning for spiritual retreat, for periods of solitary prayer and meditation, especially during his busiest times. It was this persistent yearning (one can venture to say) that, above all, shielded him from the temptations of power and worldly ambition. Toward the end of his life, while in the Tower of London, he reportedly told his daughter: "I assure thee . . . that if it had not been for my wife and you, my children, whom I account the chief part of my charge, I would not have failed long before this to have closed myself in as strait a room as this, and straiter too." More's final words on the scaffold were these: "The king's good servant, but God's first."[10]

All the recorded episodes of More's life, together with his ability to keep his endeavors in balance, amply support Bolt's chosen title for his play: *A Man for All Seasons*. More's own contemporaries and near contemporaries, I believe, would have endorsed that choice. Dean Swift placed More in the company of Socrates, Epaminondas, and the younger Cato—a stellar group whom "all the ages of the world" could not surpass. Others praised his kindness, integrity, and courage. But perhaps the finest tribute stems from his friend Erasmus, who, in a letter to Ulrich von Hutten, praised More not only for his statesmanship and literary talents but also for his conduct in everyday life, especially as a family man:

> There is not any man living so loving to his children than he, and he loves his old wife as if she were a young maid; and

such is the excellency of his temper that, whatsoever happens that could not be helped, he loves it as if nothing could happen more happily. . . . I should rather call his house a school or university of Christian religion, for there is none therein but reads and studies the liberal sciences; their special care is piety and virtue; there is no quarrelling or intemperate words heard; none seem idle . . . everybody performs his duty, yet there is always alacrity; neither is sober mirth anything wanting.[11]

What Erasmus is describing here, I believe, is a stable and balanced character—the kind of character the Indian scriptures called *sattva*, a disposition marked by equanimity and serene wisdom. Most revealing, perhaps, is the letter's reference to "sober mirth," indicating a happy and cheerful disposition that is as far removed from gloomy pedantry as from silly clowning. As one author comments (correctly, in my view): "Contrary to a strange but persistent opinion, goodness is not synonymous with gloom; sanctity is rather the companion of 'sober mirth.'" And as a corollary: "A high order of intelligence is not incompatible with religious belief and a life consistent with that belief."[12]

Gandhi and the Goals of Life

Moving briskly across a few centuries and into a very different cultural setting, we come to a man whose character was equally marked by sobriety and mirth, by a combination of high intelligence and faith: the Mahatma Gandhi. The literature devoted to the Mahatma is daunting and nearly overwhelming, and the emphases vary greatly. Many studies (perhaps the majority) devoted to him stress his political activities and public life; a large number of studies accentuate the aspects of nonviolence (*ahimsa*), civil disobedience, and transformative change relying on "soul-force" (*satyagraha*). What is seldom explored in the literature, however, is the linkage between politics and public life, on the one hand, and nonviolence and "soul-force," on the other. The former clearly seems to involve an active intervention in the world or the affairs of this world, while the latter seems to presuppose almost a nonintervention and a kind of suffering rather than acting. How is one to reconcile these different orientations or pursuits? It seems to me that the key to the secret passageway linking these dimensions can be found in another classical Indian teaching: that regarding the so-called goals of life or *purusharthas*. In his recent book devoted to the Mahatma, Anthony Parel focuses precisely on the *purusharthas*, which, in the Indian tradition, number four: pleasure (*kama*), economic and political achievement (*artha*), ethical virtue (*dharma*), and salvation (*moksha*). What Parel's book highlights, above all, is the balanced or *sattva* quality of Gandhi's character and how his entire life, including his politics, was essentially a "quest for harmony" among the goals of life.

As Parel outlines in his preface, Gandhi's deepest striving was to foster a reconciliation or reintegration of the different dimensions of human life that, in modernity, were increasingly drifting apart or colliding with one another. What Gandhi sought to uncover or revive in all his endeavors, he writes, was "a basic harmony underlying all the fundamental human strivings—the strivings for wealth, power, pleasure, ethical goodness, beauty, and spiritual transcendence." The fact that this quest was carried out in the midst of modernity—an age marked by the growing "compartmentalization of life-issues"—renders Gandhi's work "truly exemplary" for his own and subsequent generations. Part and parcel of this quest for harmony was the effort to come to terms with modern secularism. In Parel's words, Gandhi sought to forge "a moral link" between the contemplative or spiritual life—deeply embedded in Indian culture and tradition—and the "modern secular life" as manifest especially in economics and politics. Here again, he moved against the dominant current, which, as a corollary of scientific advancement, sought to emancipate politics and economics from ethical and spiritual constraints. For Gandhi, this current was lopsided and intrinsically deficient: by placing its trust entirely in scientific and economic progress and political power, the trend ignored and even denied "the need for a healthy spiritual life and for the public recognition of the sacred" as supplements to "sound economics, wise legislation, free elections, and fair adjudication." Hence, relying on classical Indian scriptures and especially on the theory of the four *purusharthas*, Gandhi aimed to establish a "working harmony" among the political, economic, ethical, aesthetic, and spiritual pursuits and thereby remedy the "malaise of modern secularism." This quest for balance, in turn, stood in the service of one of Gandhi's most cherished goals: the promotion of peace through justice, fairness, and nonviolence. "Peace within the individual, and peace between states, between religions, and between civilizations," Parel states, "depended ultimately on this harmony."[13]

Although relying on classical Indian teachings, Gandhi's endeavor was not simply nostalgic or antiquarian but involved a serious rethinking of traditional concepts so as to render them relevant to modern times. In many ancient cultures, classical teachings were sometimes ambivalent and confusing and lent themselves to very different interpretations. This was particularly true of the doctrine of the *purusharthas*. According to Parel, the most important classical texts preserved, and even insisted on, the harmonious pursuit of the goals of life; this was evident in the great *Arthashastras* and *Dharmashastras*. As K. J. Shah has convincingly shown in the case of Kautilya's *Arthashastra*, the four goals of life made sense only in their interrelation; when separated from one another, the pursuit of pleasure (*kama*) was bound to degenerate into lust and the striving for achievement (*artha*) into greed, just as virtue (*dharma*) could turn into mechanical ritual and salvation (*moksha*) into a form of escapism.[14] It was only in later periods that this harmonious relation fell apart and gave way to conflict. Parel attributes this decay mainly to the so-called renouncer (*sramana*) movements that elevated *moksha* above all else and even made *dharma* less accessible. As he writes: "In Buddhism, as in ascetic Brahminism and Jainism, *artha* and *kama* came to be marginalized to the point of being treated as negative values," adding, "The radical separation of *moksha* and *nirvana* from the other *purusharthas* had disastrous consequences for Indian civilization taken as a whole." Against this background, Gandhi emerges as a major figure—perhaps *the* major modern figure—struggling against past decay and restoring harmony to the goals of life: "He belongs to the group of forward-looking thinkers who want to explore new ways in which the theory of the *purusharthas* might be made to work." Having overcome the older *sramana* ways, what comes into view is a "new Gandhian paradigm" postulating "the coordinated pursuit of all the *purusharthas*."[15]

Again, Gandhi's effort to restore harmony was not simply backward-looking but contained several innovative features unknown to, or insufficiently developed by, the older tradition. Among these innovations were his opposition to gender biases, his critique of fatalism and fatalistically accepted caste distinctions, and finally his resolute attempt to overcome the gulf between "this-worldly" and "otherworldly" pursuits or between saints and ordinary people. Regarding the first point, Gandhi saw the distinctive quality of human beings as that of their inner spirit or true self (*purusha* or *atman*), a quality that is gender neutral. As he observed at one point: "The word *purusha* should be interpreted in its etymological sense, and not merely to mean 'man': that which dwells in the *pura* (or body) is *purusha*. If we interpret the word *purushartha* in this sense, it can be used equally for men and women."[16] A major obstacle to his restorative effort was the customary association of *karma* with fate, encouraging a fatalistic acceptance of one's condition in life. Here, a major reorientation was required. With divine help, Gandhi insisted, it was possible through struggle to turn the bad consequences of actions (bad *karma*) into a healing and liberating direction. In Parel's words: "*Purushartha* could overcome caste-related disabilities too. If only the Dalits could activate their *purushartha*, nothing in the world, neither fate nor *karma* nor caste, could prevent them from achieving their full potential." The attempt to overcome, or at least to narrow, the gulf between "this world" and nirvana proved to be the most difficult endeavor, because it involved deep metaphysical and quasi-theological quandaries. How, in effect, could the distinction between "appearance" (*maya*) and "reality" (*brahman*), between ignorance (*avidya*) and truth (*satya*), be maintained if this gulf was called into question? Struggling against both worldly and otherworldly opponents, Gandhi stood his ground, arguing that "earnest seekers after *moksha*" could not possibly remain indifferent to the social ills around them. His point, Parel notes, was "that the old distinction between saints and worldly people had lost its meaning. Now it appeared that everyone had a calling to be saints, just as everyone had a calling to be citizens."[17]

The centerpiece of Parel's study is the discussion of the different goals of life and their interpretation or reconstruction by Gandhi. The discussion throughout is erudite and brimming with instructive details. For present purposes, a few highlights of his presentation must suffice. In accord with Gandhi's own lifelong preoccupations, the discussion begins with the domain of *artha*, that is, political and economic activities. In the chapters devoted to *artha,* Gandhi is portrayed as a moderate constitutionalist, a "civic nationalist" (or civic republican) who appreciated, within limits, the role of the modern nation-state and favored a limited form of social and economic equality. To the extent that Gandhi was a nationalist, Parel emphasizes, his was not the ethnic nationalism of the devotees of "Hindutva" nor the religious nationalism of Hindu or Muslim sectarians; rather, it involved a civic-constitutional framework that alone was able to "knit together the Dalits and non-Dalits, and people belonging to different religions, ethnic and language communities." With regard to the modern nation-state, Parel presents Gandhi as upholding not an absolutist Hobbesian Leviathan but a "limited liberal" or rule-of-law state sustained by ethical legitimacy and dedicated to the preservation of "fundamental rights." What Gandhi basically added to the liberal conception was his insistence on supplementing the state with a flourishing "civil society," especially a network of nongovernmental associations. "A good society," we read, "needs both the state (acting through coercive power) and a vibrant civil society (acting through non-violent power)." Another ingredient of a good society was a balanced and equitable economic system where property was regarded not so much as an exclusive private possession but as a social or public "trust," and where individuals were expected "to cultivate the virtue of nonpossessive individualism or *aparigraha.*"[18]

The second life goal treated in Parel's text is *dharma* or virtue, and appropriately so, because the Gandhian conception of moderate constitutionalism has little or no chance of functioning without ethical banisters or moorings. It was in this domain that Gandhi's reconstructive effort was perhaps most innovative and radical. In much of traditional Indian thought, the notion of *dharma* had been linked with different social castes (*varnas*) and different stages of life (*ashramas*), with the result that separate ethical rules applied to people at different social levels and in different age groups. Gandhi completely broke with this tradition (the so-called *varnashramadharma*), denouncing it as a "hideous travesty" of the original meaning of *dharma* and of any viable ethics as such. As a corollary, "untouchability" of the lowest caste was for him an ethical monstrosity and the "greatest blot on Hinduism." In lieu of this flawed tradition, Gandhi upheld the notion of a general or universal ethics (*sadharana dharma*) that grants to all human beings "fundamental rights"—rights that are always linked with corresponding duties and need to be constantly reaffirmed through the practice of "soul-force" or "truth-force" (*satyagraha*). Another important way that Gandhi innovated the tradition was through his stress on nonviolence (*ahimsa*) or nonviolent action, although in this respect, he could rely on some Indian as well as Christian teachings. Nonviolence for Gandhi, Parel points out, was a "moral virtue" that habitually disposes individuals and groups "(a) to resist violence through non-violent means, and (b) to take active steps to resolve conflicts by peaceful techniques." Although firmly attached to this virtue, Gandhi (in Parel's view) did not rigidly adhere to it, preferring instead to distinguish between *ahimsa* as an absolute creed and as a practical policy: "Non-violence as a policy or civic non-violence is what he expects from the average citizen . . . *Satyagraha* is concerned with civic non-violence rather than with the heroic [or absolute] variety, its aim being to secure the good of society rather than the private good of the citizens."[19]

The two remaining goals of life—*kama* and *moksha*—are treated less extensively, and I limit myself to a few comments. In the domain of *kama,* an intriguing and somewhat unexpected dimension is Gandhi's relation to aesthetics and the arts (the latter being traditionally subsumed under the category of pleasure or the pleasurable). Readers here are informed of Gandhi's fondness for music, poetry, and hymn singing; they are also told that he served at one point as president of both the Association of Gujarati Literature and the Association of Hindi Literature. A more problematic and less *kama*-friendly aspect was Gandhi's attitude toward sexuality, given that he practiced nearly lifelong abstinence or celibacy (*brahmacharya*). The practice clearly marginalized *kama* in favor of virtue; by insisting so rigorously on sublimation, Parel comments, Gandhi's attitude was somewhat "inconsistent" with the harmonious pursuit of the *purusharthas*.[20] In the Indian tradition, *moksha* (salvation, liberation) was considered the highest goal and promised complete fulfillment—an idea to which Gandhi subscribed implicitly throughout his life and explicitly in the famous introduction to his 1927 autobiography, where we find this statement: "What I want to achieve—what I have been striving and pining to achieve these thirty years—is self-realization, to see God face to face, to attain *moksha*." As Parel points out, Gandhi was not really concerned with the finer metaphysical or theological points of the concept, limiting himself to its practical application in his own life, the life of a *karma yogin*. In this respect, he could find ample support and inspiration in his favorite text, the Bhagavad Gita, on which he wrote several commentaries in an effort to chart his own innovative reconstruction. "In charting his own course in the interpretation of the *Gita*," Parel states, "Gandhi wanted to avoid the Scylla of doctrinaire secularism and the Charybdis of traditional asceticism. He wanted a course that would affirm the values of the world and *purusharthas*, on the one hand, and those of world-transcending spirituality open to every human being, on the other."[21]

This balanced "middle" course is reaffirmed in the concluding chapter of Parel's book, devoted specifically to the reconciliation of "the political and the spiritual." For Parel, Gandhi was "almost alone among the great teachers of India" in striving for a reconnection between the political and the spiritual life. Departing from a long ascetic (*sramanic*) tradition, he restored *artha*, meaning politics and economics, to prominence among life's goals, circumscribed (to be sure) by the other *purusharthas*. As a mode of activity, *artha* for Gandhi meant a striving for power and wealth, but "within the bounds of ethics (*dharma*) and the requirements of a healthy spiritual life (the pursuit of *moksha*)." Restating a point made earlier in his study, Parel finds the reconnection of politics and spirituality "possible only in a free society—a civic nation presided over by a secular constitutional state" and animated by an ethically sensitive "liberal politics." As he realizes, combining *artha* with spirituality requires more than a preservation of the status quo; it involves or demands some ethical transformation. If lust for power and wealth is to make room for a saner and more just politics and economics, egotism has to be tamed and rechanneled. In the language of the Bhagavad Gita, Arjuna has to become "both a *sthitha-prajña* (person of stable wisdom) and a *bhakta* (devotee of God)." In like manner, the modern citizen is in the position of Arjuna, being called on "to engage in political pursuits in the way he did—through self-discipline and sound piety." Piety, one should note, does not refer here to any religious dogmatism but to a genuine commitment to the search for "truth" (*satya*), which is a synonym for the divine: "Life is a quest for truth, which in turn is a quest for harmony."[22]

Harmony and Strife (Agon)

Parel's book is a remarkable text, offering a wealth of insights for students of Gandhi, of India, and of contemporary politics in both East and West. Perhaps its most prominent feature is the portrayal of Gandhi as a "man for all seasons," as a person of "stable wisdom" managing to correlate worldly and otherworldly, political and spiritual pursuits. In a time of rampant ideological schisms—above all, the schism between radical agnosticism and often fanatical religious revival—the Mahatma emerges as a piously "secular" person, a man whose own deep religiosity is at ease with religious pluralism and the differentiation of public institutions from official creeds. In terms of the Indian doctrine of the *purusharthas,* Parel presents Gandhi as both a traditionalist and a creatively innovative thinker, that is, as a man whose reverence for the past is balanced by the pressing needs of the present and the requirements of the future. It is small wonder that he was a target of criticism among both nostalgic pundits and transcultural modernists and revolutionaries. Among the other admirable features of Parel's study are the discussions devoted to the Bhagavad Gita, to economic "trusteeship," and to literature and the arts. Another important aspect, not previously mentioned, is the distinction between Gandhian-style (integral) pluralism and a radical fragmentation bordering on relativism and incommensurable division—an outlook favored by Isaiah Berlin, among others. Against the latter, Parel marshals the notion of truth (*satya*) not as a possession but as a shared orientation. "*Satyagraha* would not make sense," he writes, "if conflicts did not exist. . . . But in his philosophy conflicts have a common reference point in truth. The *purusha* is open to truth, and each *purushartha* contains within itself a capacity for ultimate harmony with truth."[23]

It is precisely in this area—the relation between harmony and conflict or strife—that some afterthoughts seem appropriate, not in the sense of critical reservations or objections but augmentations of the book's arguments. In my view, the study sometimes accents harmony too strongly, at the expense of struggle and agon. Looking at its dramatic unfolding, Gandhi's life story—like that of Thomas More—was marked not by a great deal of harmony but by intense antagonism and relentless struggle. Like More, Gandhi in his political life had to endure severe hardships and ordeals at the hands of the rulers of the day; while the former languished in the Tower of London before his death, Gandhi spent nearly a third of his life in various prisons, setting an example for some of his later followers, such as Nelson Mandela in South Africa (who was jailed for twenty-eight years). Not all the hardships and sufferings were imposed by the powerful; some were self-inflicted. In an effort to promote social change or a change of heart, Gandhi, as we know, engaged in long periods of fasting, sometimes almost to the point of death. Parel's book is relatively silent on these episodes; nor does it comment on the ordeal Gandhi imposed on himself during the riots in East Bengal and Bihar at the time of the partition (and shortly before his assassination). In a desperate effort to quench the flames of violence, the Mahatma traveled on foot to remote, riot-torn villages, ignoring the frailty of his body and the dangers to himself. In the words of Sheila McDonough: "From this time until his death by assassination in 1948, Gandhi lived his final years in the midst of a sort of hell on earth," for there can scarcely be a worse fate than "outbursts of violence among the very persons one has given one's life to serving."[24]

The picture of an old man walking across rivers and half-collapsed bridges does not fit well with that of a pliant, law-abiding citizen. In Parel's book, Gandhi appears predominantly as a civic nationalist, a defender of the nation-state and its constitutional order—not far removed from the model of liberal proceduralism. Even the practice of *satyagraha*—the struggle for social change through a change of heart—is presented chiefly as a form of "constitutional agitation," as an effort to restore the constitutional rule of law. "The goal of resistance to the state," we read, "was the improved constitutional order, and not the replacement of the state by statelessness."[25] This is all well and good, but the aim to improve the constitutional order sometimes conflicts with formal or legal constitutionalism. During Gandhi's lifetime, India was part of the British Empire and hence part of the British legal and constitutional regime. His relentless campaigns for independence—including the Salt March and the later "Quit India" policy—were conducted in defiance of British law and were considered seditious and unlawful (for which the punishment was imprisonment). A similar predicament can be found in the case of Nelson Mandela, whose struggle against apartheid was launched during a time when apartheid was part and parcel of the legal system and "constitutional order" of South Africa. In the case of Thomas More, the Act of Succession and the Act of Supremacy (of king over church) were cornerstones of the English legal order at the time; because of his refusal to endorse these acts, he was charged with treason and executed. Hence, as one can see, the endeavor to "improve" an existing constitutional order involves more than a legal maneuver; it can be, and often is, a matter of life and death.

That Gandhi was not satisfied with legality and formal constitutionalism is also demonstrated by his harsh critique of the internal functioning of the British system, which was (and still is) considered by many to be the epitome of a good constitutional order. His early work *Hind Swaraj* (available in a volume edited by Anthony Parel) contains a long litany of the ills afflicting the English parliamentary regime, ranging from partisan bickering and the venality of parliamentarians to the power lust of the political elite. If such was the character of the British system, Gandhi did not want independent India to imitate it.[26] He maintained his reservations and suspicions regarding formal constitutionalism for the rest of his life. It may be quite correct, as Parel affirms, that Gandhi was not an opponent of the modern state, including the structure of the Indian state after independence; however, his approval was somewhat halfhearted and entirely contingent on the fostering of a public ethos undergirding and circumscribing the role of state structures. As Bhikhu Parekh has shown, during the last years of his life, when independent India was just emerging, Gandhi was engaged in an effort to supplement governmental structures with a civil society–based association or movement called *Loka Sevak Sangh* (Association for Service to People), entrusted with the task of promoting moral and political awakening and ethical transformation. In his conception, the two institutions of the state and the *Sangh* were to be neither entirely divorced nor conflated but to function in creative tension. In Parekh's words: while accepting the state as an "essentially *legal* institution," moral and spiritual authority—deriving from "the trust and confidence of the people"—belonged, in Gandhi's view, to civil society associations, especially the *Sangh*. Although acknowledging briefly the role of civil society in Gandhi's thought, Parel underestimates (in my view) his genuine suspicions about the modern state, dismissing Parekh and other writers focusing on these suspicions somewhat briskly as defenders of a "stateless society."[27]

What emerges here is the integral role of tension and struggle in any genuine quest for harmony. Clearly, the latter cannot simply mean adjustment or accommodation. If truth is the lodestar of the *purusharthas*—as Parel rightly claims—then cultivating them necessarily involves a struggle against untruth, injustice, and oppression. In terms of his study, the modern state for Gandhi was basically a "coercive state" or an instrument of coercion, whereas *satyagraha*, proceeding from civil society, involved resistance to unjust coercion. But can one always harmoniously combine coercion and resistance to coercion? To take a historical example: could harmony ultimately prevail between Henry VIII and Thomas More? If the relation necessarily involves tension and strife, then *satyagraha*—though preferably relying on nonviolence—cannot always be law-abiding and has to take, at least occasionally, a "heroic" stance exceeding the "average" grumbling against the state.[28] These comments seem particularly relevant for the contemporary period, when the bent toward fragmentation and diremptions (*Entzweiungen*) characterizing the modern age has reached full fruition. In this situation, any quest for harmony has to start by acknowledging or being cognizant of the prevailing differentiations and dilemmas, without necessarily acquiescing in the status quo. What follows from this acknowledgment is the realization that steps toward truth are bound to be difficult and tension ridden, requiring the truth seeker to be on guard against the pitfalls of both despair and the lure of premature totalization or synthesis. Differently phrased: holistic unity under modern circumstances can arise only out of great multiplicity—just as, in contemporary art, harmony tends to arise out of dissonance.[29]

The aspect of tension or strife actually seems to be hidden or slumbering in the traditional doctrine of the *purusharthas*, which is the cornerstone of Parel's study. The term is usually translated as "goals of life," but one may ask: whose goals? Who stands behind the different strivings or pursuits, whether they be strivings for pleasure, success, virtue, or salvation? Is the individual self in the driver's seat, and are the different goals simply modes of self-realization or ego enhancement? In this case, is everything just a matter of human contrivance? As Parel points out, *moksha* in the Indian sense means either "realization of *Brahman*" (the divine) or realization of self as *atman*, but *atman* is not the same as the empirical ego. As he also emphasizes, the point of religion—especially for Gandhi—is to bring about a transformative change "from an ego-centered way of being to a 'self'-oriented [*atman*-oriented] way of being."[30] Yet the move from one way to the other is not always smooth or harmonious; it involves a kind of transformation or rupture, a turning about or *periagoge* (never easily accomplished). Gandhi himself referred frequently to the need to "reduce himself to zero" to pursue his highest aim. From this perspective, the Buddhist emphasis on the need for self-emptying and self-denial (*sunyata, anatta*) appears intelligible and sensible and not entirely out of step with Gandhi's own path.[31] Viewed against this background, maybe the warnings of Gandhi's mentor Rajchandbhai and of the entire *sramanic* tradition against an easy compatibility of "worldly" and "transworldly" pursuits were not entirely misguided and need to be pondered by politically inclined *karma yogins*. Perhaps one even has to consider that the translation "goals of life" does not quite capture the meaning of *purusharthas*. In some sense, at least on the level of *dharma* and *moksha*, it is not a matter of humans pursuing goals or targets but rather humans being targeted and challenged in their humanity.

This aspect is also important for the Gandhian mode of political action. In much of contemporary social and political theory, "action" means the pursuit of goals by an agent or subject deliberately targeting these goals. This model undergoes a profound change in the Gandhian context. First of all, action as an ethical practice is always responsive to the situation of others, and, in the case of *satyagraha*, it frequently involves the experience of self-suffering (rather than the infliction of agendas on others). Still more importantly, action for the *karma yogin* involves a responsive self-surrender to the divine, coupled with the renunciation of selfish rewards or benefits. As Parel remarks, Gandhi was firm in maintaining that sustained *moksha*-oriented action—especially his practice of *brahmacharya*—could not possibly succeed "by mere human effort"; needed in addition to personal effort and a degree of self-reliance was "faith in God" or a striving for "God realization." In Gandhi's own words, in every genuine action, God's grace (*prabhu prasad*) and an "unreserved surrender to His grace" were crucial requisites.[32] Hence, every genuine political action of the *karma yogin* has to be both creative and receptive or passive; better still, it has to be creative while simultaneously "emptying" the agent or refusing to foreground the agent's particular will. Readers familiar with the Christian tradition will surely be reminded here of the long-standing debate among theologians whether salvation can be accomplished through human work or by grace alone.

For Gandhi (as Parel shows), the guiding inspiration on this score was always the Bhagavad Gita, and especially the concluding verses of Book 2—the *mahavakya* spelling out the condition of the "sage of stable wisdom." There we read: "When a person surrenders to me all desires [goals, pursuits] that come to the heart and by divine grace finds the joy of God, then his/her soul has indeed found peace [or harmony]." To this passage may be joined other verses: "Do your action in the peace of *yoga* and, free from selfish desires, be unmoved in success or failure. . . . In this wisdom a person goes beyond what is well done and what is not well done. Go you therefore to wisdom: wisdom is yoga in work [*karma yoga*]." As the Gita adds, in verses that were dear to Gandhi throughout his life, unselfish or self-emptying action consecrated through sacrifice brings together this world and the next: "Great is the person who, free from attachments and with a mind ruling its powers in harmony works on the path of *karma yoga*, the path of consecrated action. . . . The world is in the bonds of action, unless action is consecration."[33] In my view, this is a particularly stirring expression of the meaning of differentiated holism or integral pluralism.

8. Reason and Lifeworld
Two Exemplary Indian Thinkers

> There is a significance of perception which is not equivalent to the universe of cognition.
> —Maurice Merleau-Ponty

It was with great sadness that I learned of the passing of two leading Indian philosophers: Daya Krishna and Ramchandra Gandhi. What renders the loss particularly grievous is the fact that they were not just ordinary academics but exemplary and even iconic Indian thinkers. In a way, during much of their lives they represented two different possibilities of Indian thought, two alternative conceptions of the meaning of philosophy. On the whole, Daya Krishna identified philosophy with critical analysis and the striving for exact knowledge, whereas Ramchandra Gandhi placed himself in the tradition of the great Indian seers, the teachings of the Upanishads and the Bhagavad Gita. While the former aimed at rigorous rational truth (*episteme*), the latter explored precognitive experience and preferred to cultivate liberating insight and wisdom (*sophia*). There can hardly be a deeper gulf than this among practitioners of philosophy. Yet, when all is said and done, the two thinkers in the end were not hostile to each other and came to appreciate their respective contributions as ingredients of an integral pluralism. Thus, on a limited scale, something like a *samvada* or dialogical understanding came to prevail between them.

I was fortunate enough to be acquainted with both thinkers, though not in equal measure. With Daya Krishna I was linked through a loose bond of friendship established through periodic meetings and discussions. Repeatedly I met with him at conferences organized by the East-West Center in Hawaii; on other occasions we would meet and share a meal at conferences in Delhi, Pune, and other places in India. One particularly joyful occasion took place in Hawaii some twelve years ago when we dined together in a Hawaiian Village restaurant with a folkloric ambience. I was greatly impressed by the immense range of Daya's erudition, his familiarity with all kinds of Indian and Western texts, and his sociability and lively wit. In my view, Daya was a world-open, cosmopolitan thinker easily at home in many different places. It was, no doubt, this quality that enabled him to absorb so quickly and thoroughly some Western philosophical trends, especially the outlook and style of analytical philosophy.

My acquaintance with Ramchandra Gandhi was more limited. I met with him several times in Delhi, especially in the International Centre where he frequently stayed. I was struck by his pensive attitude and by the intensity of his search for "truth" in both the philosophical and the religious sense (*satya* and *sat-chit-ananda*). Although he was familiar with modern and contemporary Western thought, especially the Whiteheadian strand, his intellectual roots were clearly in the older Indian tradition, particularly in the "nondualist" philosophy (*Advaita Vedanta*) inaugurated by Shankara and continued by a long line of religious-philosophical thinkers.

Daya Krishna's Defense of Reason

Daya Krishna is known chiefly for his 1991 book *Indian Philosophy: A Counter Perspective*, a somewhat iconoclastic text that aims to correct a number of misconstruals of Indian thought. The chief misconception it seeks to correct or deconstruct is the notion that Indian philosophy is essentially "spiritual" and even "mystical," in contrast to the rigorous, rational character of Western philosophical inquiry. "Who does not know," Krishna writes in a somewhat mocking vein, "that Indian philosophy is spiritual? Who has not been told that this is what specifically distinguishes it from Western philosophy, and what makes it something unique and apart from all the other philosophical traditions of the world?" In Krishna's view, this conception is entirely untenable and at odds with major strands of traditional Indian thought (including Nyaya, Vaisheshika, and Carvaka). Hence, he concludes that this "spiritual" characterization is "completely erroneous." Another closely related misconception is the claim that Indian thought is basically marked by a practical objective: the orientation toward spiritual liberation or *moksha*. Krishna calls this the "Bhattacharya model." According to this model, he writes, "Indian philosophy is the essential theoretic counterpart to that which, when practically realized or verified, is called sādhanā (practice) or *yoga*. . . . In the language of Bhattacharya, it is philosophic reflection alone which makes us aware of certain possibilities which demand to be actualized, even though the process of actualization itself is not philosophical in nature." This means that the cognitive propositions of philosophy have no independent status and can be verified only in practical application.[1]

Among other misconceptions challenged in the text are the alleged authoritative status of the Vedas and Upanishads in traditional Indian thought and the claim that Indian philosophy comes packaged in distinct "schools" attached to specific doctrines or dogmas and is thus impervious to further questioning. Against all these erroneous construals Krishna upholds a view of philosophy that is basically congruent with Socratic and Western analytical self-understanding. This outlook, we read, "thinks of Indian philosophy as philosophy proper and not as something radically different from what goes under that name in the Western tradition." Above all, this view denies "that Indian philosophy has anything to do with *moksha* and asserts that the alleged association is due to a complete misunderstanding of the actual situation." This denial has important corollaries summed up by Krishna's statement that Indian philosophy, properly conceived, "is neither exclusively spiritual nor bound by unquestionable, infallible authority, nor constricted and congealed in the frozen moulds of the so-called 'schools' which are supposed to constitute the essence of Indian philosophy by those who have written on the subject." The basic aim of Krishna's text is to liberate Indian philosophy from prevailing prejudices and "mummified" straightjackets in order to render it a viable partner in worldwide intellectual inquiries: "Indian philosophy will become contemporarily relevant only when it is conceived as philosophy proper."[2]

In the ensuing chapters of the book, the iconoclastic or deconstructive implications of Krishna's approach become palpably evident and have led to no small amount of controversy. Here it must suffice to mention a few main points. One prominent theme (previously mentioned) concerns the role of spiritual liberation (*moksha*) in traditional Indian thought. Relying on a number of texts, Krishna has no difficulty showing that such liberation "is not the exclusive concern of Indian philosophy; nor is it its predominant concern either." It is time, he insists, that the "myth" of *moksha*'s central role be dispelled and Indian philosophy be "treated seriously as philosophy proper." Another major theme involves the authoritative or privileged status of the Vedas and Upanishads. Although frequently asserted and even presented as distinctive of Indian philosophy, Krishna finds the claim mired in confusion and dogmatic double-talk. When one asks "whose authority is being invoked or denied, one does not find from the texts or the tradition any clear or definite answer." According to Krishna, similar questions can be asked, and similar obscurity prevails, regarding the status and meaning of the Nyaya-Sutras and the Samkhya-Karika, reputed to be the oldest known text of the Samkhya School of philosophy. Two chapters (easily the most contentious) are devoted to the status and meaning of Advaita Vedanta as inaugurated by Shankara. The first chapter charges Shankara with building his theory of nondualism (*Advaita*) on dualist premises (deriving from the Samkhya School). The second takes aim at the idea of Vedanta itself, asking "Does it really mean anything?"—a question resolutely answered in the negative. Although acknowledging that Vedanta is "the most dominant, alive and continuous tradition of Indian philosophizing," Krishna concludes that it is "only a word full of emotional significance, good for propagandistic purposes but, basically, signifying nothing." Hence, the term "needs to be banished from the realms of thought, if we are to be serious about thinking."[3]

Although best known and most widely cited, *Indian Philosophy* was not Krishna's only "counter perspective" or effort at critical reconstruction. A few years later, his book titled *New Perspectives in Indian Philosophy* offered a critical reexamination of the entire tradition of Indian thought from the Vedas and Vedanta to Mimamsa, Nyaya, and Navya Nyaya. There is no point in reviewing the entire course of the critical analyses here; it must suffice to distill the central animus or motivations inspiring the work. Foremost among these motivations is the desire to rejuvenate Indian philosophy by liberating it from ingrained habits of rote learning and sterile repetition. In Krishna's words, the chief aim of his book, and especially its discussion of Vedanta, is "to outline a strategy for creative thinking in general and philosophizing in particular." What he finds distressing in Indian thought is a certain backward-looking tendency, a proclivity to view philosophy in the "rear-view mirror" without a corresponding effort to renew thinking by bringing it to bear on ongoing issues and discussions. From the angle of many traditional pandits, philosophizing simply means "an articulation of that which has already been thought as if there were no imperfections or incompleteness in it, or as if it was a finished picture or product of thought." Deliberately invoking Kantian language, Krishna stresses the need to strengthen the critical impulses in philosophy. His book, he notes hopefully, will contribute to "making us free from our 'dogmatic slumbers' and making us aware of the need for a fresh look at the philosophical traditions of India, so that they may become alive once again and be pursued with renewed vigor once more."[4]

Another animus permeating the book is a certain antiparochialism or incipient universalism opposed to the erection of intellectual or geographic boundaries. This opposition applies to domestic or intracivilizational developments, where, with regard to the traditional schools of thought (*darshanas*), Krishna emphasizes their dialogical interaction rather than their doctrinal separation. His antiparochial élan, however, is most clearly evident with respect to cross-cultural or intercultural relations. Complaining about the "monadic self-sufficiency" of traditional Indian philosophy, Krishna finds it "unbelievable" that "hardly any attempt has been made to see its inner connections with developments of thought in other civilizations." Lack of connection in philosophy carries over into the realms of social, political, and legal thought, as well as the domains of the natural sciences and the arts. In all these fields, the "insulated" character of Indian tradition has been underscored by "the almost total absence of any awareness of the way it has been influenced by thought current in sister civilizations, or the way it might have influenced them." For example, the Persian, Greek, Central Asian, and Chinese civilizations were "in active interaction for long periods of time" with the Indian civilization, and "it is extremely unlikely that they were not influenced by one another." Significantly, Krishna lists the Arabic and Islamic civilizations among those influencing and being influenced by Indian thought. "From at least 1200 A.D. onwards," he writes, "Islam may be said to have a definitive presence in North India"—a presence that has been largely sidelined or ignored. "The histories of thought in the second millennium A.D. in this country show hardly any awareness of it or of the possible influence it might have had on the varied fields of intellectual life in India."[5]

The broad civilizational and intercivilizational issues raised in *New Perspectives* were not just a passing concern for Krishna. At the time he wrote that book, he was involved in an ambitious project of cross-cultural and even transcultural reflection whose result appeared under the title *Prolegomena to Any Future Historiography of Cultures and Civilizations*. Published by the Delhi Centre for Studies in Civilizations under the general editorship of D. P. Chattopadhyaya, the book reveals Krishna as a self-reflective thinker oriented toward global and world-historical horizons. Drawing some inspiration from the historical reflections of Kant and the later Husserl, Krishna finds the clue of civilizational development in the growth and maturation of reflective consciousness, although this accent is modified in several ways (which I discuss later). In his words: "Thinking about civilizations is thinking about 'man' [human being] itself; it sees 'man' as the 'creator-builder' of civilizations through a vast collective effort lasting over millennia. . . . In this process, man 'creates' and 'builds' itself also." In the course of history, he adds, nature steadily gives way to culture and natural inclinations to reflective, civilized dispositions: "The 'naturally' built institutions of society and culture undergo a radical transformation through the development of self-consciousness and increasing intervention on its part in the way they function before its intervention." For Krishna, the progressive advancement of civilization through creative intervention reflects in the end "the transcendental seeking of man" (in Husserl's terms, the maturation of transcendental consciousness). "The successive embodiments in which the living consciousness articulates itself," we read, "provide a clue not only to the meaning or purpose which is evidenced in them but also . . . to the seeking which is expressed through the successive evidences. There is, thus, a visible and invisible history to be captured." Switching into a more linguistic or narrative idiom, Krishna adds that the maintenance and transmission of culture are "symbolic in character and concerned with the understanding and interpretation of the symbols in which it is embodied."[6]

It is important to note at this point that civilizational narratives cannot be viewed in complete isolation from a world-historical angle. Actually, on this level, one can notice both centrifugal and centripetal tendencies. Thus, alongside a search for "relative autonomy and independence" one also finds "a desire to relate oneself to a larger whole of which one would like to be a member as this would not only give one an added importance, but also the feeling of belonging to an unending quest of 'man' to which one might significantly contribute by his/her independent effort." As Krishna's study makes abundantly clear, cultural identity—when seen from an intercivilizational and world-historical perspective—is highly fluid and tenuous. In his words: "The idea of the new frontier has become proverbial since the American experience"; yet, though not sufficiently recognized, "there has always been a shifting frontier in the history of civilizations." Underscoring his strong antiparochial (and incipiently universalist) stance, Krishna adds: "The point is that a civilization is not bound to the place of its origin nor even to the peoples amongst whom it may have arisen.... It is almost like the invisible spirit which moves from one place to another and is confined to no particular place, though there may be temporary illusions that it belongs only to a particular people or place or time." Reinforcing this point further, so that it emerges almost like the motto of a world-historical teleology, Krishna continues: "Civilizations thus have to be disengaged from their entanglement and identification not only with geographical regions and particular peoples but also with some unchanging foundation lying at their beginning without which they will cease to be what they are."[7]

To be sure, the absence of cultural or civilizational "essences" does not involve the denial of historical experiences in which particular geographic regions and particular people played a recognizable role. Can one still speak—Krishna asks pointedly—of "an Indian, Chinese or West Asian or European civilization"? The answer to this question resides in two considerations. The first relates to the fact that "civilizations are not just a matter of the past but of the future as well," and the historical development of many civilizations gives evidence of "significant turns" and even "radical breaks" that later merged with their past and became an integral part of their history. The second, more crucial consideration has to do with the fact that "all civilizations are basically human achievements" that have to be seen in "a unitary manner as part of a common human enterprise" endowed with "a claim to universality relevant for all humankind." Viewed from this angle, civilizations can be seen as variations on a common enterprise or, better still, as participants in a shared and competitive endeavor. Civilizations, Krishna writes, must be regarded as shareholders in a common endeavor, a striving "which has been carried on by successive generations over long periods of time, and which, though sometimes interrupted, has never been given up for long by human beings who have been even vaguely aware of what they have inherited from their past." What is crucial for Krishna, in this context, is the fact of inter-civilizational contacts and the evidence of intercivilizational learning over time. "The significant factor," he writes, "is not that civilizations have developed an identifiable personality of their own over millennia but that they have continually borrowed from each other's achievements and deficiencies." Properly told, the story of civilizations has been "both a cooperative and competitive enterprise" in which there has been "an element of rivalry along with a deeper awareness that they are all engaged in the common enterprise of 'man' on this planet which is as unending as time itself."[8]

No doubt, the account of civilizational maturation presented in the book is captivating and uplifting. As it happens, however, the story of humankind's growing self-consciousness and self-constitution is intersected by a number of comments that put pressure on the story's linearity. One comment concerns the very notion of self-constitution itself. One of the important insights to emerge from his study, Krishna remarks in the preface, is that of "the empirical *a priori* which normally is supposed to be a contradiction in terms in the analytic philosophical tradition dominant in Western philosophy." Somewhat further along, he returns to the notion of concrete or "immanent *a priori* conditions" of historiography, observing that "unless we become aware of them, we would not see the constraints that the historical enterprise itself involves." Clearly, this idea of "immanent" conditions is hard to reconcile not only with assumptions of the "analytic philosophical tradition" but also with the transcendental trajectory of a universal historiography of civilizations. The problem resurfaces more clearly toward the end of the book. There, reflecting again on human identity, Krishna writes: "The simple truth is that the essential unchangeability of consciousness [which] has been accepted as an unquestioned and unquestionable axiom by all [is yet] strangely and paradoxically refuted every moment by the experiences of each and everyone, including the thinker himself." This happens "because of the 'illusion' generated by self-consciousness which cannot see consciousness as an 'object' even if it tries to do so." The refutation becomes particularly clear if one turns from philosophy to the domains of "polity, economy, and society," as Krishna does in the concluding section. In his words, there are indeed "internal" factors in the story of civilization, including "the life of the imagination and what is called 'spirit.'" Yet there is another dimension. The "unasked question" here is, "what happens to 'man' who is the center of all this drama and whether history with all the changes in polity, economy, and society will leave his 'essence' untouched, or transform and transmute him in a sense that is difficult to grasp as the very activity of thinking and understanding seems to be structured in such a way as to determine and give form to itself by conceiving of everything, including itself, as constituted by the differences that distinguish and define them as 'this' rather than 'that.'"[9]

Ramchandra Gandhi and Assemblage

The preceding comments show Krishna as a circumspect and multifaceted thinker, though without jeopardizing or erasing his emancipatory posture.[10] It seems to me that Daya Krishna's work stands basically in the tradition of "critical" philosophy intimated by Socrates and later deepened by a string of thinkers from Descartes to Kant (and, in part, Husserl). Wedded to the project of human intellectual as well as social liberation, the tradition forms the linchpin of Western modernity and probably of worldwide modernity today. The merits of this modern project (so-called) in terms of human advancement are manifest, but its premises are no longer unquestioned. During the twentieth century, a number of thinkers inquired precisely into the "immanent" conditions of the possibility of cognition and consciousness, that is, the conditions undergirding the Cartesian cogito and transcendental subjectivity. Some thinkers, following Ludwig Wittgenstein, explored the embeddedness of thought in language, that is, its dependence on semantic, syntactical, and performative criteria. Other thinkers, especially American pragmatists, underscored the practical and context-bound parameters of human cognition. Still others, especially Martin Heidegger and Alfred North Whitehead, delved into the ontological and quasi-metaphysical premises of human reasoning and being-in-the-world. What all these thinkers have in common is the turn from rational knowledge (*episteme*) to the precognitive reservoir of experience and understanding—a reservoir that, without being irrational or simply mystical, constantly eludes and transgresses the limits of cognitive grasp and control. In many respects, Ramchandra Gandhi has always placed himself in this philosophical genre.

Ramchandra's philosophical leanings are clearly outlined in one of his early works titled *Two Essays on Whitehead's Philosophic Approach*. There, Ramchandra takes his point of departure chiefly from Whitehead's *Modes of Thought* (1938), which, together with *Adventures of Ideas* (1933), is among that philosopher's later writings. In *Modes of Thought*, Whitehead distinguishes between two types of philosophizing that he calls "philosophic assemblage" and "speculative philosophy." In his preface, Gandhi expresses his conviction that Whitehead's own pursuit of speculative or systematic philosophy is likely to be "seriously misunderstood" if it is not seen in relation to his discussion of philosophic assemblage, "which is an activity in many ways diametrically opposed to the agenda of speculative philosophy, yet complementary to it." The distinction is explained more clearly in subsequent contexts. For Whitehead, doing speculative or systematic philosophy is "an attempt to construct a coherent system of ideas which would be adequately explanatory of the nature of ultimate reality and therefore of the totality of existence." To an extent, Whitehead himself pursued such an agenda. However, in *Modes of Thought* and other late writings, he acknowledges an "inherent deficiency" in system building and recommends "assemblage" as a corrective device. Basically, the deficiency of system building resides in the fact that it unavoidably limits the scope of inquiry "by trying to force every kind of experience into a particular systematic pattern." It is thus necessary to find a way of "widening our philosophical horizons," based on the recognition that our experience is broader than our systematic grasp. In Whitehead's own words, there is in all systematic thought a profound tendency of exclusion, of the "putting aside of notions, of experiences, and of suggestions, with the prim excuse that, of course, we are not thinking of such things." In *Modes of Thought*, he calls this the "pedantry" of systematic philosophy.[11]

In a way, Whitehead's notion of assemblage constitutes a kind of "immanent *a priori*" (as invoked by Daya Krishna), but not in the sense of a Kantian condition of possibility. According to *Modes of Thought*, assemblage constitutes the "first chapter in philosophic approach," but only in an inchoate, experiential manner; it allows for "a free examination of some ultimate notions as they occur naturally in daily life." In Ramchandra's reading, what Whitehead is suggesting is "not a Kantian inquiry" designed to uncover "the *a priori* system of presuppositions of experience," for the simple reason that assemblage is "not a systematic inquiry." From a certain angle, assemblage is akin to a commonsense mode of reasoning because common sense shuns apodictic convictions and is full of "shifts of interest and standpoint." What Ramchandra finds particularly appealing in the commonsense approach is its tolerance of diversity and its taste for overflowing abundance. "Commonsense is open-minded," he states; "it has freer access to a variety of philosophical ideas." In the ordinary course of experience and thinking, we are not tempted "to downgrade the importance of an experience or idea for the sake of vested metaphysical interests." Where common sense is somewhat deficient in comparison with assemblage is in its inability to bring diverse experiences together in a loose web of significance; in fact, the interrelatedness of meanings "takes commonsense by surprise," especially when familiar notions resurface in unfamiliar contexts without sharp rupture. "The aphoristic profundity of mystics and poets and some philosophers," Gandhi writes pointedly, "consists in just this ability of theirs to reveal unsuspected relationships between familiar notions of large and adequate metaphysical generality."[12]

As these comments indicate, assemblage for Gandhi is a source of inspiration, a resource of innovative discovery and disclosure that can never be exhaustively mapped by cognitive reason. In Whitehead's own words, the achievement of assemblage is "novelty and disclosure," not "coherence and systematization"; when approached in a tentative, experimental way, aspects "hitherto dismissed as casual irrelevancies" are lifted into "coordinated experience" or a web of significance. In contrast to the orderly overview provided by cognitive rationality, assemblage in its best moments yields "chance flashes of insight" in areas that are "large, ill-defined, and not controlled by any explicit boundary." Ramchandra speaks in this context of "the anarchic poetic approach of assemblage," which on occasion provides us with the "surprise of a revelation." At another point, he refers to assemblage as "the natural response of our reflective consciousness to a world that exceeds us on all sides," a response cultivated especially (though not exclusively) by poets and mystics. Being attentive to ongoing experience is a lifelong endeavor; in a similar manner, the work of philosophical assemblage is unending and cannot reach final completion. As Gandhi emphasizes, following Whitehead, completeness and finality are the ideals of systematic philosophy, which ultimately is a subject for specialists. Philosophic assemblage, in contrast, is an ordinary, nonacademic practice; more than that, it is "a habit of mind—the habit of striving after adequate generality of understanding which should receive the attention of every educated mind in its 'escape from its own specialization.'" As Gandhi adds (picking up a theme dear to Daya Krishna): "It is the essence of civilization to cultivate this habit of escaping from the narrowness of understanding." Indeed, quoting Whitehead: "It is civilization. . . . Civilized beings are those who survey the world with some large generality of understanding."[13]

Apart from relying on Whiteheadian philosophy, Gandhi's *Two Essays* also invokes the testimony of Wittgenstein, William James, and some (unspecified) phenomenologists and existentialists as pointing in the same direction.[14] Given this philosophical background, it is hardly surprising that Gandhi was led to a consideration of religion or religiosity—the latter seen not as a dogmatic belief system nor as an academic specialty but as a mode of experience. Just as, in Whitehead's account, assemblage is not the antithesis but the corollary and presupposition of philosophical inquiry, religious experience for Ramchandra constitutes a recessed matrix and penumbra of philosophical thought, and hence a legitimate topic of reflection. The main result of his reflections in this area was a series of essays published in 1976 under the title *The Availability of Religious Ideas*. Although acknowledging that religion or religious experience can be approached in different ways—for instance, as a set of shared beliefs in a community or as an academic subject matter—the introduction to the book insists that the same experience is not antithetical to, but rather a legitimate partner of, philosophy—more specifically, the philosophy of religion. As Ramchandra points out, in light of these considerations, one might define the philosophy of religion, or an essential aspect of it, as follows: "We might say that one is doing philosophy of religion when one seeks to understand the character of philosophical problems in relation to dominant, fundamental, religious ideas, and vice versa." Understanding religious experience in this manner rests on the assumption or belief "that philosophical reflection and religious ideas are [not mutually exclusive but] available to one another in a mutually illuminating way," quite outside the range of communally shared doctrines or specialized academic research programs.[15]

Among the "available" religious ideas discussed in the book are such notions as the soul, immortality, God, prayer, the mystical, the miraculous, and others—an array of themes whose subtle exploration far exceeds the scope of these pages. What I want to highlight here are some basic guideposts orienting the study. One crucial guidepost is the idea of a certain "givenness" of experience, the idea that dimensions of experience are given to and not constituted by consciousness; this givenness can be further qualified as relational and nonatomistic. "The central philosophical conviction which sustains practically the whole of this book," Ramchandra writes, "is that in the most fundamental sense of the word 'given,' what is given for philosophical reflection is the communicative form of human life." Self-consciousness itself emerges from this primary communicative relationality; likewise, ethics or morality is wholly derived from the "principles of caring" (echoes of Heidegger?) inherent in this communicative situation. Significantly, for Gandhi, relational communication extends to the realm of the divine, which implies "the possibility of calling upon God without being under an obligation to first establish his reality," that is, "the possibility and legitimacy of agnostic prayer." Another closely connected guidepost of the study is the primacy of being and doing over knowing and reasoning. In Gandhi's words, contrary to popular misconceptions, *"being a human being* or *being myself* is not an experience of mine to which I have an inward [cognitive] access" or that I can understand by introspection. Following Wittgenstein and others, one must say "that consciousness is a mode of being, not a mode of knowing, and that the character of concepts like 'I,' 'You,' 'He' etc. can only be grasped by appropriate [semantic] analysis." This argument carries over to the idea of the soul, which Gandhi describes as "the idea of that as which we imaginatively see one another in acts of addressing one another."[16]

Another important guidepost—perhaps overshadowing all the

rest—is the notion of an inexhaustible assemblage, an elusive "wholeness" resisting cognitive grasp. Commenting on a possible meaning of the "mystical," Ramchandra writes: "There is the notion of the totality of all actual and possible states of affairs which is implicated in the notion of any particular set of actual and possible states of affairs." The decisive consideration here is that "nothing at all—nothing descriptive—can be said about the totality or system of all actual and possible states of affairs, for such a totality must be inclusive of all objects of description." What follows is that the notion of totality or of a totalizing system is "a notion of the mystical—an essentially incomprehensible and yet ineliminable notion." Closely akin to totality is the notion of "absolute nothingness," which, Gandhi says, is "implicated in every affirmative existential judgment to the effect that something, *as opposed to nothing*, exists." This idea of absolute nothingness is a corollary of comprehensive being and, as such, is again "incomprehensible and yet ineliminable." Based on the inevitable excess of assemblage over cognition—evident in the totality of being and radical nothingness—Gandhi rejects a positivist (or "ontic") immanentism neglectful of this excess. "Underlying all the essays of this book," he writes, "is a rejection of what might be called 'the immanentist view of the world and human life.'" This view expresses itself in statements such as "This world is all that there is" or "This life of mine, terminated by my death, is all there is of 'me.'" In opposing this view, Gandhi minces no words: "I argue that the immanenist view of the world and human life is unacceptable not because it is a demonstrably false philosophical view, but because it is essentially unintelligible" (both religiously and philosophically).[17]

Ramchandra's critique of positivist immanentism does not amount to an endorsement of rigid transcendentalism—an alternative that would split asunder heaven and earth, the divine and the human, the sacred and the secular. In addition to these polarities, his thinking is opposed to all other dualisms, such as those between subject and object, self and other, friend and enemy. For this reason, his thought finds its proper place in the tradition of Advaita Vedanta, where *advaita* can be translated as "nondualism" (without complete synthesis), as differentiated unity or holistic difference (or what I call integral pluralism). In Gandhi's own words: "Dualism is the conviction that self and not-self are everywhere pitted against one another," that is, "individual human beings against one another and against human collectivities; human collectivities against one another and against individual human beings." But the range of dualism reaches even further into all areas of reality, pitting "living species against one another; the human species against all other living species; all life against matter; all existence against nothingness." Relentlessly pursued, the upshot of dualism is the "temptation of annihilation" and "despairing destructiveness"—a temptation "now unfurling in all societies on an unprecedented scale," prompting a readiness "to destroy all life and civilization of earth."[18]

In the Indian context, dualistic destructiveness reached a pinnacle of frenzy in the town of Ayodhya, the reputed birthplace of Lord Rama and the site of an old mosque, the so-called Babri or Babari masjid (named after the Muslim conqueror Babar). At the height of the Hindu-Muslim conflict, Ramchandra visited Ayodhya to gain some firsthand experience; the result was a series of reflections published in 1992 under the title *Sita's Kitchen: A Testimony of Faith and Inquiry*. What he discovered on his visit was evidence—generally acknowledged—that materials from an older Hindu temple had been used in the construction of the Babri mosque. But he also discovered something that was not generally known: that the precinct of the temple-mosque also contained remnants of a still older shrine designated *Sita-ki-rasoi*, reputed to have been the kitchen of Rama's wife and consort Sita. The discovery triggered in him a deeper insight into the meaning of nondualism or *advaita*—a meaning where heaven and earth, sacred and mundane, are conjoined or entwined. The name "Sita's Kitchen" (or, rather, its Hindi original), he writes, suggests "an ambience of domesticity and divinity which happily includes the notion of an actual kitchen where Godhead-incarnate Sita cooked delicious and nutritious food for the Raghava household [of her husband]," but which also "stretches all the way beyond that architectural idea to the archetypal notion of the earth as the Divine Mother's laboratory of manifestation and field of nourishment for all self-images of self." For Ramchandra, the status of Sita far exceeds her role as Rama's wife and consort. As he states, in the spirit of Vaishnava religiosity, she is "only in manifestation" his consort; in actuality, she is "Mahalakshmi, Godhead," and her kitchen is "the entire field of her self-imaging *Shakti* [divine energy], powerfully represented on earth. [For] it is on earth, in the embrace of the Divine Mother, that all are born, all creatures great and small, all forms manifest, noble or evil; and all are nourished."[19]

Transgressing the bounds of Hindu religiosity, Ramchandra's reflections on Ayodhya have a genuinely ecumenical cast. During his stay there he remembered, perchance, his student days in Oxford and his visits to the university's oldest church, St. Mary's. As it happens, that church had recently installed a mural painting showing Mahatma Gandhi in a cross-legged posture with upraised arms. In Ramchandra's interpretation, the raised hands can be seen as highlighting Gandhi's nondualism and rejection of exclusive identities, for "he was a Hindu, but insisted that he was simultaneously also a Muslim, Christian, Jew, Buddhist, Jaina, etc.—a believer in the truth of all faiths." He also "loved fellow human beings as himself, and had no difficulty in honoring their deepest concerns as his own." Viewed against this background, the mural in St. Mary's carries a strong interfaith significance: it "draws attention to the neglected dimension of Christ's teaching that man does not live by bread alone, but by every word that proceeds from the mouth of God." At this point, the old church in Oxford is subtly transfigured into "a non-dualist church of Atman-Brahman-Mary," a church whose generous "kitchen" is able, without exclusivist denial, to offer "the full range of truth's cuisine to spiritually starved humanity." In addition to Christian resonances, the Ayodhya experience reminded Ramchandra of crucial Buddhist insights, especially the notion of the interconnection and nonseparateness of all beings: "The Buddha's teaching of the inter-relatedness of all evanescent items and their situatedness within non-initiative emptiness (*sunyata*) or nirvana is also wholly consonant with [the site's] vision of the vibrant interdependence of all forms of life and their location within the nourishing embrace of Mother Earth."[20]

The greatest significance of Ayodhya for Gandhi, however, resides in its status as a testimonial of Hindu-Muslim nondualism or *advaita*. In his words: "Ayodhya today presents an aspect of otherness to Muslims which is as stark as the aspect of otherness under which Hindus see the Babari mosque towering over the city of Rama." Here, "otherness" does not mean separateness or polarity but rather difference or differential entwinement, a holistic or integral kind of pluralism. To be sure, this entwinement has been strained and wounded by recent excesses of violence, when thoughtful Hindus and Muslims were "marginalized as bombs of hatred erupted in the sky." Yet the long history of Indian spirituality also carries a healing balm that needs to be revived and cultivated. "Indian spiritual self-knowledge," Gandhi writes, "cannot become self-realization without encounter with non-Indian spiritual traditions, and without sharing space and time with them." This consideration is particularly relevant to the site of the temple-mosque. There, "held in topographical and historical embrace by the birthplace and kitchen zone of Ayodhya," the Babari mosque can be seen as evidence "not of Hindu humiliation but of its venturesome *sādhanā* (spiritual quest) of self-realization." At this point, Ramchandra's *Sita's Kitchen* contains a passage that can be read as a paean to religious and cultural pluralism and nondualism:

> The Babari edifice is a testifying tree which bears the flowers of nearly five hundred years of Islamic piety, and of nearly fifty years of Hindu *bhakti*. It could have grown only in the sacred soil of Sita's Kitchen, and cannot be transplanted anywhere else. Certainly the tree bears thorns too, thorns of medieval and modern vandalism. But it can give shade to pilgrims weary of hatred in the name of the sacred for at least another half a millennium. . . . Hindus and Muslims must forgive each other's trespasses in Ayodhya, if they wish their trespasses against each other all over India to be forgiven.[21]

Figure and Ground

The preceding discussion has brought out some of the similarities as well as the significant differences between the two Indian thinkers. Both thinkers, one might initially say, link philosophy with a form of liberation and emancipation (*swaraj*), but they do so with very distinct emphases. As I indicated, Daya Krishna stands mainly in the tradition of critical philosophizing; hence, his accent tends to be on intellectual or rational liberation, on the refinement of self-consciousness through critical analysis and the demolition of unexamined prejudices. Ramchandra Gandhi's main concern is with the deepening and maturing of experience rather than rational cognition; hence, his philosophical trajectory points more in the direction of what might be called "ontological" freedom or liberation, where freedom means not just the removal of external constraints but the transgression of the ego in favor of *advaita* (or the nonduality of being). The two modes of philosophizing cannot easily be reconciled. In the traditions of both Western and Eastern philosophizing, the two modes have often stood in stark opposition and intense rivalry. However, it may be possible to detect in this case a kind of nondualism and intellectual mutuality (*samvada*).

On another occasion, reflecting on the relation between Western and Indian philosophizing, I invoked some arguments advanced by Indian poet and philosopher A. K. Ramanujan. In an essay titled "Is There an Indian Way of Thinking?" Ramanujan distinguishes between text and context and, more specifically, between "context-free" and "context-sensitive" modes of philosophizing. As a trained linguist, he traces the distinction back to the difference between two kinds of grammatical rules: those that are context free, in the sense of being universally applicable, and those that are context sensitive, in terms of being closely tied to their concrete application. Moving boldly from grammar, Ramanujan finds an analogous distinction between cultures: "I think cultures [may be said to] have overall tendencies," he writes, "tendencies to *idealize,* and think in terms of, either the context-free or the context-sensitive kind of rules. . . . In cultures like India's, the context-sensitive kind of rule is the preferred formulation." In an effort to buttress this view, his essay provides a number of historical examples, ranging from Manu's legislation (where rules are typically contingent on caste and status) to the great Indian epics *Ramayana* and *Mahabharata* (where each individual story is embedded in a larger metanarrative that contextualizes and gives meaning to each tale). Proceeding to the modern and contemporary period, Ramanujan offers some striking comments on modernization (or Westernization) and comparative development theory. In contrast to the context sensitivity of Indian culture, his essay portrays modernity as wedded to decontextualization: "One might see 'modernization' in India as a movement from the context-sensitive to the context-free in all realms: an erosion of contexts, at least in principle. Gandhi's watch (with its uniform autonomous time) replaced the almanac."[22]

For Ramanujan, another key for grasping cultural differences resides in literary theory and especially in the vocabulary of literary tropes. In the case of Indian literature and thought, he notes a tendency to privilege "metonymy" (where a part "stands in" for a larger whole) over other expressions. For example, the term "man" or "human being" does not designate a creature separate from nature but one that "stands in" for nature and the cosmos. Seen as "man in nature" or "man in context," he observes, the human being is conceived as being "continuous with the context s/he is in." The same point can be made with the help of Peircean semiotics. In semiotic terms, he argues, Indian thought accords primacy to indexical signs over symbolic expressions, where "indexes" are signs in which signifiers and signified "belong to the same context," that is, the signifier is not externally related to the signified (in a subject-object dualism) but is itself the intrinsic carrier of signification. (Thus, one might say that a figure of Shiva or Rama or Sita does not symbolize something else but rather "indicates" its own meaning.) Turning to the fields of logic and sociology, Ramanujan explicates context sensitivity by pointing to the pervasive Hindu concern with *jati*, that is, with "the logic of classes, of genera and species, of which human *jatis* are only an instance." Each *jati* or class "defines a context, a structure of relevance, a rule of permissible combinations, a frame of reference." By contrast, contextual relevance and any reference to particular circumstances are sidelined in context-free or universalizing social arrangements.[23]

In my earlier discussion of Ramanujan's text, I expressed my admiration but also voiced some reservations. My qualms were basically of two kinds. First of all, the distinction elaborated by Ramanujan not only applies to the relation between India and the West but also can be found in the Indian context itself—the incipient "dialogue" between Daya Krishna and Ramchandra Gandhi being a prominent example. Second, the opposition between text and context, or between context freedom and context sensitivity, still seems to suggest a kind of dualism in which the two frameworks can be neatly separated from each other, neglecting their intimate entwinement and mutual implication. For this reason, I prefer to turn to the image of "figure" and "ground," an image introduced by Gestalt psychology but radically reformulated by Maurice Merleau-Ponty. In his *Phenomenology of Perception*, Merleau-Ponty criticizes traditional rationalist philosophy—what he calls "intellectualism"—for trying to articulate a universal and apodictic type of knowledge severed from perceptual experience. Practiced in this manner, he notes, philosophy no longer seeks to account for concrete perception but aims "to coincide with and understand the perceptual process" epistemologically. The basic yardstick for this kind of undertaking is modern science and its cognitive achievements. In Merleau-Ponty's words: "The real sin of intellectualism lies in having taken as its datum the determinate universe of science," that is, a universe of objects governed by external cause-and-effect relations. Against this epistemological stance, his text pits the experience of precognitive perception, an experience thematized by phenomenology in the wake of Husserl's work. From the phenomenological angle, there is "a significance of perception which is not equivalent to the universe of [rational] cognition, a perceptual domain which is not yet the 'objective' world, a perceptual being which is not yet determinate being."[24]

As Merleau-Ponty acknowledges, it was Gestalt theory that pointed a way beyond intellectualism. As that theory has shown, "the alleged signs of [physical] distance," such as the apparent size of an object or the number of objects interposed between it and us, are expressly known only in "analytic cognition," which turns away from phenomena in favor of their objective presentation. In challenging this approach, Gestalt theory brought to the fore "the tensions which run like force lines across the visual field" and "which breathe into it a secret and magic life by exerting here and there forces of distortion, contraction, and expansion." Yet, despite these achievements, Gestalt psychology has not lived up to its promise. By retreating into sense-data empiricism, the theory construes bodily stimuli as external "causes" rather than seeing them as "signs or reasons." With this construal, Merleau-Ponty notes, we are back in "explanatory psychology," whose ideal was never abandoned by Gestalt theory "because, as psychology, it has never broken with [positivist] naturalism." At this point, a bolder step is needed, a "complete reform of understanding" that would allow us "to translate phenomena accurately." *Phenomenology of Perception* is uncompromising in staking out the different path to be followed. If we wish to grasp phenomena properly, we read, "the objective thinking of classical logic and philosophy will have to be questioned, the categories of the [empirical] world laid aside . . . and a true 'phenomenological reduction' undertaken." Once such steps are taken, what comes into view is the role of a "*non-positing* consciousness," a consciousness "not in possession of fully determinate objects." At the same time, what emerges is a new figure-ground relation that cannot be reduced to a cause-and-effect nexus. Here, figure-ground means "a *logic lived through* which cannot account for itself," an "*immanent meaning* which is not clear to itself and becomes fully aware of itself only through experiencing certain natural signs."[25]

The path sketched in *Phenomenology of Perception* was pursued and elaborated in Merleau-Ponty's subsequent writings, especially in a series of essays published as *Sense and Non-Sense*. As the translators of the book point out in their preface, Merleau-Ponty drew inspiration from recent developments in philosophy and the human sciences—including Husserl's phenomenology, Heidegger's existential ontology, and the insights of Gestalt psychology—in order to articulate his own complex account of "order in the perceptual world." From the later Husserl, he learned that rationality and meaning are not "given beforehand" but are emergent qualities of perception. Likewise, with Gestalt theorists, he assumed that "we *discover* meanings by responding to solicitations already in our experience." The main insight he adopted from them was that "whenever I perceive, I perceive a figure on a ground." Thus, a spot on a page "appears to be *on* the page," in the sense that the paper is perceived as present behind the spot. However, a more subtle relation is involved: "Whatever appears suggests in its very appearance something more which does not appear, which is concealed." For this reason, "the figure can be said to have a meaning since . . . it refers beyond what is immediately given." Reformulated in a more philosophical vein, this insight resonates with Heidegger's notion of the relation between revealment and concealment, between presence and absence (what Merleau-Ponty later calls the "visible" and the "invisible"). Without pursuing these ontological implications, the preface leaves no doubt about Merleau-Ponty's affinity with Heidegger's work. "Following Heidegger," it states, he "calls the activity of organizing the world by responding to it from within 'being-in-the-world' or 'ek-sistence.'"[26]

Heideggerian affinities are particularly evident in an essay dealing with the recessed ontological status of human beings (labeled, or perhaps mislabeled, "The Metaphysical in Man"). What Heidegger portrayed as the constitutive openness of human *Dasein* to "being" (in its many forms), Merleau-Ponty describes as the basic human responsiveness to a broad range of experiences exceeding the grasp of rational-scientific cognition. As in *Phenomenology of Perception*, scientific knowledge is presented here as a limited mode of reasoning embedded—as in the figure-ground relationship—in a broad welter of uncharted and precognitive experience. In its ideal aspiration, Merleau-Ponty observes, science always "takes for granted an absolute observer in whom all points of view are summed up," thus offering "a true projection of all perspectives." This projection, however, is not possible in the properly human world, and especially in the context of human interactions. Far from being an emblem of pure rationality, interhuman relations involve an ambivalent mutual exploration—namely, "the taking up by each, *as best one can,* of the acts of others, reactivating from ambiguous signs an experience which is not strictly one's own." At this point, we are no longer confronting external objects but enter into "communication with ways of being." Seen from this angle, the lived world is not just a string of data amenable to "systemic" cognition; rather, it "recovers its texture," that is, its density as well as its depth. In Merleau-Ponty's words, existential phenomenology is not merely an inquiry seeking to "complete the edifice of [scientific] knowledges"; rather, it offers a "lucid familiarity" with the limits of these knowledges while remaining "acutely aware" of their worth. This familiarity is not "a little truth" for which we have to "make room in some nook or cranny of the 'system'"; it is the condition of our being-in-the-world.[27]

The preceding excursions into the writings of Ramanujan and Merleau-Ponty were undertaken for a point: to find a bridge correlating the different philosophical agendas of Daya Krishna and Ramchandra Gandhi. Clearly, these agendas cannot be neatly synchronized or synthesized (especially not in an overarching "system"). At the same time, however, their philosophical orientations are not simply antithetical or mutually exclusive. In my view, and as I have tried to show, the two agendas may be said to reflect a differentiated nondualism or integral pluralism, allowing for at least a limited form of dialogue (*samvada*). My own preference is to see this nondualism in terms of the figure-ground relationship as articulated by Merleau-Ponty. Whereas Daya Krishna, in the majority of his writings, aimed at the progressive refinement of consciousness and critical rationality (largely in the tradition of Kant and Husserl), Ramchandra Gandhi sought pathways to the exploration of precognitive experience (enlisting for this purpose the testimony of Whitehead and William James, as well as older Indian wisdom traditions). As it seems to me, both agendas aim at human freedom or liberation (*swaraj*), but they do so on different levels: the levels of human reason (freedom from prejudice) and of ontological being (freedom from self-centeredness), respectively. These two levels are surely in tension with each other, but they do not ultimately contradict each other (as both Whitehead and Ramchandra agreed). Most important, the two perspectives are linked in their opposition to the reigning "realist" creed of dualism, the Hobbesian war of all against all. In Ramchandra's words (echoing the teachings of his grandfather): this creed ultimately reflects the temptation of "annihilation and despairing destructiveness," a temptation "now unfurling in all societies on an unprecedented scale," prompting a readiness "to destroy all life and civilization on earth."[28]

Appendix A

Return of the Repressed
Merleau-Ponty Redivivus

Psychoanalysts speak of the "return of the repressed," meaning the unexpected upsurge of memories or experiences sidelined for a long time. This sidelining and its overturn are not limited to individual psychic states but extend deep into culture. Bach's compositions, for example, were eclipsed for nearly two hundred years until rescued from oblivion by Mendelssohn-Bartholdy. In less dramatic fashion, similar reversals happen in literary and philosophical contexts. A prominent example in recent times is Maurice Merleau-Ponty, whose work (following his death in 1961) was sidelined for almost half a century by successive waves of structuralism, poststructuralism, deconstruction, and antihumanism. In his case, it is true, the sidelining did not amount to complete erasure; in fact, many so-called postmodern thinkers freely appropriated his ideas, usually without crediting their source. Indications are that the practice of overt neglect is coming to an end. According to two distinguished writers on the subject, interest in and scholarship on Merleau-Ponty is now "expanding at an extraordinary rate."[1] Diana Coole's book illustrates this renewed upsurge of interest—an upsurge that is liable to salvage some of his best insights after the spell of postmodern "anti-humanism."[2]

For Coole, Merleau-Ponty's writings anticipated many arguments of later structuralism and poststructuralism, but without going to the extreme of celebrating the "death of the subject" or the erasure of human experience—a celebration bound to expunge political agency and social responsibility. As she writes, the main reason for rereading Merleau-Ponty is "not that he was already a poststructuralist, but that he was trying to integrate elements now associated with poststructuralism with other traditions that maintain a more robust sense of politics, experience, and agency." The basic task for her today is "to excavate a politics after poststructuralism," a politics that does not "dissolve the political and agentic into the ethical, the aesthetic, or the discursive" (11). In Coole's account, both structuralism and poststructuralism—despite their advances over "philosophies of the subject"—tended to neglect "agent's practical motivations and experiences," a neglect that demonstrated the "lamentable deficit of their anti-humanism" (199). It was Merleau-Ponty's goal (or at least his persistent attempt) to dislodge capacities for agency from "subjectivity" and hence to rid agency "of its subjectivist pedigree and locate it instead in the perceiving body" (175). In contrast to many interpreters, Coole does not discern a basic break or rupture in his thought that neatly distinguishes between "his early and his late work," between "his humanism and anti-humanism," or simply between "phenomenology and structuralism." Instead, she insists on a certain continuity whereby "the early work stakes out a route for overcoming subjectivism and the later writings simply continue this project" in the direction of a steady "deepening of inquiry" on the levels of self-interrogation and world interrogation (182, 185).

Coole's book is divided into three main parts, with the first part highlighting the basic issues or problems triggering Merleau-Ponty's thinking, the second part delineating his phenomenological approach, and the last part exploring his later turn to "ontology" under such labels as "chiasm" and "flesh of the world." Coole's starting point is important. In contrast to abstract theorists picking logical puzzles at random, Merleau-Ponty was deeply enmeshed in the agonies of his time, especially in what he perceived as the dilemmas or the "crisis" features of Western modernity. Crucial among these features for him was modern "rationalism" deriving from Descartes—a rationalism that split experience into subject and object, consciousness and "extended matter," and that basically granted to the former primacy or mastery over the latter. In struggling with this perceived crisis, Merleau-Ponty was, of course, in the company of a host of other thinkers, including Max Weber, some Western Marxists, and the founders of the Frankfurt School. The opening chapters instructively discuss his affinities with, as well as his differences from, his contemporaries. One of the distinctive marks from early on was his focus on the "lifeworld" as generative matrix of thought (a notion derived from Husserl). In Coole's words, his main approach was "to challenge the primacy of reason with the primacy of perception," a perception anchored in the lifeworld. From the angle of this matrix, he challenged both Western "liberal" and Soviet-style "communist" regimes as being "equally implicated in modern rationalism," since both "oscillate between (abstract) Kantian moralism and Cartesian positivism" (33–34). In this context, Coole discusses some early (and more overtly political) writings such as *Humanism and Terror* and *Adventures of the Dialectic*. In these writings, she notes, liberalism is identified as "a form of idealism that rips principles from their material context while reducing politics to an impotent moralism" or "humanism" (51). At the same time, orthodox communism is critiqued as a dogmatic and vulgar materialism foreclosing "processes of interrogation" and reducing dialectics to a "massive positivity" (69, 75).

The distinctive qualities of Merleau-Ponty's approach emerge more clearly in the book's second part titled "In Pursuit of the Interworld." Coole turns here to Merleau-Ponty's reading of Husserl and his move from transcendental to "genetic" phenomenology, a move expected to yield "a new type of reflection" able to tackle the problems of modernity (98). Special attention is given to *Phenomenology of Perception* and related writings that are said to proceed "in an increasingly anti-humanist direction" by making little or no reference to a constitutive ego (103). Contrary to one of Michel Foucault's allegations, Merleau-Ponty at this point no longer practiced "a philosophy of self-certainty and a metaphysics of presence" (104); distancing himself from a "subjectivist, humanist, and idealist philosophy," his phenomenology steadily acquired "dialectical, posthumanist, yet existentialist" overtones (107). In Coole's reading, what prompted this change was, at least in part, his encounter with Gestalt theory, Weberian sociology, and facets of structuralism (especially Saussure and Marcel Mauss). Gestalt theory in particular, she notes, was a way to reach the "interworld," for in application to social life, Gestalt means "the particular way in which men . . . co-exist" (127). Another influence at this point was Machiavelli (freed from Machiavellian opportunism), a thinker who allowed Merleau-Ponty to glimpse "an ambiguous interworld where collective life is swept along in a maelstrom of conflict and cooperation and politics operates on several more or less opaque and precognitive levels" (154). On the basis of these encounters, Merleau-Ponty came to define the political philosopher as an engaged intellectual involved in a "concrete politics of change where responsibility has to be accepted for choices and commitments made." In a similar way, the political actor was seen as practicing an "active/passive agency, of construction and learning, of intervention and listening," in a process oriented toward "indefinite verification" (147, 149).

The concluding part turns to Merleau-Ponty's later work under the title "Politics of the Body, the Flesh of the Political." The immediately preceding chapter already introduced some of the key themes under the labels of "negativity," "agency," and "ontology." Regarding negativity, Merleau-Ponty breaks with Sartre's notion of a radical non-being or "nothingness," conceiving it instead as a "chiasm" or decentering "shift" (*écart*). In Coole's words, this shift is "not an ontological void" but only a "hiatus," a "dehiscence that opens my body in two"; as such, it is a "productive difference, not a fatal lack," "a passivity that bears an activity" (174). Seen in this manner, the shift brings into view a new, no longer subject-centered agency in which negativity and action are joined in "immanent generativity" (177). Such generativity, in turn, is anchored in a recessed negative-positive "ontology" (largely indebted to Heidegger), where "Being" refers to a "becoming, self-disclosing truth" and ultimately points to the lifeworld as generative matrix (161–162). Given the increasing use of the terms "flesh" or "flesh of the world" in his later writings, Merleau-Ponty's ontology has been the target of critical feminist readings (by Judith Butler, Elizabeth Grosz, and others), and these readings are the topic of one of the concluding chapters. The final chapter returns to the book's central aim: the recovery of political agency after the interlude of antihumanism. Crucial guideposts here are Merleau-Ponty's development of a "thick theory of intersubjectivity" and his portrayal of the "flesh of the political" as a "field of forces," where flesh and force field are closely intertwined. Both the phenomenology of flesh as humanly experienced and the aspect of the force field, she comments, are needed to convey "this interlacing," which is "chiasm" (237).

Coole's book is clearly important in the present intellectual situation: the aftermath of structuralism and poststructuralism. Without dismissing the needed deflation of "subjectivity" and a self-centered humanism, the text opens the road to a renewal of politics and political agency—an agency operating (if one wishes) in the "middle voice," in the *écart* between passivity and activity, between receptivity and innovative praxis. Coole demonstrates admirably the many contributions Merleau-Ponty's work can make to this renewal, especially through his elaborations on the "interworld" and the ontology of the "flesh." Along the way, she offers some insightful comments on his relations with distinguished contemporaries. Particularly valuable are her observations on the importance of Heidegger's legacy. Merleau-Ponty, she notes, followed Heidegger's lead by infusing existence with temporality and by attempting to rethink humanity "from the non-anthropological perspective of Being." At the same time, he departed from that legacy by maintaining closer contact with worldly experience and concrete politics (182, 252). Given Merleau-Ponty's emphasis on the lifeworld, his approach seems to resemble that of Habermas, but not on closer inspection. "Even in modernity," Coole states, "Merleau-Ponty's lifeworld is outrun to a considerably lesser extent than Habermas's, largely because it is anchored in embodied, perceptual processes rather than in [purely] linguistic, communicative practices" (143). Above all, the phenomenologist was never willing to reduce the lifeworld to a realm of unreflective and "unmediated certainty." Also insightful and instructive are the book's comments on Merleau-Ponty's relation to Sartre, especially the Sartre of *Being and Nothingness*. As indicated before, consciousness for Sartre was a rupture, an emblem for pure negativity or nothingness. In contrast, without abandoning the negative, Merleau-Ponty treated it as an enabling potency, as "the productive condition of reversibility" (174). As we read in *The Visible and the Invisible,* the *écart* is "not a void" but is "filled precisely by the flesh as the place of emergence of a vision, a passivity that bears an activity."[3]

Given Merleau-Ponty's double move—his embrace *and* transgression of antihumanism—his relation to the generation of structuralists and poststructuralists is particularly significant. Tension clearly prevails between the phenomenologist and Foucault in his more structuralist-epistemological phase, which tended to erase the "subject" in favor of anonymous forces and a "genealogy" of power. However, as Coole notes, Foucault himself became increasingly aware of "the difficulties inherent in maintaining a politics without relatively efficacious agents or an account of intersubjectivity." She can rely here on the testimony of Gilles Deleuze, to the effect that the later Foucault "came to understand subjectivation in terms of folding" and that his main mentors at that point were "undoubtedly Merleau-Ponty and Heidegger" (230, 232). More complicated is the relation to Deleuze himself, given the latter's more resolute antihumanism, evident in his stress on "nonhuman forces of the cosmos" and an impersonal force field "without a subject" (237). The relation is rendered even more strained by Deleuze's radical rejection of negativity and his embrace of an apparently seamless "immanence" inhabited only by "positive" forces. Can such a seamless immanence even be thought without reference to a difference from or with that immanence? Moreover, does reliance on anonymous force fields not imply an ascent to that "aerial view" or "view from nowhere," which Merleau-Ponty consistently criticized? Noticing the tension, Coole suggests an avenue of reconciliation. Clearly, she states, Deleuze's rejection of the negative seems to put him "on a collision course with Merleau-Ponty as well as Sartre." Yet, on inspection, his concerns were similar to those Merleau-Ponty expressed when critiquing an "embalmed dialectic." Thus, despite Deleuze's dismissal of the intentionality implicit (for him) in the notion of "flesh," Coole submits that "his invocation of the 'being of the problematic' is strikingly reminiscent of Merleau-Ponty's later ontology" (170).

I find congenial the balanced judgment and evenhanded tenor pervading Coole's book. Among many other places, this tenor is clearly evident in her discussion of feminist critiques that Merleau-Ponty's notion of the "flesh" is either male gendered or gender neutral. As she rightly maintains (203), if transferred to the ontological plane, gender differences tend to become "essentialized"—something most feminists surely want to avoid. The best one can do in this field is to both affirm and deny such differences in accordance with pragmatic objectives. My reservations about the book are limited and involve mostly matters of emphasis. I do not believe that Merleau-Ponty ever meant to "substitute force field for flesh," as one passage suggests (238). A bit more pronounced are my qualms regarding the treatment of "exemplary action" or praxis. Coole associates such action perhaps too closely with political "leaders," including both "liberal statesmen" and "Marxist revolutionaries." As she writes, both types "exhibit the particular qualities of living their times well and of trying continuously to clarify the lines of force and negativities of the present." Borrowing a leaf from Max Weber, the leading figures are said to display "a vocation for politics" and to exhibit the qualities of "Weber's charismatic politician" (149–150). Although perhaps in tune with some of Merleau-Ponty's early inclinations (at the time of *Adventures*), these statements hardly reflect his subsequent seasoning and especially his later ontology of the "flesh." Like the rest of us, he had plenty of sobering experiences with both liberal statesmen and revolutionaries. Above all, the statements fail to resonate with his persistent democratic leanings and with a politics carried on in the ordinary lifeworld.

An important dimension of Merleau-Ponty's thought—but one too frequently neglected or sidelined—is its ethical sensibility. Coole's text is diligent in rescuing this dimension from oblivion. Turning to one of his early essays (reprinted in *Sense and Non-Sense*), she obverses that Merleau-Ponty "confirms the intersubjective nature of ethical relations and associates them with an ethos of keeping promises, respecting others, communication, and generosity" (257n46). A distinctive (and appealing) feature of her book is its persistent emphasis on what she calls an "interrogative ethics." As she writes at one point: "Interrogation is an originary structure of existence for Merleau-Ponty and enjoys ontological status. But . . . it also acquires normative significance inasmuch as an interrogative ethos emerges as a possible alternative to modernity's rationalist way of being-in-the-world" (169). On one level, Merleau-Ponty's ethical sensibility approximated him to Emmanuel Levinas, despite the latter's frequent (often lopsided and unfair) attacks on his compatriot. One basic difference, however, resides in Levinas's sharp separation between ethics and politics, between private and public domains. In the politico-ethical realm, Coole writes (correctly, I believe), "we can never rely upon simply personal responsibilities" because "our lives are commingled through and through in their interiority and exteriority," and "we all inhabit the dense flesh of the world." This realization leads her to an important point: "Rather than suggesting something like Levinas's ethics of the gift, which is indifferent to reciprocity and predicated on the radical separation of self and other, Merleau-Ponty brings us back to a dialectical world whose exemplary ethico-political attitude I have labeled an interrogative ethos." The broader import of this argument is that "it is as crucial to avoid reducing politics to ethics as it is to separate them definitively" (247). This is surely one of the many salient lessons that Merleau-Ponty's work, mediated through Coole's reading, teaches us.

Appendix B

Disclosure and Critique
Critical Reason and Its Horizons

The fate of reason today hangs in the balance. This is no small matter. Ever since its historical beginnings, reason or rationality has been the central focus and point of honor of Western modernity—a focus enshrined in Descartes' cogito, Enlightenment rationalism, and Kantian (and neo-Kantian) critical philosophy. The result of this focus was an asymmetrical dichotomy: separated from the external world of "matter" (or nature), the cogito assumed the role of superior taskmaster and overseer—a role fueling the enterprise of modern science and technology. During the past century, the edifice of Western modernity has registered a trembling due to both internal and external contestations. Subverting the modern asymmetry, a host of thinkers—ranging from practitioners of American pragmatism to adherents of European life philosophy and phenomenology—has endeavored to restore precognitive "experience" (including sense perception and affect) to its rightful place. In the context of French postmodernism, a prominent battle cry has been to dislodge logocentrism (often equated with anthropocentrism). In the ambience of recent German philosophy, the battle lines have been clearly marked, pitting the champions of modern rationalism, represented by Jürgen Habermas, against the defenders of experiential "world disclosure," represented by Martin Heidegger. The book *Critique and Disclosure: Critical Theory between Past and Future* by Nikolas Kompridis endeavors to shed new light on this controversy, with the aim not of bringing about a cease-fire but of providing resources for arriving at better mutual understanding.[1]

One should note that Kompridis does not exactly assume a position above the contestants (he repeatedly rejects the "view from nowhere"). As the book's subtitle indicates, his point of departure is "critical theory" as championed by the Frankfurt School, and his intention is to nudge that theory beyond a certain rationalist orthodoxy in the direction of possible "future" horizons. Although he appreciates some of its merits—such as the "linguistic turn" and the emphasis on "communicative" rationality—Kompridis finds Habermas's reformulation of the Frankfurt program on the whole unhelpful and debilitating. In his words: "For all there is to recommend it, Habermas's reformulation has produced a split between new and old critical theory so deep that the identity and future of critical theory are at risk" (17). The main reason is that the "normative gain" deriving from the linguistic turn remains attached to narrow rationalist premises that have "needlessly devalued" the theory's potential. In Kompridis's view, Habermas's evolving thought exhibits a break or rupture (quite apart from the linguistic turn): namely, a move toward pure "theory" that happened soon after the publication of *Knowledge and Human Interests*. "That turn to theory," he writes, "refashioned the project of critical theory as a *strenge Wissenschaft*, less bound by or beholden to the historical and existential exigencies of modernity," thereby undermining modernity's intrinsic "relation to time" (232–233). As a result of this refashioning, critical theory was catapulted in the direction of an abstractly rational universalism disdainful of cultural and practical modes of pluralism. The upshot was a growing "insensitivity to particularity," justifying the suspicion that the basic concepts of communicative rationality had from the start been "rigged in favor of the universal." But, the book adds sharply, "a provinciality-destroying reason is a meaning-destroying reason" and the latter is "a history-destroying reason" (234).

Considerations of this kind serve to buttress the book's basic thesis that Habermas's reformulation is "in need of urgent reassessment if critical theory is to have a future worthy of its past" (17). In Kompridis's view, critical theory's renewal has to rely on alternative resources, including insights "central to the German tradition from Hegel to Heidegger and Adorno" and phenomenological explorations of the "life-world" (28–29). In this context, a crucial resource is Heidegger's notion of "world disclosure," articulated variously under the labels *Erschlossenheit*, *Lichtung*, and *Ereignis*. The basic point of the notion of disclosure is that "we operate 'always already' with a pre-reflective, holistically structured, and grammatically regulated understanding of the world" (32–33), which means that our thinking and reasoning are always embedded in a precognitive experiential setting. In Heidegger's own terms: if there is to be any understanding of something "as something," then "our understanding must itself somehow *see as disclosed that upon which it projects*."[2] The implications of this insight are obviously immense and are bound to reverberate through all modes of philosophizing, including critical theory. Kompridis is by no means naive about the obstacles facing the recuperation of Heideggerian insights. As he writes: "The idea that Heidegger's thought can contribute to the renewal of critical theory is more likely to be greeted with disbelief (if not derision) than with curiosity." As is well known, "Heidegger's person and his thought have played the role of critical theory's 'other': he is the very antithesis of the critical intellectual as critical theorists imagine 'him'" (32). Not daunted by these obstacles, Kompridis wagers that the benefits of the recuperation outweigh the possible drawbacks. "Rather than regarding it as a threat to reason, as Habermas does," he states, "I will argue that disclosure presents us with the possibility of a new, practice-altering conception of reason, a conception upon which the basis for an alternative model of critical theory can emerge" (38).

The second part of the book, titled "Dependent Freedom," seeks to retrieve crucial aspects of Heidegger's work and rescue them from various misreadings, especially Habermas's charges of "methodological solipsism" and a relapse into "subjectivity." As Kompridis tries to show, the salient difference between *Being and Time* and Habermas's own project is "not between subject-centeredness and intersubjectivity" but between the former's focus on "semantic" criteria—how something becomes mutually intelligible—and the latter's stress on "justificatory" and "context-transcending" criteria (44–46). The difference can also be articulated in terms of the primacy granted, respectively, to "meaning" and universal "validity." A central Heideggerian teaching in this context is his notion of "solicitude" and especially of "anticipatory-liberating solicitude"—a notion that clearly conflicts with subject-centeredness. For Kompridis, the notion accentuates how "our freedom for self-determination . . . is both dependent on and facilitated, not just impeded, by our relation to others," which means that "the condition under which the other and I can realize our freedom are conditions that must be cooperatively established, preserved, and enlarged" (49). Another important Heideggerian term is *Entschlossenheit,* or "resoluteness." As Kompridis insists, contra Habermas, the term is "not synonymous with decision or decisiveness, or a manly readiness to take action"; rather, it resonates "with *Erschlossenheit,* with disclosure or disclosedness." Hence, a better translation would be "unclosedness," which draws attention to "the receptive [though not purely passive] character" of our activity (58). Refreshingly unconventional are also Kompridis's comments on *das Man.* Countering widespread prejudices, he argues that Heidegger's category "displays no more contempt for 'average everydayness' . . . than is to be found in Rousseau's *Second Discourse,* Emerson's 'Self-Reliance,' Thoreau's *Walden,* or Mill's *On Liberty.*" Specifically, Heidegger is *not* advocating "an interpretation of 'authenticity' in terms of radical individuality" but rather is guided by an interest "in recovering the everyday, rescuing its semantic resources from daily degradation" (71–74).

The third part discusses some of the main strategies employed by critical theorists to debunk Heideggerian "disclosure" by removing it to a realm outside of reason. Kompridis conveniently lists Habermas's main objections: that Heideggerian ontology "dictates history," that disclosure "precludes the very possibility of learning," and that it is not prior to but "subordinate" to validity claims. For Kompridis, "all of these criticisms fail, often by their own lights," such that Habermas's meta-critique of disclosure "turns out to be rather incoherent." One strategy used to obviate disclosure is to relegate it to a purely "aesthetic" domain, that is, the "value sphere" of art and literature stipulated by Habermas; in that sphere, rational validity "goes on holiday" (98). The strategy fails for the simple reason that disclosure undercuts the division of value spheres: "The very idea of an independent sphere of value organized around the world-disclosing practices of art and literature is incoherent" (109). Similarly misguided is the identification of disclosure with an "extraordinary" event or capacity. In Kompridis's words, what is neglected here is that "the success of everyday practice depends on the world-illuminating, problem-solving power of disclosure." Hence, Habermas's misconstrual reflects precisely "an inattentiveness to the presence of the extraordinary in the everyday"

(112–113). Other tactics found in critical theory's arsenal are the "debunking strategy," directed mainly at the notion of "ontological difference" (which silently remains presupposed), and the "annexing strategy," whereby disclosure is somehow assimilated to validation. What all these strategies miss is what Kompridis calls the "test of disclosure," for the latter is tested "not against the world as it is, but as it might be; [hence] any new disclosure of meaning and possibility is *underdetermined* by the 'world'" (142).

In the fourth part, the book defends a broad conception of philosophy transgressing the boundaries of a narrow rationalism and proceduralism. From the procedural angle, Kompridis asserts, philosophy is restricted to "a definition of argument so narrowly 'professional' as to be unphilosophical"; in fact, a history of philosophy employing the procedural criterion "would be a very short, colorless history" (149). A main target of critique in this context is Habermas's definition of philosophy as a stand-in (that is, a place-keeper for science) and as an interpreter—a definition that Kompridis considers lopsided and untenable: "The more it is scrutinized, the more this whole mixed-up conception of philosophy . . . appears to be the product of an expert-culture mentality, exhibiting that mentality's tendency to think in terms of highly distinct 'specializations' and roles within an insufficiently examined division of labor" (161). A corollary of proceduralism is the rigid distinction of philosophy from literature. Again, Kompridis's response is pointed: "*Pace* Habermas, what distinguishes philosophy from literature is *not* that the former is a problem-solving enterprise while the latter is a world-disclosing enterprise"—a spurious distinction, "since there is no way to separate world-disclosure from problem-solving in the relevant instances" (178). Above all, what proceduralism and the focus on rationalist theory occlude is philosophy's integral relation to praxis and the practical disclosure of a possible future. Taking a leaf from American pragmatism, Kompridis states that "philosophy receives its concept of itself from the needs of its time, and it is from the quality of philosophy's response to these needs that it can be in a position to react responsibly as an agency of critical enlightenment" (167).

The exploration of possible horizons occupies the remainder of the book. For Kompridis, Habermasian thought is not sufficiently open to these horizons because it tolerates only "change that is both familiar to us and controllable by us." To be sure, openness, or *Erschlossenheit*, needs to be distinguished from random plasticity, from "contemporary culture's drunken infatuation with the promise of limitless freedom" (192–193). At that point, Hannah Arendt's theory of action becomes relevant, with its accent on radical but ongoing and sustainable transformation. In the same manner, Heideggerian disclosive praxis can fruitfully be invoked. In this domain, the charge of "fatalism" often leveled against him serves as a "distorting lens." In one of his most innovative moves, Kompridis links disclosure and "letting be" not with passivity but with a "receptivity" sustaining nondomineering action. "Both Heidegger's early and later writings," he observes, "offer a promising starting point for understanding how cooperative, accountable practices of reflective disclosure can facilitate new cultural beginnings, initiate new practices, and found new institutions." What is required here is a rethinking of "agency," away from the deeds of heroic overmen and pointing in a new and "unfamiliar direction": a direction "not only decentering but also reconfiguring what it means to be an agent." Such rethinking makes it possible to see "human beings as cooperative facilitators rather than heroic creators of new beginnings" (202–203). As has to be admitted, Heidegger did not always live up to the potential of his thought (as shown in his temporary attachment to an ideology that demanded "closed, not open minds"). Intimately associated with this receptive mode of agency is Heidegger's view of human interaction informed by "solicitude." Going beyond narrow formulations of "recognition," recognizing the other from Heidegger's angle involves "a struggle in which one's own self-understanding . . . [is] at stake. That is why such a struggle for recognition is at once cognitive and affective" (210). In contrast to a purely cerebral or "notional" construal, "genuine experiences of self-decentering involve and challenge all of our cognitive and affective capacities, *our whole sensibility*" (214).

In the concluding sixth part, the focus is entirely on open possibilities "in times of need." Kompridis complains first of all about the prevailing cultural skepticism and the apparent "exhaustion of utopian energies": "Skepticism and despair seem to have outstripped hope" (245–247). This situation is detrimental to philosophy per se, but especially to an outlook that claims to be "critical" of unexamined conditions. "Critique," he states, "is unavoidably 'utopian,' not in the sense that it depends on the availability of a fully determinate utopia, but in that it depends on the openness and receptivity of the future to utopian thought" (252). The recovery of this dimension requires the restoration of trust and confidence in available possibilities. Returning to the book's central theme, and differentiating between prereflective and reflective disclosure, Kompridis at this point defines *disclosure* as a kind of "intimate" or "immanent" critique, and he defines *critique* as the practice of reflective disclosure. In his words: "The goal of critique should aim at the self-decentering disclosure of meaning and possibility. . . . Ultimately the test of any newly disclosed possibilities is the degree to which they can initiate self-decentering learning that makes a cooperative new beginning possible" (255). Again, beginning anew here does not coincide with a rupture that is entirely forgetful of the past. Invoking both Herbert Marcuse and Walter Benjamin, Kompridis stresses the need to "preserve the *unclosedness* of the past" precisely in order to preserve the openness of the future. (A similar point can be found in Heidegger's notion of "the future of the past.") Such an outlook, he writes, protects against both reactionary nostalgia and vanguardist euphoria: "It is absolutely essential to the success of possibility-disclosing critique that it lets itself be permeated with the *potential* of what could be different," and this means "letting oneself suffer one's time, making oneself vulnerable to it by letting oneself be marked by it" (270–272). By way of conclusion—and invoking Heidegger's writings on Hölderlin—Kompridis asserts the need to revive the legacy of a "suppressed romanticism": "In my view, romanticism is not just some superseded period of cultural history; it is the frequently unacknowledged position from which we engage in a critical, time-sensitive interpretation of present" (275).

This is an important and timely (or time-sensitive) book, both in philosophical and in practical political terms. Today, a few years after the book's publication, its plea for a recovery of trust in the future has gained unexpectedly broad resonance. Philosophically, the book signals the end of a period marked by divergent, even opposite tendencies: on the one hand, the postmodern fascination with extraordinary rupture (or rapture), and on the other, the streamlining of critical theory in the mold of a rule-governed, rationalist normalcy. The book's basic aim—one that I heartily endorse—is to rescue critical thought from these limiting parameters and thus to nurture openness to new possibilities. My sympathy with this aim is in part motivated by my own similar endeavors to open critical theory to Heideggerian insights.[3] Like Kompridis, I was chagrined by Habermas's abandonment of his earlier practical, engaged outlook in favor of abstract theorizing; Kompridis's comments on the flaws of such theorizing are pointed and basically on target. Of late, it is true, Habermasian thought seems to have undergone a certain mellowing, softening the harsh edges of his abstract universalism and moving him closer again to hermeneutics and even modes of religious thought (although the name of Heidegger remains banished from his discourse). Despite such recent modifications, Kompridis's book performs a valuable function by nudging rank-and-file critical theorists away from certain "orthodox" school positions that Habermas himself seems ready to abandon.

These are numerous other features of the book—a veritable cornucopia—with which I heartily agree. One has to do with the reformulation of praxis in terms of a decentered receptivity and open engagement with others. This reformulation gives a crucial new impulse to conventional "action theory," pushing it beyond the confines of self-centered activism and passive self-erasure. In my own thinking, I have tended to view Heideggerian solicitude and "letting be" as prime examples of what is often called the "middle voice." The accent on receptivity or receptive generosity also reveals important dimensions of a Heideggerian ethics—dimensions that are usually sidelined or ignored. This neglect is astonishing in view of such salient Heideggerian terms as "solicitude" and especially "anticipatory-liberating solicitude," as Kompridis correctly observes. The topics of receptivity and engaged solicitude have a clear bearing on the traditional notion of interhuman recognition—a notion that, in the past, has often been confined to a purely cerebral level. The reformulation of this concept in terms of a reconnection of cognition with affect and sensibility can obviously rely on the Heideggerian category of *Stimmung*, but beyond that, it can rely on a longer tradition stretching from Spinoza to Emerson, Merleau-Ponty, and Stanley Cavell. Extremely valuable in this context are also Kompridis's comments on the broader social import of self-decentering. As he writes, such self-decentering "is *not* about overcoming our partial view of things in order to arrive at the single right answer to a moral problem. It is not about a 'transcendence' of our parochial self in order to achieve an impartial or objective view of things; it is about an enlargement of self, opening it up to what was previously closed" (213). In conformity with these comments, Kompridis's view of "utopia" does not involve a bland universalism or cosmopolitanism. What Heideggerian disclosure brings into view, he states, is the need to change a monistic conception of being "into a pluralistic one, such that we acquire an increased sensitivity to the presence and endangered state of plural 'local worlds'—plural understandings not subsumable under a single notion of being." What this underscores is "the interdependent relationship between intelligibility, plurality, and possibility" (219–220).

Despite my general agreement with the book's orientation, I cannot refrain from voicing some reservations. Although lucidly written, the presentation is often somewhat rambling and repetitive; a tightening of structure might have strengthened its argument. More serious are reservations having to do with the portrayal of Heidegger's thought. Despite his initial rejection of the Habermasian charges of solipsism and a relapse into the "philosophy of the subject," Kompridis surprisingly ends up echoing these charges in a slightly revised form. The section "Dependent Freedom" castigates the "conspicuous lack of a normatively robust conception of intersubjective accountability and recognition" (48). In large measure, this lack is blamed on Heidegger's allegedly self-centered conception of *Entschlossenheit* and the "call of conscience." Despite his own translation of *Entschlossenheit* as "unclosedness," and in the face of a quoted passage in which Heidegger describes the "call of conscience" as a call that comes "from me and yet from *outside and beyond me*," Kompridis states: "Regrettably Heidegger chose to develop the meaning of 'resoluteness' one-sidedly, as an openness or receptivity to a 'call' whose disclosed meaning should be understood *independently* of our relation to others. Thus he made monophonic and monological a call that is inherently polyphonic and dialogical" (51). From here it is only a short step to the claim that Heidegger decided to "suppress that half of the 'call' that emanates from outside the self," with the result that *Being and Time* culminates in "a solipsistic rather than a 'fundamental' ontology," hovering at "the precarious edge of subjectivism" (52–53). A similar revindication concerns Habermas's charge of decisionism. Although strongly asserting that "*Entschlossenheit* is not synonymous with decision," Kompridis in effect revokes his assertion by stating that "Heidegger undermines the illuminating power of his own analyses by uncoupling *Entschlossenheit* from *Dasein*'s positive dependence on others and thus from positive solicitude" (65). Painting with a broad brush, even Heidegger's famous "turning" (*Kehre*) is interpreted as "the successful suppression of dependence on others" (67).

In my view, assertions of this kind could easily be corrected by a closer reading of Heidegger's texts, especially his *Beiträge* and some lecture courses presented during the 1930s (and only recently made available). Less easily resolvable is the central issue announced in the book's title: the relation between critique and disclosure. As one can gather from the subtitle and numerous other statements, the basic tendency is to subordinate disclosure to critique, that is, to make disclosure serviceable to critical theory. As Kompridis states at one point: "What I propose to draw from Heidegger does *not* require abandonment of Habermas's best critical insights; rather, it means reassessing them and recombining them with Heidegger's in order to re-envision the future of critical theory" (31–32). Yet, taking into account the sustained criticisms of Habermas throughout the book, how plausible or persuasive is this aim? In his most exacting or developed formulations, Kompridis defines *critique* as reflective disclosure and *disclosure* as intimate critique (238, 255). But what about prereflective disclosure? Would it not be more plausible and sensible to assign critique to what some writers call "secondary reflection" (and Kompridis calls "reflective disclosure")? Ever since the time of Kant, modern philosophy has been defined (or has defined itself) preeminently as critique—a primacy the book seems to accept. In my opinion, however, Heidegger's work does not entirely subscribe to this tradition; it is not primarily critical but rather ontological and phenomenological, honoring Merleau-Ponty's notion of the primacy of "perceptual faith." Looked at from this angle, a better title might have been *Disclosure and Critique*.

Appendix C

On Love with Distinction
A *Chinese Debate*

> I should be able to love my country and still love justice.
> —Albert Camus

In Chinese philosophy today, an important issue is being debated: whether ethics requires us to give precedence to universal principles or sanctions particular attachments or loyalties. Specifically, the issue revolves around the ethical legitimacy of "filial piety" and a special fondness for particular persons (called "love with distinction").[1] The following reflections are offered with some hesitation. Although I have immersed myself in Chinese thought, I am neither a Sinologist nor an expert on Confucian thought. So, regarding Chinese matters, I am a stranger or perhaps a distant lover, a friend from distant shores. But then it was Confucius himself who invited distant friends or lovers to draw near and participate in the conversation, saying "that friends should come to visit one from afar, is this not after all delightful?" (*Analects* 1:1). So, I am sufficiently encouraged by Confucius to overcome my hesitation and present these (quite limited) comments.

As I understand it, the Chinese debate raises a profound and complex question: whether filial piety, as conceived in traditional Confucian thought, is intimately tied up with ethics or whether it signals a derailment into corruption, injustice, or immorality. As can readily be seen, the central issue of this debate—though prompted by specific Confucian texts—is not narrowly limited to the Chinese setting but has a broader, perhaps even universal significance. From the literature available to me, I gather that the debate about filial piety and, more broadly, about love with distinction, often shades over into a familiar conundrum: the relation between particularism and universalism. Some of the scholars praising love with distinction do so precisely because of its attention to particularity, to particular human beings, in opposition to vague generalities or generalizations. Scholars denouncing filial piety do so because of the same particularism, the same neglect of general or universal standards (above all, the standards of morality and justice). If this is the character of the debate—or at least a certain dimension of it—my position is difficult. Coming from abroad and not being an "insider" of the Confucian tradition, I may be suspected of leaning toward moral universalism and away from (Chinese) particularism. But things are not that simple; they rarely are.

In the exchange between Chinese philosophers Liu Qingping and Guo Qiyong, I intuitively find much that is appealing in the former's argument, perhaps because, as an outsider, I have been influenced by Enlightenment ideas and especially by Frankfurt-style "critical theory" (with its emphasis on rational distantiation or decontextualization). Thus, even without being fully aware of it, my intellectual habitus resonates with a universal register of discourse—a register displayed by Liu when he writes that "Confucius puts the particular affection of filial piety above the universal principles of justice and honesty," and for both Confucius and Mencius, "particular affection could override universal principles." One should note that Liu does not entirely reject filial piety or love with distinction, but only their primacy over universal justice. "I do not entirely negate," he writes, "the significance of kinship love or family life, but advocate that [such] affection should take its proper place in human life as a whole." What he calls "post-Confucianism" is hence not a total rejection of the Confucian tradition but involves a simple reversal of priorities. What post-Confucianism does, he states, "is merely to turn the old framework of traditional Confucianism upside-down: to make the universal dimension of humane love, which was secondary in the old framework, primary in the new one, and to make the particular dimension of filial piety, which was primary in the old framework, secondary in the new one." By doing so, the proposed framework will "creatively transform traditional Confucianism from a particularistic doctrine into a universalistic idea."[2]

These are powerfully stirring words, especially for a reader familiar with the Enlightenment tradition and its privileging of universal ideas over particularistic loyalties. Seen from this angle, traditional Confucianism appears hopelessly quaint and parochial; above all, the emphasis placed on love with distinction seems to be the mark of a bygone era out of step with the demands of our globalizing and universalizing age. But perhaps there is a need to be cautious; perhaps particular loyalties or affections cannot be surrendered without loss to universal principles. Perhaps it is the case that universalism and particularism are always mutually embroiled and cannot be simply rank ordered. Guo Qiyong seems to be fully aware of this embroilment. His paper emphatically pays tribute to the centrality of "humaneness" (*ren*) in Confucian thought, but without relinquishing the aspect of filial piety or love with distinction. For Guo, there is a process of maturation linking filial piety with universal humaneness. As he writes, "the beginning of love for one's parents is followed by love for other people which is followed by things." Hence, there exists "an order of love" whereby "one can gradually extend one's love for parents to brothers, relatives, townspeople and clan, and further to all nations of the world." Citing Zhu Xi and Wang Yangming, Guo adds that humanity or humaneness "must have a 'starting point' which resides in filial piety and brotherly love," for "if one does not love one's own parents, brothers, and sisters, we cannot imagine that the person will love the parents, brothers, and sisters of others, finally forming one body with Heaven, Earth, and the myriad things."

In stressing this process of maturation, I believe, Guo Qiyong is not far removed from Aristotelian ethics. The linkage becomes even clearer in the emphasis on actual conduct—the *praxis* of love—vis-à-vis the mere theoretical cognition of virtues or rightness. For Aristotle, ethics is not merely a mode of knowledge but something that has to be practiced, and this practice is inevitably learned and cultivated in concretely lived situations. Although we know theoretically, or in our minds, about the existence of a universal humanity, ethical conduct toward others has to be guided by our "heart/mind (*hsin*)," that is, by our thought and affection or our affectionate thought, which is a concretely lived affection or a love with distinction. Following again Zhu Xi and Wang Yangming, Guo observes that "the operation of the humane heart/mind is the concrete practice of humanity in real life. The reason that it begins with loving one's parents and relatives is that, compared with loving people and loving things, it has [practical, though perhaps not ontological] superiority and priority." As he adds in an instructive (and again quite Aristotelian) passage: "The operation of the humane heart/mind in concrete practice, or the realization of universal love in the specific historical time and space, needs a procedure, order, or sequence, because real life and concrete practice cannot take place all at once in a vacuum. . . . A tree must first produce a shoot, and only then can it grow the trunk, branches, and leaves."

Though hailing from afar, I find much of Guo's argument quite congenial. Over the years, I have become weary of universal "lovers" of humanity or humankind; I have found that in their everyday conduct, such lovers are often quite unloving or uncaring toward their fellow beings and sometimes even neglectful of their rudimentary responsibilities toward them. Philosophically and existentially, I detect a certain deficit of "humaneness" (*ren*) in an abstractly celebrated universalism—an unwillingness to accept our "human condition," that is, our "finitude" or our finite embeddedness in time and place. As one may recall, Martin Heidegger, in commenting on human finitude, speaks of our "thrown" condition as "beings-in-the-world," a condition that does not at all equal confinement or imprisonment but rather constitutes the precondition for our longing or striving for the more-than-finite (or infinite). Readers construing Heideggerian finitude as a vindication of parochialism or narrowly local attachments fail to take seriously the centrality of the notion of "care for Being," where the latter carries a more than local (or in some sense "transcendental") significance. At the same time, however, "care for Being" evaporates into a vacuous chimera unless it is instantiated in practical conduct, in the active care for fellow beings and ultimately the care for "Heaven, Earth, and the myriad things."

Seen from this angle, filial piety and universal care are not strictly separable; they certainly resist the idea of universal lineation or rank ordering. In his defense of post-Confucianism, Liu Qingping adopts a resolute priority scheme in which universal justice always trumps filial piety and love with distinction. His main charge leveled at "traditional" Confucians is that they prefer the opposite arrangement, allowing local particularism to triumph over universalism. I am not sure that Guo is willing to subscribe to this kind of rank ordering (his paper is not entirely clear on this issue). Perhaps, to escape the lure of rank orders, it may be advisable to turn again to Aristotle, more specifically to his notions of the "mean" (*mesotes*) and prudent judgment (*phronesis*). As Aristotle would have recognized, there may be a tension between local and more general attachments and responsibilities. The task is to navigate carefully between different attachments and responsibilities and, if possible, find a "mean" or middle point. This navigation, in turn, has to be guided by thoughtful and carefully balanced judgment, the judgment of a reasonable and broadly educated person (*phronimos*). I am not sure whether the Confucian tradition has a notion that parallels the idea of prudent judgment (perhaps the notion of *quan*, or "flexibility," comes close). But I know that Confucianism is famous for the "Doctrine of the Mean" (*chung-yung*), about which Tu Weiming has written that it is not "a categorical imperative in the Kantian [universalist] sense" but rather a "standard of inspiration" or an "experienced ideal" needing to be cultivated in practical conduct.[3]

By way of conclusion, I want to add a further caveat (which perhaps exceeds the Aristotelian framework): in some cases, competing demands may collide so harshly that there is no midpoint, no possibility of finding a "mean" through prudent judgment. At this juncture we enter the realm of tragedy beyond resolution. Greek tragedy presents us with the exemplary case of Antigone, who was forced to choose between the general "law of the land" and her own deeper family loyalty, her love with distinction for her dead brother; since there was no way to reconcile these loyalties, her fate was sealed. In the Confucian tradition, perhaps the case of Emperor Shun and his relation to his father is similar. Shun realized and accepted that it was up to the "law of the land" to apprehend his father as a murderer. For himself, however, the situation was different: his task was not to apprehend but to love his father, and he could do so only by exiling them both from the law of justice and retreating into a land of love beyond law. (I am troubled by Shun's treatment of his brother, as recorded in Mencius, but will not comment on it here.) Turning to more modern (Western) literature, I find exemplary the case of Tolstoy's *Anna Karenina*. By the rules of law and morality, Anna was bound to her husband and her children, and there is no indication that she was ready to willfully disregard these rules and her obligations as a wife and mother. However, something happened to her: without seeking or soliciting it, a deep passion entered her life, a very special love with distinction that shattered all rules and ultimately her life. At this point, one can see that love with distinction, though very particular and singular, carries its own limitless horizon, an infinity that ruptures conventional norms. Paul Ricoeur speaks of the "supra-ethical" status of genuine love with respect to justice and general morality.[4] It is, I believe, part of our "humaneness" (*ren*) to recognize and honor this "distinct" status.

Notes

1. Integral Pluralism

1. The thesis that modernity is marked by "disenchantment" and the growing differentiation or segregation of "value spheres" is chiefly associated with the work of Max Weber. Compare especially his "Politics as a Vocation" and "Science as a Vocation," in *From Max Weber: Essays in Sociology*, trans. and ed. H. H. Gerth and C. Wright Mills (New York: Oxford University Press, 1946), 77–156.

2. On this point, see my *The Promise of Democracy: Political Agency and Transformation* (Albany: State University of New York Press, 2010).

3. See Claude Lefort, *Democracy and Political Theory*, trans. David Macey (Minneapolis: University of Minnesota Press, 1988), 19.

4. The most forceful articulation of this point has been advanced by Samuel P. Huntington, "The Clash of Civilizations?" *Foreign Affairs* 72 (1993): 22–49; see also his *The Clash of Civilizations and the Remaking of World Order* (New York: Simon and Schuster, 1996).

5. William James, *A Pluralistic Universe* (1909; reprint, New York: Longmans, Green, 1932), 34, 36–37, 71, 76. The text was initially presented in 1908 as the Hibbert Lectures at Manchester College in England. Subsequent references are to this edition unless otherwise noted.

6. Ibid., 25. In stark opposition to this theistic view, the text advances the bold vision of a "finite God" participating with other beings in the ongoing creation or remaking of the world. As James states, he has come to accept the notion "that there is a God, but that he is finite, either in power or in knowledge, or in both at once. These, I need hardly tell you, are the terms in which common men have usually carried on their active commerce with God" (ibid., 311).

7. Ibid., 212–213, 237. In articulating his view of radical empiricism, James repeatedly pays tribute to the work of Henri Bergson; he also clearly anticipates arguments developed later in phenomenology. In the judicious words of Richard Bernstein: James "sought to show that we are not confronted with an epistemological dichotomy where there is experience or consciousness, on one side, and reality or things known, on the other. There is only 'pure experience' which functions in different contexts and in different

ways. . . . James sees how much of modern philosophy has been trapped within the limiting and distortive confines of Cartesian dualism . . . [He] was evolving an understanding of human individuals as 'lived bodies' within which we make functional distinctions between 'mental' and 'physical' poles. In this respect he anticipates Maurice Merleau-Ponty's phenomenological description of the 'lived body' and 'the primacy of perception.'" "Introduction" to *A Pluralistic Universe* (Cambridge, Mass.: Harvard University Press, 1977), xxvi–xxvii.

8. James, *A Pluralistic Universe*, 322–324, 326–327. On this issue, compare Richard Madsen and Tracy B. Strong, eds., *The Many and the One: Religious and Secular Perspectives on Ethical Pluralism in the Modern World* (Princeton, N.J.: Princeton University Press, 2003). Unfortunately, neither the editors nor most of the contributors come to terms with the metaphysical dimension raised by James. See also my "Conversation across Boundaries: E Pluribus Unum?" in *Dialogue among Civilizations: Some Exemplary Voices* (New York: Palgrave Macmillan, 2002), 31–47.

9. James, *A Pluralistic Universe*, 314–315.

10. Raimon Panikkar, *A Dwelling Place for Wisdom,* trans. Annemarie S. Kidder (Louisville, Ky.: Westminister/John Knox Press, 1993), 146–147. He adds: "Pluralism contends neither that truth is singular nor that there are many truths. If truth were only singular, we could not accept the positive tolerance of a pluralistic attitude and would have to assume that pluralism allows error. If there were many truths, we would become trapped in plain contradictions" (146). For a critique of Panikkar's pluralism, see Gerald J. Larson, "Contra Pluralism," in *The Intercultural Challenge of Raimon Panikkar,* ed. Joseph Prabhu (Maryknoll, N.Y.: Orbis Books, 1996), 71–87. For a defense along the lines of Alfred North Whitehead, see John B. Cobb Jr., "Metaphysical Pluralism," ibid., 46–57; for Panikkar's response, see "A Self-Critical Dialogue," ibid., 227–291, especially 247–262.

11. William E. Connolly, *Pluralism* (Durham, N.C.: Duke University Press, 2005), 10, 41, 79. Apart from James, Connolly also invokes the testimony of contemporary scientists such as Ilya Prigogine and Stephen Dolfram, known for the formulation of chaos theory and natural systems of disequilibrium (83–87). Compare also Kennan Ferguson, *William James: Politics in the Pluriverse* (Lanham, Md.: Rowman and Littlefield, 2007).

12. Jean-François Lyotard, *The Postmodern Condition: A Report on Knowledge,* trans. Goeff Bennington and Brian Massumi (Minneapolis: University of Minnesota Press, 1984), 15–17. As Lyotard explicitly stresses in his preface, postmodernism is meant to strengthen "our sensitivity to differences" and "our ability to tolerate the incommensurable" (xxiv–xxv). In this context, compare my "The Politics of Nonidentity: Adorno, Postmodernism, and Edward Said," in *Alternative Visions: Paths in the Global Village* (Lanham, Md.: Rowman and Littlefield, 1988), 47–69.

13. Richard Rorty, *Contingency, Irony, and Solidarity* (Cambridge: Cambridge University Press, 1989), 44, 73. Basically, "irony" here signals a retreat into individual privacy, while "solidarity" is a concession to external social needs. For a critique of Rorty's position, see Richard J. Bernstein, "Rorty's Liberal Utopia" and "One Step Forward, Two Steps Backward: Rorty on Liberal Democracy and Philosophy," in *The New Constellation: The Ethical-Political Horizons of Modernity/Post Modernity* (Cambridge: Polity Press, 1991), 230–292.

14. For the distinction between pluralism and plurality, see Kenneth L. Schmitz, "The Unity of Human Nature and the Diversity of Cultures," in *Relations between Cultures*, ed. George F. McLean and John Kromkowski (Washington, D.C.: Council for Research in Values and Philosophy, 1991), 305–322.

15. James, *A Pluralistic Universe*, 213, 271, 321–322, 329–330. At another point, James very clearly spells out the aspect of embroilment and continuity: "Our 'multiverse' still makes a 'universe'; for every part, though it may not be in actual or immediate connexion, is nevertheless in some possible or mediated connexion, with every other part however remote, through the fact that each part hangs together with its very next neighbors in inextricable interfusion. The type of union, it is true, is different here from the monistic type of *Alleinheit*. It is not a universal co-implication or integration of all things *durcheinander*. It is what I call the strung-along type, the type of continuity, contiguity, or concatenation" (325).

16. Raymond D. Boisvert, *John Dewey: Rethinking Our Time* (Albany: State University of New York Press, 1998), 5–10, 20–21.

17. John Dewey, "The Development of American Pragmatism" (1925), in *The Essential Dewey*, vol. 1, *Pragmatism, Education, Democracy*, ed. Larry A. Hickman and Thomas M. Alexander (Bloomington: Indiana University Press, 1998), 6. Following this line of argument, Dewey perceives in pragmatism "a metaphysical implication," namely, "the conception of a universe whose evolution is not finished, of a universe which is still, in James's term, 'in the making,' 'in the process of becoming,' of a universe up to a certain point still plastic" (8). In another context, in *The Public and Its Problems* (1927), Dewey spells out the political consequences of a static monism: "The belief in political fixity, of the sanctity of some form of state consecrated by the efforts of our fathers and hallowed by tradition, is one of the stumbling blocks in the way of orderly and directed change." See "Search for the Public," in *The Essential Dewey*, 1:291.

18. Connolly, *Pluralism*, 43, 48, 64–65, 74, 77. See also William E. Connolly, *The Ethics of Pluralization* (Minneapolis: University of Minnesota Press, 1995); David Campbell and Morton Schoolman, eds., *The New Pluralism: William Connolly and the Contemporary Global Condition* (Durham: Duke University PRess, 2008); and Stephen K. White, *The Ethos of a Late-Modern Citizen* (Cambridge, Mass.: Harvard University Press, 2009).

19. Raimon Panikkar, *The Intra-Religious Dialogue* (New York: Paulist Press, 1978), 89, 91–92.

20. Martin Heidegger, *Identität und Differenz*, 4th ed. (Pfullingen: Neske, 1957), 57 (my free translation). In contrast to this kind of embroilment, Heidegger sees the trademark of traditional metaphysics precisely in the deductive subsumption of beings under a monistic idea: "The basic character of metaphysics resides in the unification of beings in supreme universality" (52). Compare also William E. Connolly, *Identity/Difference: Democratic Negotiations of Political Paradox* (Ithaca, N.Y.: Cornell University Press, 1991); Luce Irigaray, *Thinking the Difference: For a Peaceful Revolution*, trans. Karin Montin (London: Athlone Press, 1994); Douglas L. Donkel, ed., *The Theory of Difference: Readings in Contemporary Continental Thought* (Albany: State University of New York Press, 2001); and Heinz Kimmerle, *Philosophien der Differenz* (Würzburg: Königshausen und Neumann, 2000).

21. Maurice Merleau-Ponty, *Phenomenology of Perception*, trans. Colin Smith (London: Routledge and Kegan Paul, 1962), vii, ix, 364, 448. As Merleau-Ponty adds: "My life must have a significance which I do not constitute. There must strictly speaking be an intersubjectivity: each one of us must be both anonymous in the sense of absolutely individual, and anonymous in the sense of absolutely general. Our being in the world is the concrete bearer of this double anonymity" (448)—or the bearer of an uncharted embroilment.

22. Maurice Merleau-Ponty, *The Visible and the Invisible, Followed by Working Notes*, ed. Claude Lefort, trans. Alphonso Lingis (Evanston, Ill.: Northwestern University Press, 1968), 160, 172–174, 248, 263. Note that for him, the dimensions of the "visible" and the "invisible," of immanence and transcendence, are entwined in the same way: "The visible itself has an invisible inner texture, and the invisible is the secret counterpart of the visible; it appears only within it" (215).

23. See in this context Claude Lefort, "Flesh and Otherness," in *Ontology and Alterity in Merleau-Ponty*, ed. Galen A. Johnson and Michael B. Smith (Evanston, Ill.: Northwestern University Press, 1990), 3–13.

24. Note that James's *A Pluralistic Universe* was composed almost a decade after his Gifford Lectures and gives more emphasis to lateral connections and concatenations. In contrast, although Taylor favors a more holistic perspective, he stops short of clearly embracing (what I call) integral pluralism. There is a further difference: while James leans in the direction of an "immanent" religiosity, Taylor's recent tendency is to stress a radical "transcendence" and to denounce (what he calls) a purely "immanent frame." See Taylor's *A Secular Age* (Cambridge, Mass.: Harvard University Press, 2007), especially 309–310, 539–593. On this issue, I am inclined (with Panikkar and Merleau-Ponty) to favor an undecidable embroilment of immanence-transcendence.

25. Anthony Parel, *Gandhi's Philosophy and the Quest for Harmony* (Cambridge: Cambridge University Press, 2006). Gandhi was an integral

pluralist in another domain particularly crucial on the Indian subcontinent: the relations between different religions and faith traditions (Hindu, Buddhist, Muslim, Jain, and others). Compare in this context my "Gandhi and Islam: A Heart-and-Mind Unity?" in *Peace Talks—Who Will Listen?* (Notre Dame, Ind.: University of Notre Dame, 2004), 132–151. Gandhi is often taken to task for allegedly showing insufficient concern for the plight of the Untouchables or Dalits. In his defense, one could probably say that, for him, the remedy resided in a revision of the entire caste system rather than a partial dismantling of it. Still, in this case, his holism may have overshadowed his pluralism.

2. The Concept of the Political

1. Joseph Lieberman, "Democrats and America's Enemies," *Wall Street Journal*, May 22, 2008, 17.

2. There is, to be sure, a vast literature on Carl Schmitt today, but the friend-enemy distinction is rarely the central focus. Compare George Schwab, *The Challenge of the Exception: An Introduction to the Political Ideas of Carl Schmitt between 1921 and 1936*, 2nd ed. (New York: Greenwood Press, 1989); Heinrich Meier, *Carl Schmitt and Leo Strauss: The Hidden Dialogue* (Chicago: University of Chicago Press, 1995); J. W. Bendersky, *Carl Schmitt: Theorist for the Reich* (Princeton, N.J.: Princeton University Press, 1983); Jacob Taubes, *Ad Carl Schmitt: Gegenstrebige Fügung* (Berlin: Merve Verlag, 1987); D. Dyzenhaus, ed., *Law as Politics: Carl Schmitt's Critique of Liberalism* (Durham, N.C.: Duke University Press, 1998); Chantal Mouffe, *The Challenge of Carl Schmitt* (London: Verso, 1999); William Scheuerman, *Carl Schmitt: The End of Law* (Lanham, Md.: Rowman and Littlefield, 1999); G. Balakrishnan, *The Enemy: An Intellectual Portrait of Carl Schmitt* (London: Verso, 2000); J. W. Müller, *A Dangerous Mind: Carl Schmitt in Post-War European Thought* (New Haven, Conn.: Yale University Press, 2002); Reinhard Mehring, ed., *Carl Schmitt: Der Begriff des Politischen, Ein Kooperativer Kommentar* (Berlin: Akademie Verlag, 2003). The present chapter does not deal with Schmitt's work in toto but only with the friend-enemy distinction.

3. Carl Schmitt, *Der Begriff des Politischen* (Munich: Duncker und Humblot, 1932). The basic thesis of the text was published earlier as "Der Begriff des Politischen," *Archiv für Sozialwissenschaft und Sozialpolitik* 58 (1927): 1–33.

4. George Schwab, introduction to Carl Schmitt, *The Concept of the Political*, expanded ed., trans. George Schwab (Chicago: University of Chicago Press, 2007), 6. In a book published a year after *Der Begriff* and after the "seizure of power," Schmitt formulated a triad of categories borrowed in part from National Socialist rhetoric: state, movement, and people. See his *Staat,*

Bewegung, Volk: Die Dreigliederung der politischen Einheit (Hamburg: Hanseatische Verlagsanstalt, 1933). The same triad was mentioned in the preface to the second edition (1934) of *Political Theology*; see Carl Schmitt, *Political Theology: Four Chapters on the Concept of Sovereignty*, trans. George Schwab (Chicago: University of Chicago Press, 1985), 3. However, the modification did not affect the status of sovereignty or the friend-enemy distinction. On the whole, I agree with Schwab when he writes that, at least during this period, "Schmitt opted for a strong state that would ensure order, peace, and stability. . . . Schmitt's political theory can be summarized in the following propositions: By virtue of its possession of a monopoly on politics, the state is the only entity able to distinguish friend from enemy and thereby demand of its citizens the readiness to die" (introduction to *Political Theology*, 1).

5. Carl Schmitt, *Le categorie del "politico,"* ed. Gianfranco Miglio and Pierangelo Schiera (Bologna: Società editrice il Mulino, 1972), 23–24, quoted by Schwab, introduction to *Concept of the Political*, 6. To be sure, by "state," Schmitt never meant a mere bureaucratic machinery but rather a living unity guided by a personalized sovereign able to distinguish between friend and enemy. From this angle, one can also understand his 1970 statement that "today one can no longer define the political in terms of the state; on the contrary, what we take to be the state today must inversely be defined and understood from the political" (i.e., the friend-enemy distinction). Carl Schmitt, *Political Theology II: The Myth of the Closure of Any Political Theology*, trans. Michael Hoelzl and Graham Ward (1970 [German]; Cambridge: Polity Press, 2008), 45. On this basis, Tracy Strong observes that one possible consequence of Schmitt's concept of the political is a kind of "right-wing Leninism, where the Party is replaced by the *Volk* and the sovereign becomes the Party-in-action" (provided personal leadership is not bureaucratically smothered). See Strong's foreword to *Political Theology*, xxviii.

6. Compare in this context D. Diner and M. Stollers, eds., *Hans Kelsen and Carl Schmitt: A Juxtaposition* (Tel Aviv: Schriftenreihe des Instituts für deutsche Geschichte, University of Tel Aviv, 1999); and D. Dyzenhaus, *Legality and Legitimacy: Carl Schmitt, Hans Kelsen, and Hermann Heller* (Oxford: Clarendon, 1997). To an extent, the above comparison is meant tongue-in-cheek; in Schmitt's case, purity was no doubt diminished by an ideological (antiliberal) animus that influenced his text. Still, Schmitt occasionally uses the language of "purity," such as when he writes: "The exception is that which cannot be subsumed; it defies general codification, but it simultaneously reveals a specifically juristic element—the decision in absolute purity." *Political Theology*, 13.

7. Schmitt, *Concept of the Political*, 19, 22–25, 39–41. The text links the rise of associational pluralism in Germany with the teachings of Otto Gierke and Hugo Preuss, in France with the syndicalist movement, and in England with the pluralist theories of G. D. H. Cole and Harold Laski.

8. Ibid., 25–26.
9. Ibid., 28, 32.
10. Ibid., 33–34, 46, 71.
11. Ibid., 28–29.
12. Ibid., 27, 54, 66.
13. Ibid., 79. It is this anti-ideological or antifanatical quality of Schmitt's work that, in our time of terror wars, has become attractive to many Western intellectuals (even those at odds with his political affiliations). This sympathy has been greatly reinforced by the publication of the English translation of Schmitt's *Der Nomos der Erde* (first published in 1950); see Carl Schmitt, *The Nomos of the Earth in the International Law of the Jus Publicum Europaeum,* trans. G. L. Ulmen (New York: Telos Press, 2003). Compare Maurice Merleau-Ponty, *Humanism and Terror,* trans. John O'Neill (Boston: Beacon Press, 1969).
14. Schmitt, *Concept of the Political,* 27, 63, 67–68. The loose reference to Hegel involves the master-slave relation and the struggle for "recognition." But the passage entirely omits any mention of the crucial Hegelian emphasis on mediation and reconciliation.
15. Ibid., 64–65. One misses in the above catalog the name of Friedrich Nietzsche. As Tracy Strong states in his foreword to *Political Theology,* following Heinrich Meier, "Schmitt never engaged in a full-fledged confrontation with Nietzsche" (xix). Compare Heinrich Meier, *Carl Schmitt and Leo Strauss: The Hidden Dialogue,* trans. J. Harvey Lomax (Chicago: University of Chicago Press, 1995), 65n72. Leaving this aside, Schmitt's anthropology clearly relies on a stark antinomy between optimism and pessimism, between conceptions of human nature as essentially good or evil. What this dichotomy bypasses is a nonessential view treating human beings as potentially good *and* evil. Curiously, Schmitt acknowledges this option in a footnote, citing Irenaeus, but without comment: "Men are free and endowed with the opportunity to choose [between good and evil]; therefore, it is not true that some men are good by nature and others evil by nature" (*Concept of the Political,* 64n33).
16. Schmitt, *Concept of the Political,* 35, 38, 49. At one point, Schmitt refers to a "normal" or nonexceptional situation, but without noting any consequences for the political. "The endeavor of a normal state," he writes, "consists above all in assuring total peace [total peace?] within the state and its territory. To create tranquility, security and order and thereby establish the normal situation is the prerequisite for legal norms to be valid" (ibid., 46).
17. Leo Strauss, "Notes on Carl Schmitt, *The Concept of the Political,*" trans. J. Harvey Lomax, in *Concept of the Political,* 100. He adds: "If it is true that the 'systematics of liberal thought' has 'still not been replaced in Europe today by any other system,' it is to be expected that [Schmitt] too will be compelled to make use of elements of liberal thought in the presenta-

tion of his views. The tentativeness of Schmitt's statements results from this compulsion" (101).

18. Ibid., 101, 103–106.

19. Ibid., 106. For Strauss, Hobbes's attempt to escape from the state of nature is evidence of his incipient liberal progressivism, an aspect absent in Schmitt's account. "Hobbes," he writes, "to a much higher degree than Bacon, is the author of the ideal of 'civilization'; by this very fact he is the founder of liberalism. . . . Hobbes's foundation for the natural-right claim to the securing of life pure and simple sets the path to the whole system of human rights in the sense of liberalism. . . . In an unliberal world Hobbes forges ahead to lay the foundation of liberalism against the—*sit venia verbo*—unliberal 'nature' of man" (107). The claim is sharpened in a subsequent passage: Liberalism "forgets the foundation of culture, the state of nature, that is, human nature in its dangerousness and endangeredness. Schmitt returns, contrary to liberalism, to its author, Hobbes, in order to strike at the root of liberalism in Hobbes's express negation of the state of nature. Whereas Hobbes in an unliberal world accomplishes the foundation of liberalism, Schmitt in a liberal world undertakes the critique of liberalism" (108). As is well known, Strauss later presented Hobbes as the author of the modernist derailment of political thought; see his *The Political Philosophy of Hobbes,* trans. Elsa M. Sinclair (Chicago: University of Chicago Press, 1952). On this point, Strauss and Schmitt obviously diverged, since the latter considered Hobbes chiefly as an antiliberal thinker; see his *The Leviathan in the State Theory of Thomas Hobbes,* trans. George Schwab and Erna Hilfstein (1938 [German]; Westport, Conn.: Greenwood Press, 1996). Still later, Strauss assigned the blame for inaugurating the derailment of modern political thought to Machiavelli rather than Hobbes.

20. Strauss, "Notes on Carl Schmitt," 110–112, 114–115, 117. Adding more concrete contours to the "moral" dimension of the friend-enemy polarity, Strauss writes: "Thus warlike morals seem to be the ultimate legitimation for Schmitt's affirmation of the political, and the opposition between the negation and the positing of the political seems to coincide with the opposition between pacifist internationalism and bellicose nationalism," or else "between the 'authoritarian and anarchistic theories'" (112–113).

21. Ibid., 115, 118–121. Strauss adds: "The polemic against liberalism can therefore only signify a concomitant or preparatory action: it is meant to clear the field for the decisive battle" (121). Unsurprisingly, Strauss's concluding comments repeatedly refer not so much to *The Concept of the Political* as to another (admittedly more complex and ambivalent) writing: Schmitt's *Political Theology.*

22. The strategy of reversal is most clearly manifest in the text that, in a way, inaugurated the postmodern movement: Jean-François Lyotard, *The Postmodern Condition: A Report on Knowledge* (Minneapolis: University of

Minnesota Press, 1984). The strange attraction of Schmitt's work for many Continental writers on the Left was first noted and critically dissected by Norberto Bobbio in his book *Right and Left: The Significance of a Political Distinction,* trans. Allan Cameron (Chicago: University of Chicago Press, 1996), especially 18–19. See also the comment by Metz that "it is the former left wing that today is clamoring for a strong, decisionist state." Johann Baptist Metz, *The Passion for God,* trans. J. Matthew Ashley (New York: Paulist Press, 1998), 146.

23. I find it convenient to distinguish three main phases of Derrida's development: an early phase bearing the imprint of Husserl and Heidegger, a middle phase shaped by the encounter with Nietzsche, and a later phase dominated by the thought of Emmanuel Levinas.

24. Jacques Derrida, "Force of Law: The 'Mystical Foundation of Authority,'" in *Deconstruction and the Possibility of Justice,* ed. Drucilla Cornell, Michel Rosenfeld, and David G. Carlson (New York: Routledge, 1992), 6, 8, 13. The text repeatedly makes brief references to Schmitt's work, portraying him as "that great conservative Catholic jurist" (30) and as a thinker who still recognized the crucial role of "war and *polemos*": "War is another example of this contradiction internal to law (*Recht* or *droit*). There is a *droit de la guerre* (Schmitt will complain that it is no longer recognized as the very possibility of politics)" (39). The fascination with war and violence often found in Continental thought has been ably criticized by Hannah Arendt in *On Violence* (New York: Harcourt Brace Jovanovich, 1970). See also John Keane, *Reflections on Violence* (London: Verso, 1995), and my "On Violence: Post-Arendtian Reflections," in *Peace Talks—Who Will Listen?* (Notre Dame, Ind.: University of Notre Dame Press, 2004), 111–131.

25. Derrida, "Force of Law," 14–16, 24–25, 27. Repeatedly, it is true, Derrida seeks to soften the polarity by emphasizing a certain relationship or mediation. As he states: "Everything would still be simple if this distinction between justice and law (*droit*) were a true distinction. . . . But it turns out that *droit* claims to exercise itself in the name of justice and that justice is required to establish itself in the name of a law that must be 'enforced.' Deconstruction always finds itself between these two poles" (22). But the opposition of "two poles" is precisely the heart of polarity. The veering toward dualism and a quasi-theological transcendence is discussed and rebuked by Dominique Janicaud in "The Theological Turn of French Phenomenology," in *Phenomenology and the "Theological Turn,"* ed. Dominique Janicaud et al. (New York: Fordham University Press, 2000), 16–103. Compare also my "Small Wonder: Finitude and Its Horizons," in *Small Wonder: Global Power and Its Discontents* (Lanham, Md.: Rowman and Littlefield, 2005), 13–32.

26. Alain Badiou, *Infinite Thought: Truth and the Return to Philosophy* (New York: Continuum, 2003), 48–50, 56.

27. See ibid., 82; Alain Badiou, *Abrégé de métapolitique* (Paris: Seuil,

1998), 114; "Entretien de Bruxelles," *Les Temps Modernes* 526 (May 1990): 19; "Politics and Philosophy," interview in *Angelaki* 3 (1998): 125. As Hewlett comments: "For Badiou, true politics is something quite specific, short-lived, and momentous, which often involves a resolution or revolt of a collective, egalitarian and emancipatory nature, an irruption of positive political energy that may well take the form of an uprising or at least some sort of revolt against the established order." Nick Hewlett, *Badiou, Balibar, Rancière: Rethinking Emancipation* (London: Continuum, 2007), 50.

28. Hewlett, *Badiou, Balibar, Rancière,* 60; Badiou, *Abrégé de métapolitique,* 134–135.

29. Jacques Rancière, "Ten Theses on Politics," *Theory and Event* 5 (2001): 8; *La Mésentente* (Paris: Galileé, 1995), 139; *La Haine de la démocratie* (Paris: Seuil, 2005), 48.

30. In Hewlett's words: "Rancière's theory is a theory of the subject similar to Badiou's, in that subjects must believe in their actions and statements and make them true by creating the revolutionizing criteria by which they are judged." *Badiou, Balibar, Rancière,* 107.

31. Claude Lefort, *Democracy and Political Theory,* trans. David Macey (Minneapolis: University of Minnesota Press, 1988), 9, 11, 20. Lefort is not alone in formulating a conception of the political and a distinction between the political and politics that are at odds with Schmitt's thesis. For comparable attempts, see Paul Ricoeur, "The Political Paradox," in *History and Truth,* trans. Charles A. Kelbley (Evanston, Ill.: Northwestern University Press, 1965), 247–270; Sheldon S. Wolin, *Politics and Vision* (Boston: Little, Brown, 1966), 43; and my "Rethinking the Political: Some Heideggerian Contributions," in *The Other Heidegger* (Ithaca, N.Y.: Cornell University Press, 1993), 49–76.

32. Lefort, *Democracy and Political Theory,* 11, 218. He adds, "the elaboration attested to by any political society . . . therefore involves an investigation into the 'world,' into Being as such" (219). For a comparison of Lefort and Heidegger, see my "Post-metaphysical Politics: Heidegger and Democracy," in *The Other Heidegger,* 77–105. See also Claude Lefort, "Flesh and Otherness," in *Ontology and Alterity in Merleau-Ponty,* ed. Galen A. Johnson and Michael B. Smith (Evanston, Ill.: Northwestern University Press, 1990), 3–13.

33. Lefort, *Democracy and Political Theory,* 16–17. Compare Ernst Kantorowicz, *The King's Two Bodies: A Study in Medieval Political Theory* (Princeton, N.J.: Princeton University Press, 1957).

34. Lefort, *Democracy and Political Theory,* 16, 19–20, 225. Note that "empty place" in this context does not designate a mere vacuum but rather the latent promise of liberation and equality. In the stirring words of Agnes Heller: "An empty seat awaits the Messiah. If anyone does occupy it, we can be sure we would have then a perverse or hypocritical Messiah. . . . Poli-

tics cannot make use of an empty podium; yet as long as the podium is left where it is, exactly in the middle of the room. . . . politicians will always [have to] take its existence into account." Agnes Heller, "Politik nach dem Tod Gottes," in *Instanzen/Perspekiven/Imaginationen,* ed. Jörg Huber and Alois M. Mueller (Zurich: Museum Press, 1995), 94.

35. See my "The Law of Peoples: Civilizing Humanity," in *Peace Talks—Who Will Listen?* 42–63.

36. John Dewey, "Creative Democracy—The Task before Us" (1939), in *John Dewey: The Later Works, 1925–1953,* ed. Jo Ann Boydston (Carbondale: Southern Illinois University Press, 1981–1990), 14:228. Compare my *In Search of the Good Life: A Pedagogy for Troubled Times* (Lexington: University Press of Kentucky, 2007). Consider also Nietzsche's observation: "How much respect has a noble person for his enemies! And such respect is already a bridge to love." Friedrich Nietzsche, "Toward a Genealogy of Morals," in *The Portable Nietzsche,* ed. Walter Kaufmann (New York: Viking Press, 1968), 452.

3. The Secular and the Sacred

This chapter is dedicated to Raimon Panikkar.

1. Carl Schmitt, *Political Theology: Four Chapters on the Concept of Sovereignty,* trans. George Schwab (Cambridge, Mass.: MIT Press, 1985), 5. The book first appeared in German in 1922 and was revised in 1934. Here and elsewhere, I have slightly altered Schwab's translation for purposes of clarity. The original sentence reads in German: "Souverän ist, wer über den Ausnahmezustand entscheidet." Schwab's translation reads: "Sovereign is he who decides on the exception." However, the "he" could certainly also be a "she." In his foreword to the book, Tracy Strong looks at different possible meanings of the sentence and concludes: "Schmitt is saying that it is the essence of sovereignty *both* to decide what is an exception *and* to make the decisions appropriate to that exception" (xii).

2. Ibid., 36.

3. See, for example, Creston Davis, John Milbank, and Slavoj Zizek, eds., *Theology and the Political: The New Debate* (Durham, N.C.: Duke University Press, 2005); Hent de Vries and Lawrence E. Sullivan, eds., *Political Theologies: Public Religions in a Post-Secular World* (New York: Fordham University Press, 2006). The latter book, which is nearly 800 pages, contains only one chapter dealing tangentially with Carl Schmitt: Marc de Wilde, "Violence in the State of Exception: Reflections on Theological-Political Motifs in Benjamin and Schmitt," 188–200. Both books are completely silent on the alternative or "new" kind of "political theology" developed in Germany partly in response to Schmitt: that of Jürgen Moltmann and Johann Baptist Metz. I refer to these writers (to whom I am in many ways indebted) later in this

chapter. Nor do the books mention the different versions of "liberation theology." Jean Bethke Elshtain's *Sovereignty, God, State, and Self* (New York: Basic Books, 2008) contains some brief comments on Schmitt (114–117).

4. Schmitt, *Political Theology*, 36–37. In an instructive fashion, Schmitt exempts the work of Thomas Hobbes from the (later) rationalistic tendencies: "In addition to the decisionistic cast of his thinking, Hobbes remained personalistic and postulated an ultimate concrete deciding agency . . . and also elevated his state, the Leviathan, into an immense person and thus point-blank into mythology. This he did despite his nominalism and natural-scientific approach and his reduction of the individual to an atom. For Hobbes, this was no anthropomorphism—from which he was truly free—but a methodical and systematic consequence of his legal thinking" (47).

5. Ibid., 41–42, 48.

6. Ibid., 49–51. What Schmitt completely ignores here is that the entire story of modernity can be read in a very different light: namely, as the incipient unfolding of a different conception of the divine and a correspondingly different self-understanding of humanity. Seen in this light, the alleged "transfer" of theological concepts to political theory appears much more complex and less unilateral than Schmitt suggests. In our time, in particular, the experience of Auschwitz and other atrocities has rendered the idea of an omnipotent, sovereign deity (who does not seem to care) incoherent and nearly intolerable. See chapter 4 for the delineation of a religion of service and of God as "suffering servant" rather than absurd emperor. Along the same lines, one can no longer think of secularity as the simple antithesis to religion; rather, it is embroiled with and a necessary complement to faith, linked with the latter in differentiated correlation.

7. Ibid., 53–54.

8. Ibid., 55–56.

9. Ibid., 56–58. Notwithstanding the extremism of the Spaniard, Schmitt later devoted a longer study to his thought. See his *Donoso Cortés in gesamteuropäischer Interpretation* (Cologne: Greven, 1950). See also Schmitt's *Roman Catholicism and Political Form*, trans. G. L. Ulman (1923 [German]; Westport, Conn.: Greenwood Press, 1996).

10. Schmitt, *Political Theology*, 59, 61–62. As he adds: "In his radical intellectuality Cortés directed his attention always only at the theology of his opponent" (62). Although sharing the diagnosis and some of the antiliberal animus of the Catholic counterrevolutionaries, Schmitt does not find their remedies or strategies entirely suitable to contemporary conditions. In this respect, Tracy Strong seems correct when he writes in his foreword to *Political Theology* that, for Schmitt, "the Right has gotten the *problem* of modern politics correct, even if what it sometimes proposed to do about it (as with Maistre, Bonald, and Cortes) has not always been on target or on the only target" (xxxii).

11. See Hans Blumenberg, *The Legitimacy of the Modern Age*, trans.

Robert M. Wallace (1966 [German]; Cambridge, Mass.: MIT Press, 1983); also *Säkularisierung und Selbstbehauptung* (Frankfurt: Suhrkamp, 1974). Compare in this context Michael A. Gillespie, *The Theological Origins of Modernity* (Chicago: University of Chicago Press, 2008).

12. See Carl Schmitt, *Political Theology II: The Myth of the Closure of Any Political Theology*, trans. Michael Hoelzl and Graham Ward (1970 [German]; Cambridge: Polity Press, 2008). In his postscript, Schmitt remarks: "I do not want to create the impression . . . that I wish to engage in a confrontation with a book [Blumenberg's] that opens up astonishing horizons, theologically, anthropologically, and cosmologically, and whose insights were very fruitful for me. Neither starting nor attempting such a confrontation would be appropriate" (121). Despite this disclaimer, however, Schmitt levels a serious charge against Blumenberg: "Autism is inherent in this argument. Its immanence, directed polemically against a theological transcendence, is nothing but self-empowerment. Of course, Blumenberg also speaks the language of a philosophy of values [which also involves] . . . the loss of value. . . . Thus questions of legitimacy and legality are dissolved into a universal convertibility of values" (120). Curiously, Schmitt's critique of immanentism and his defense of transcendence come to grief when confronted with Peterson's reliance on a strong Augustinian transcendentalism.

13. Surprisingly, *Political Theology II* is dedicated to the Catholic theologian and "canonist" Hans Barion, who had written some essays more or less siding with Peterson. Note, however, that *Political Theology II* was written and published in the aftermath of Vatican II and the so-called *aggiornamento* introduced by Pope John XXIII, an accommodation welcomed by neither Barion nor Schmitt.

14. Schmitt, *Political Theology II*, 76–78, 80, 91–92, 98–102. For the sake of brevity, this presentation is highly condensed and bypasses some of the nuances of early church history.

15. Ibid., 80, 109n2, 115.

16. By Johann Baptist Metz, see *Faith in History and Society*, trans. J. Matthew Ashley (New York: Crossroad, 2007); *A Passion for God: The Mystical-Political Dimension of Christianity*, trans. J. Matthew Ashley (New York: Paulist Press, 1989); *Theology of the World*, trans. William Glen-Doepel (New York: Herder and Herder, 1969). By Jürgen Moltmann, see *God for a Secular Society: The Public Relevance of Theology* (Minneapolis: Fortress Press, 1999); *On Human Dignity: Political Theology and Ethics*, trans. M. Douglas Meeks (Minneapolis: Fortress Press, 1984); *The Crucified God*, trans. R. A. Wilson and John Bowden (New York: Herder and Herder, 1974). By Gustavo Gutierrez, see *A Theology of Liberation*, trans. Sister Caridad and John Eagleson (Maryknoll, N.Y.: Orbis Books, 1973); *The Power of the Poor in History*, trans. Robert R. Barr (Maryknoll, N.Y.: Orbis Books, 1983). See also Juan Luis Segundo, *Liberation of Theology*, trans. John Drury (Maryknoll,

N.Y.: Orbis Books, 1976); Leonardo Boff, *Introducing Liberation Theology,* trans. Paul Burns (Maryknoll, N.Y.: Orbis Books, 1987).

17. See Jürgen Moltmann, "Covenant or Leviathan? Political Theology at the Beginning of Modern Times," in *God for a Secular Society,* 40–41, 43–44. In a similar vein, Johann Baptist Metz argues that critique of the privatization of faith does not necessarily lead to an endorsement of a unified public religion or to "hostility to the Enlightenment and to democracy—as it did with Carl Schmitt and his sources, as it did with Donoso Cortés and with the French traditionalists.... A critical rapprochement between religion and politics on modernity's ground in no way leads necessarily to a decisionist theory of the state." In this context, Metz also rebukes Schmitt's tendency to essentialize human sinfulness, a tendency that forms "the starting point for his fundamental political axiom of the friend-enemy constellation." See Metz, "Monotheism and Democracy: Religion and Politics on Modernity's Ground," in *A Passion for God,* 141–142, 146.

18. See Claude Lefort, *Le travail de l'oeuvre: Machiavel* (Paris: Gallimard, 1972); *The Political Forms of Modern Society,* ed. John B. Thompson (Cambridge, Mass.: MIT Press, 1986).

19. Claude Lefort, *Democracy and Political Theory,* trans. David Macey (Minneapolis: University of Minnesota Press, 1988), 11, 17. The formulation harkens back to Martin Heidegger's "ontic-ontological" difference and his notion that the truth of "Being" is simultaneously revealed and concealed. As Lefort adds: "Democratic society is instituted as a society without a body, as a society which undermines the representation of an organic totality. I am not suggesting that it therefore has no unity or defined shape; on the contrary, the disappearance of 'natural' determination (linked to a prince or a nobility) leads to the emergence of a purely 'social' society in which the people, the nation and the state take on the status of universal categories and in which any individual or group can claim the same status. But neither the state, the people or the nation represent substantial entities" (18).

20. Ibid., 16, 241–242, 244; Jules Michelet, *Histoire de France* (Paris: Lacroix, 1870); Jules Michelet, *Historical View of the French Revolution,* trans. C. Cocks (London: Bohn, 1960); Ernst Kantorowicz, *The King's Two Bodies: A Study in Medieval Political Theology* (Princeton, N.J.: Princeton University Press, 1957).

21. Lefort, *Democracy and Political Theory,* 248–249. As one may recall, the issue of the visible and the invisible was treated extensively by Lefort's friend Maurice Merleau-Ponty; see *The Visible and the Invisible, Followed by Working Notes,* ed. Claude Lefort, trans. Alphonso Lingis (Evanston, Ill.: Northwestern University Press, 1968). For some of Lefort's sustained reflections on Merleau-Ponty's work, see his "Flesh and Otherness," in *Ontology and Alterity in Merleau-Ponty,* ed. Galen A. Johnson and Michael B. Smith (Evanston, Ill.: Northwestern University Press, 1990), 3–13.

22. Lefort, *Democracy and Political Theory*, 232.

23. Ibid., 222–223. "To simplify the argument to extremes," he continues, "what philosophical thought cannot adopt as its own, on pain of betraying its ideal of intelligibility, is the assertion that the man Jesus is the Son of God; what it must accept is the meaning of the advent of a representation of the *God-Man,* because it sees it as a change which recreates humanity's opening onto itself. . . . Any society which forgets its religious basis is laboring under the illusion of pure immanence and thus obliterates the locus of philosophy; . . . philosophy is bound up with religion because they are both caught up in an adventure to which philosophy does not possess the main key" (223–224).

24. Raimon Panikkar, *Worship and Secular Man* (Maryknoll, N.Y.: Orbis Books, 1973), 1. See my essay "Rethinking Secularism—with Raimon Panikkar," in *Dialogue among Civilizations: Some Exemplary Voices* (New York: Palgrave Macmillan, 2002), 185–200. See also Talal Asad, *Formations of the Secular: Christianity, Islam, Modernity* (Stanford, Calif.: Stanford University Press, 2003).

25. Panikkar, *Worship and Secular Man*, 2, 7.

26. Ibid., 2, 7, 10–13.

27. Ibid., 3–4, 18, 20–22.

28. Ibid., 28–30, 35–36.

29. Ibid., 42, 47, 49–52. See also his *The Cosmotheandric Experience*, ed. Scott Eastham (Maryknoll, N.Y.: Orbis Books, 1993).

30. Raimon Panikkar, "Religion or Politics: The Western Dilemma," in *Religion and Politics in the Modern World*, ed. Peter H. Merkl and Ninian Smart (New York: New York University Press, 1983), 44–46.

31. Ibid., 45–47, 49–50.

32. Raimon Panikkar, *Christophany: The Fullness of Man*, trans. Alfred DiLascia (Maryknoll, N.Y.: Orbis Books, 2004), xiv. See also his *The Experience of God: Icons of Mystery*, trans. Joseph Cunneen (Minneapolis: Fortress Press, 2006).

33. Panikkar, *Christophany*, 125.

34. Ibid., 128.

35. Ibid., 130. Compare in this context Paul Ricoeur, *Living Up to Death*, trans. David Pellauer (Chicago: University of Chicago Press, 2009).

4. Postsecular Faith

1. John Dewey, "A Common Faith" (Terry Lectures, Yale University, 1934), in *John Dewey: The Later Works: 1925–1953*, ed. Jo Ann Boydston (Carbondale: Southern Illinois University, 1986), 9:125–145. In his lectures, Dewey steered a course between theism and nontheism, between Spinozistic naturalism and Emersonian transcendentalism or spiritualism. For a

sensitive discussion of Dewey's religiosity, see Steven C. Rockefeller, *John Dewey: Religious Faith and Democratic Humanism* (New York: Columbia University Press, 1991); Steven C. Rockefeller, "Dewey's Philosophy of Religious Experience," in *Reading Dewey: Interpretations for a Postmodern Generation*, ed. Larry A. Hickman (Bloomington: Indiana University Press, 1998), 124–148.

2. On the notion of "postsecular," see the comments by Jürgen Habermas: "The expression *post-secular* does not merely acknowledge publicly the functional contribution that religious communities make to the reproduction of desired motives and attitudes. Rather, the public consciousness of post-secular society reflects a normative insight that has consequences for how believing and unbelieving citizens interact with one another politically. In post-secular society, the realization that 'the modernization of public consciousness' takes hold of and reflexively alters religious as well as secular mentalities in staggered phases is gaining acceptance." Jürgen Habermas, "On the Relations between the Secular Liberal State and Religion," in *Political Theologies: Public Religions in a Post-Secular World*, ed. Hent de Vries and Lawrence E. Sullivan (New York: Fordham University Press, 2006), 258. See also my "Rethinking Secularism—with Raimon Panikkar," in *Dialogue among Civilizations: Some Exemplary Voices* (New York: Palgrave Macmillan, 2002), 185–200.

3. See Max Weber, "Politics as a Vocation" and "The Social Psychology of the World Religions," in *From Max Weber: Essays in Sociology*, trans. and ed. H. H. Gerth and C. Wright Mills (New York: Oxford University Press, 1958), 78–79, 294–295. I bypass here the issue of "charismatic" legitimacy.

4. William James, *The Varieties of Religious Experience: A Study in Human Nature*, 36th impression (London and New York: Longmans, Green, 1928), v, 2–3, 27–28. As James insisted, religious emotions are ordinary "human" emotions like others: "If there were such a thing as inspiration from a higher realm, it might well be that a neurotic temperament would furnish the chief condition of the requisite receptivity" (27).

5. Ibid., 28–29, 31.

6. Charles Taylor, *Varieties of Religion Today: William James Revisited* (Cambridge, Mass.: Harvard University Press, 2002), 3–5, 7. More recently a revised and greatly expanded version of his Gifford Lectures was published under the title *A Secular Age* (Cambridge, Mass.: Belknap Press, 2007). Basically, the expanded version does not conflict with the earlier text.

7. Taylor, *Varieties of Religion Today*, 9–11, 13–14. Taylor cites at this point W. K. Clifford, *The Ethics of Belief and Other Essays*, ed. Leslie Stephen and F. Pollock (London: Watts, 1947), and William James, *The Will to Believe, and Other Essays in Popular Philosophy* (Cambridge, Mass.: Harvard University Press, 1979).

8. Émile Durkheim, *Les formes élémentaires de la vie religieuse*, 5th ed.

(Paris: Presses Universitaires Françaises, 1968); for an English version, see *The Elementary Forms of Religious Life*, trans. Carol Cosman (Oxford and New York: Oxford University Press, 2001).

9. Taylor, *Varieties of Religion Today*, 65–67, 77, 99; Ernst Kantorowicz, *The King's Two Bodies* (Princeton, N.J.: Princeton University Press, 1997).

10. Taylor, *Varieties of Religion Today*, 93–94, 96.

11. Ibid., 111–112, 115–116. James's later text, *A Pluralistic Universe*, corrected to some extent the emphasis of his Gifford Lectures on "individual men in their solitude." See *A Pluralistic Universe* (1909; reprint, New York: Longmans, Green, 1932). See also chapter 1.

12. Taylor, *Varieties of Religion Today*, 23–24.

13. James L. Heft, ed., *A Catholic Modernity? Charles Taylor's Marianist Award Lecture* (New York and Oxford: Oxford University Press, 1999), 18–19, 35. For a discussion of this text and other writings by Taylor, see my "Global Modernization: Toward Different Modernities," in *Dialogue among Civilizations*, especially 97–100.

14. Paul Ricoeur, "Ye Are the Salt of the Earth," in *Political and Social Essays*, ed. David Stewart and Joseph Bien (Athens: Ohio University Press, 1974), 105, 115–117, 123. See also my "Religious Freedom: Preserving the Salt of the Earth," in *In Search of the Good Life: A Pedagogy for Troubled Times* (Lexington: University Press of Kentucky, 2007), 205–219. In one of his late writings, Ricoeur returned to the question of religious faith, placing the emphasis strongly on a religion of service in opposition to a religion of domination. See Ricoeur, *Vivant jusqu'à la mort, suivi de Fragments* (Paris: Editions du Seuil, 2007), especially 89–91; in English, *Living up to Death*, trans. David Pellauer (Chicago: University of Chicago Press, 2009).

15. See, for example, Abraham Heschel, "The Theology of Pathos," in *The Prophets* (New York: Harper and Row, 1962), 2:1–11. The legacy saw an intense revival during the Nazi regime. Thus, prior to being executed, Dietrich Bonhoeffer noted that "only a suffering God can help," which means that Christ helps not by virtue of his omnipotence but by virtue of his suffering. Dietrich Bonhoeffer, *Letters and Papers from Prison*, 4th enlarged ed., ed. E. Bethge, trans. R. H. Fuller et al. (London: SCM Press, 1971), 361 (letter of July 16, 1944). Curiously, Whitehead, the philosopher of process, also subscribed to this notion when he wrote: "God is the great companion—the fellow sufferer who understands." Alfred North Whitehead, *Process and Reality: An Essay in Cosmology* (New York: Macmillan, 1929), 532.

16. Among the proponents of this perspective, Gustavo Gutierrez is well known for his defense of Bartolemé de Las Casas and his role as protector of the Indians against imperial Spain, which was then the embodiment of paleo-Durkheimian ambitions. See Gustavo Gutierrez, *Las Casas: In Search of the Poor of Jesus Christ*, trans. Robert R. Barr (Maryknoll, N.Y.: Orbis

Books, 1993); Gustavo Gutierrez, *A Theology of Liberation,* trans. and ed. Sr. Caridad Inda and John Eagleson (Maryknoll, N.Y.: Orbis Books, 1973).

17. John D. Caputo, *The Weakness of God: A Theology of the Event* (Bloomington: Indiana University Press, 2006), 38. The turning away from "strong" theology does not mean a retreat into isolated inwardness but implies a call to service in the promised "kingdom": "The kingdom of God is a kingdom of base, ill-born, powerless, despised outsiders who are null and void in the eyes of the world . . . yet precisely for that reason the ones whom God called" (48).

18. Richard Kearney, *The God Who May Be: A Hermeneutics of Religion* (Bloomington: Indiana University Press, 2001), 108. Again, dispossession here does not entail private retreat but a reorientation to the "kingdom": "The kingdom is precisely that which can never be fully possessed in the here and now, but always directs us toward an advent still to come—an alternative site from which to begin afresh" (108). Kearney's reference to "self-emptying" or *kenosis* finds a parallel in Vattimo's *After Christianity,* where salvation history is linked with a certain "secularization": "If it is the mode in which the weakening of Being realizes itself as the *kenosis* of God, which is the kernel of the history of salvation, secularization shall no longer be conceived of as abandonment of religion but as the paradoxical realization of Being's religious vocation." Gianni Vattimo, *After Christianity,* trans. Luca D'Isanto (New York: Columbia University Press, 2002), 24. Vattimo also comments on the continued relevance of the "church" or religious community in a "postmodern" setting (9).

19. James, *A Pluralistic Universe,* 34.

20. William E. Connolly, *Pluralism* (Durham, N.C.: Duke University Press, 2005), 70–71, 74.

21. Ibid., 48, 59, 64. Connolly adds: "The public ethos of pluralism pursued here, solicits the active cultivation of pluralist virtues by each faith and the negotiation of a positive ethos of engagement between them. . . . I am thereby a proponent of civic virtue. But the public virtues embraced are pluralist virtues" (65). See also his "Pluralism and Faith," in de Vries and Sullivan, *Political Theologies,* 278–297.

22. Connolly, *Pluralism,* 48.

23. Jonathan Sacks, *The Dignity of Difference: How to Avoid the Clash of Civilizations* (London and New York: Continuum, 2002), viii, x–xi. As he adds at another point: "Judaism was the first religion to wrestle with the reality of global dispersion. . . . For almost 2,000 years, scattered throughout the world, they continued to see themselves and be seen by others as a single people—the world's first global people" (13). See also my "The Dignity of Difference: A Salute to Jonathan Sacks," in *Small Wonder: Global Power and Its Discontents* (Lanham, Md.: Rowman and Littlefield, 2005), 209–217.

24. Sacks, *The Dignity of Difference,* viii, xi, 13, 18–19. Together with

George Soros, Sacks challenges the reigning "market fundamentalism," the idea that we can leave the market entirely to its own devices. As he notes, global capitalism today is "a system of immense power, from which it has become increasingly difficult for nations to dissociate themselves" (28). Although benefiting some segments of the population, its social effects in terms of maldistribution constitute "a scar on the face of humanity" (20). Entering into specifics, Sacks reports that the average North American consumes "five times more than a Mexican, ten times more than a Chinese, thirty times more than an Indian." Nearly one-fourth of the world's population lives beneath the poverty line, and almost a billion people are malnourished and lack access to medical care (28–29). In light of recent economic developments, see Kevin Phillips, *Bad Money: Reckless Finance, Failed Politics, and the Global Crisis of American Capitalism* (New York: Viking, 2008).

25. *Al-Qur'an: A Contemporary Translation,* by Ahmed Ali (Princeton, N.J.: Princeton University Press, 1984), 54 (Sura 3:31), 537 (Sura 90:13–16). Compare also this Hadith: "When the Prophet was asked which form of Islam was best, he replied: 'To feed the people and extend greetings of peace to them—be they of your acquaintance or not.'" *Words of the Prophet Muhammad: Selections from the Hadith,* ed. Maulana Wahiduddin Khan (Delhi: Al-Risala Books, 1996), 57.

26. *The Bhagavad Gita,* trans. Juan Mascaró (London: Penguin Books, 1962), 56–58, 62 (Book 3:7, 20; Book 4:11); see also *Buddhist Peacework: Creating Cultures of Peace,* ed. David W. Chappell (Boston: Wisdom Publications, 1999).

27. Richard Falk, "A Worldwide Religious Resurgence in an Era of Globalization," in *Religion in International Affairs: The Return from Exile,* ed. Fabio Petito and Pavlos Hatzopoulos (New York: Palgrave Macmillan, 2003), 186, 194–195.

28. Ibid., 198–199, 202, 205. I stress "legitimacy" to connect this conclusion with the beginning of the chapter. See also Richard Falk, *Religion and Human Global Governance* (New York: Palgrave, 2001).

5. Religion and the World

This paper was first presented as keynote address at a conference on "Religion in the Quest for Global Justice and Peace" held in Kuala Lumpur, Malaysia, July 24–28, 2008.

1. The reference here is to the story in Matthew 22:19. I tend to agree with those interpreters who read the story not as a defense of a "two-swords" theory but as an indication by Jesus of the relative insignificance of Caesar's coin when compared with the abundance of God's love.

2. The term *ramarajya* has sometimes been employed by Mahatma Gandhi. However, for him, the term designated a society ruled by justice and

goodness (*Ram*), not by a Hindu government. Regarding the abuse of the term by defenders of "Hindutva," see Prabha Dixit, "The Ideology of Hindu Nationalism," in *Political Thought in Modern India,* ed. Thomas Pantham and Kenneth L. Deutsch (New Delhi: Sage Publications, 1986), 122–141.

3. Asma Afsaruddin, "Mawdudi's 'Theo-Democracy': How Islamic Is It?" *OM* 87 (2007): 324–325.

4. See "The Cambridge Declaration of the Alliance of Confessing Evangelicals," http://www.alliancennet.org/intro/CamDec.html. Compare also Stephen Prothero, *American Jesus: How the Son of God Became a National Icon* (New York: Farrar, Straus and Giroux, 2003).

5. See H. Richard Niebuhr, William Pauck, and Francis Miller, *The Church against the World* (New York: Willet, Clark, 1935), 123–124, 128. See also R. Laurence Moore, *Selling God: American Religion in the Marketplace of Culture* (New York: Oxford University Press, 1994); William E. Connolly, *Capitalism and Christianity, American Style* (Durham, N.C.: Duke University Press, 2008).

6. Regarding the "death of God" theology, see Thomas J. J. Altizer and William Hamilton, *Radical Theology and the Death of God* (Indianapolis: Bobbs-Merrill, 1966); Thomas J. J. Altizer, *Living the Death of God: A Theological Memoir* (Albany: State University of New York Press, 2006). Regarding a "becoming God," see Hans Jonas, *Mortality and Morality: A Search for God after Auschwitz* (Evanston, Ill.: Northwestern University Press, 1996). For the legacy of the "suffering servant," see chapter 4, especially note 15.

7. John D. Caputo, *The Weakness of God: A Theology of the Event* (Bloomington: Indiana University Press, 2006), 23–41; Richard Kearney, *The God Who May Be: A Hermeneutics of Religion* (Bloomington: Indiana University Press, 2001), 108–110.

8. William James, *The Varieties of Religious Experience: A Study in Human Nature,* 36th impression (London and New York: Longmans, Green, 1928), 28–29, 31. See also chapter 4.

9. For a strong critique of the "privatization of religion," see Stanley Hauerwas, *The Peaceable Kingdom* (Notre Dame, Ind.: University of Notre Dame Press, 1983), 12–15. As Hauerwas writes: "The essential Christian witness is neither to personal experience, nor to what Christianity means to 'me,' but to the truth that this world is the creation of a good God who is known through the people of Israel and the life, death, and resurrection of Jesus Christ. Without such a witness we only abandon the world to the violence derived from the lies that devour our lives" (15). By the same token, Hauerwas also critiques what I call the "politicization" of religion: "As Christians, we must maintain day in and day out that peace is not something to be achieved *by our power.* Rather peace is a gift of God that comes only by our being a community formed around a crucified savior—a savior who teaches us to be peaceful" (12). Compare in this context John Howard Yoder,

The Priestly Kingdom: Social Ethics as Gospel (Notre Dame, Ind.: University of Notre Dame Press, 1984), especially the chapter titled "The Christian Case for Democracy" (151–171); and Stanley Hauerwas and Romand Coles, *Christianity, Democracy, and the Radical Ordinary* (Eugene, Ore.: Cascade Books, 2008).

10. Chandra Muzaffer, *Rights, Religion and Reform: Enhancing Human Dignity through Spiritual and Moral Transformation* (London and New York: Routledge Curzon, 2002), 104.

11. Mohandas Gandhi, *Satyagraha* (Ahmedabad: Navajivan, 1958), 6; Mohandas Gandhi, *An Autobiography; The Story of My Experiments with Truth* (London: Longmans, 1949), 370–371.

12. Reinhold Niebuhr, *Moral Man and Immoral Society: A Study in Ethics and Politics* (1932; reprint, New York: Charles Scribner's Sons, 1960), xi–xii.

13. Ibid., xii, xv, xx–xxi, xxiii, 3. As Niebuhr adds: "As individuals, men believe that they ought to love and serve each other and establish justice between each other. As racial, economic, and national groups they take for themselves, whatever their power can command" (9). In a similar vein, see also Reinhold Niebuhr, *The Children of Light and the Children of Darkness* (New York: Scribner's Sons, 1944), and *Christian Realism and Political Problems* (New York: Scribner's Sons, 1953).

14. Hans J. Morgenthau, *Scientific Man vs. Power Politics* (Chicago: University of Chicago Press, 1946), 2, 32, 43–45, 71, 193, 206.

15. Hans J. Morgenthau, *Politics among Nations: The Struggle for Power and Peace*, 4th ed. (1948; reprint, New York: Knopf, 1967), 4, 25–27, 34–35. See also Hans J. Morgenthau, *In Defense of the National Interest* (New York: Knopf, 1951); Kenneth W. Thompson, *Political Realism and the Crisis of World Politics* (Princeton, N.J.: Princeton University Press, 1960).

16. Martin Luther King Jr., *I Have a Dream: Writings and Speeches that Changed the World*, ed. James M. Washington (New York: HarperCollins, 1992), 90. As King stated in his Nobel Prize acceptance speech in 1964: "I refuse to accept the view that mankind is so tragically bound to the starless midnight of racism and war that the bright daybreak of peace and brotherhood can never become a reality. I refuse to accept the cynical notion that nation after nation must spiral down a militaristic stairway into a hell of thermonuclear destruction. I believe that unarmed truth and unconditional love will have the final word in reality" (ibid., 110).

17. Mohandas K. Gandhi, *Hind Swaraj and Other Writings*, ed. Anthony J. Parel (Cambridge: Cambridge University Press, 1977), 28; Mohandas K. Gandhi, *India's Case for Swaraj* (Ahmedabad: Yeshanand, 1932), 369.

18. John Dewey, "Democracy Is Radical," in *The Essential Dewey*, vol. 1, *Pragmatism, Education, Democracy*, ed. Larry A. Hickmann and Thomas M. Alexander (Bloomington: Indiana University Press, 1998), 338. As he adds:

"There is no opposition in standing for liberal democratic means combined with ends that are socially radical."

19. Chandra Muzaffer, "Islam: Justice and Politics," in *Rights, Religion and Reform*, 173.

20. Jacques Derrida, "Force of Law: The 'Mystical Foundation of Authority,'" in *Deconstruction and the Possibility of Justice*, ed. Drucilla Cornell, Michel Rosenfeld, and David G. Carlson (New York: Routledge, 1992), 26. For an equation of justice with rational principles (especially the principle of equal liberty), see John Rawls, *A Theory of Justice* (Cambridge, Mass.: Harvard University Press, 1971).

21. Aristotle, *Nicomachean Ethics*, trans. Terence Irwin (Indianapolis: Hackett, 1985), 34–35, 118 (1103a31, 1103b1, 1129b17).

22. Ibid., 14–15 (1097a35, 1097b15).

6. Hermeneutics and Cross-Cultural Encounters

1. Hans-Georg Gadamer, *Truth and Method*, 2nd rev. ed., trans. Joel Weinsheimer and Donald G. Marshall (New York: Crossroad, 1989), 198–199 (translation slightly altered).

2. Ibid., 241.

3. Ibid., 254, 257, 259–260.

4. Ibid., 267–269.

5. Ibid., 367–370.

6. Ibid., 306.

7. Ibid., 295. This midpoint is well captured by Nikolas Kompridis when he stresses the importance of resisting "two extremes: thinking of ourselves either as standing completely outside our traditions, in no way affected by or indebted to them, or as identical with our traditions, fatefully bound to or enclosed within them." See his *Critique and Disclosure: Critical Theory between Past and Future* (Cambridge, Mass.: MIT Press, 2006), 7. On this issue, see also my "Hermeneutics and Deconstruction: Gadamer and Derrida in Dialogue," in *Critical Encounters: Between Philosophy and Politics* (Notre Dame, Ind.: University of Notre Dame Press, 1987), 130–158, and my "Self and Other: Gadamer and the Hermeneutics of Difference," *Yale Journal of Law and the Humanities* 5 (1993): 101–124.

8. Gadamer, *Truth and Method*, 293. Continuing this line of thought, Gadamer (293–294) perceives in hermeneutical understanding an anticipation or "fore-conception of completeness" (*Vorgriff der Vollkommenheit*) aiming at the disclosure of "truth" (and hence bypassing any kind of relativism).

9. Ibid., 307–309.

10. Ibid., 309, 324.

11. Ibid., 329.

12. Hans-Georg Gadamer, "Hermeneutics as Practical Philosophy" (1972),

in *Reason in the Age of Science,* trans. Frederick G. Lawrence (Cambridge, Mass.: MIT Press, 1981), 93, 101–102.

13. Ibid., 90–92. The same volume also contains Gadamer's important essay "What Is Practice [*Praxis*]? The Conditions of Social Reason" (1974), 69–87. Although perhaps unduly sidelining Heidegger's influence, Richard Bernstein is surely correct in saying that Gadamer's hermeneutics stands firmly in "the tradition of practical philosophy that has its sources in Aristotle's *Nicomachean Ethics* and *Politics,*" where understanding takes the "form of *phronesis.*" See his *Beyond Objectivism and Relativism: Science, Hermeneutics, and Praxis* (Philadelphia: University of Pennsylvania Press, 1983), xiv–xv.

14. Hans-Georg Gadamer, *Das Erbe Europas: Beiträge* (Frankfurt: Suhrkamp, 1989), 28–31. As he adds: "And here it may be one of the special advantages of Europe that—more than elsewhere—her inhabitants have been able or were compelled to learn how to live with others, even if the others are very different."

15. Ibid., 31–34.

16. Ibid., 35, 46–48.

17. Thomas Pantham, "Some Dimensions of the Universality of Philosophical Hermeneutics: A Conversation with Hans-Georg Gadamer," *Journal of Indian Council of Philosophical Research* 9 (1992): 132.

18. See Charles Taylor, "Gadamer on the Human Sciences," in *The Cambridge Companion to Gadamer,* ed. Robert J. Dostal (Cambridge: Cambridge University Press, 2002), 126–142; Charles Taylor, "Interpretation and the Sciences of Man," in *Philosophy and the Human Sciences: Philosophical Papers 2* (Cambridge: Cambridge University Press, 1985), 15–57.

19. Charles Taylor, "Conditions of an Unforced Consensus on Human Rights," in *The East Asian Challenge for Human Rights,* ed. Joanne R. Bauer and Daniel A. Bell (Cambridge: Cambridge University Press, 1999), 124–144.

20. Charles Taylor, "The Politics of Recognition," in *Multiculturalism and "The Politics of Recognition,"* ed. Amy Gutmann (Princeton, N.J.: Princeton University Press, 1992), 66–68, 72–73. See also Paul Ricoeur, "Hermeneutics and the Critique of Ideology," in *Hermeneutics and the Human Sciences,* ed. and trans. John B. Thompson (Cambridge: Cambridge University Press, 1981), 63–100.

21. In this respect, see especially John Dewey, "Search for the Great Community" from *The Public and Its Problems* (1927), in *John Dewey: The Later Works, 1925–1953,* ed. Jo Ann Boydston (Carbondale: Southern Illinois University Press, 1988), 2:325–327. See also David Foot, *John Dewey: America's Philosopher of Democracy* (Lanham, Md.: Rowman and Littlefield, 1998).

22. John Dewey, "Nationalizing Education" (1916), in *John Dewey: The*

Middle Works, 1899–1924, ed. Jo Ann Boydston (Carbondale: Southern Illinois University Press, 1975), 10:202–204.

23. Ibid.

24. Maurice Merleau-Ponty, "Dialogue and the Perception of the Other," in *The Prose of the World,* ed. Claude Lefort, trans. John O'Neill (Evanston, Ill.: Northwestern University Press, 1973), 133.

25. Ibid., 133–134.

26. Ibid., 134–135. On the issue of identity and noncoincidence, see the exemplary study by Bhikhu Parekh, *A New Politics of Identity: Political Principles for an Interdependent World* (New York: Palgrave Macmillan, 2008).

27. Merleau-Ponty, "Dialogue and the Perception of the Other," 137–138. As he adds: "We are trying to awaken a carnal relation to the world and the other that is not an accident intruding from outside upon a pure cognitive subject . . . or a 'content' of experience among many others but our first insertion into the world and into truth" (139). As should be clear, "truth" here refers to a "disclosive" truth, not a propositional truth. On this distinction, see Kompridis, *Critique and Disclosure,* and my *Between Freiburg and Frankfurt: Toward a Critical Ontology* (Amherst: University of Massachusetts Press, 1991); see also appendix B.

28. Merleau-Ponty, "Dialogue and the Perception of the Other," 139–140.

29. Ibid., 140–141; Maurice Merleau-Ponty, "Everywhere and Nowhere," in *Signs,* trans. Richard C. McCleary (Evanston, Ill.: Northwestern University Press, 1964), 139. See also John Dewey, "Search for the Great Community," in *The Public and Its Problems* (1927; reprint, Athens: Ohio University Press, 1954), 143–184.

7. A Man for All Seasons

1. With his talent for pithy formulations, Alasdair MacIntyre has singled out some dominant "stock characters" of the modern age: chiefly the "manager" in charge of anonymous rule systems, the "therapist" managing people's inner lives, and the "aesthete" devoted to privatized consumption. See *After Virtue: A Study in Moral Theory,* 2nd ed. (Notre Dame, Ind..: University of Notre Dame Press, 1984), 11–12, 23–24, 34–35.

2. See *The Bhagavad Gita,* trans. Juan Mascaró (New York: Penguin Books, 1962), 54 (Book 2, verses 61, 64).

3. Anthony Parel, *Gandhi's Philosophy and the Quest for Harmony* (Cambridge: Cambridge University Press, 2006).

4. Robert Bolt, *A Man for All Seasons: A Play of Sir Thomas More* (London: Methuen Drama, 1995), 83.

5. Ibid., 101.

6. On More's public career, see Gerard B. Wegemer, *Thomas More on*

Statesmanship (Washington, D.C.: Catholic University of America Press, 1996); Peter Ackroyd, *The Life of Thomas More* (New York: Nan A. Talese, 1998); Ernest E. Reynolds, *The Field Is Won: The Life and Death of Saint Thomas More* (Milwaukee: Bruce, 1968).

7. Quoted in J. W., introduction to Sir Thomas More, *Utopia and A Dialogue of Comfort* (London: Dent and Sons, 1951), viii–ix.

8. For the text of the dialogue, see More, *Utopia and A Dialogue of Comfort*, 143–423. As J. W. points out in his introduction, the tribulation mentioned in the text seemingly refers to an impending invasion by the Turks; however, the actual danger stemmed from a tyrannical king. As More himself stated: "There is no born Turk so cruel to Christian folk as is the false Christian that falleth from the faith" (xi).

9. Robert M. Adams, preface to Sir Thomas More, *Utopia: A New Translation, Background, Criticism*, trans. and ed. R. M. Adams (New York: Norton, 1975), vii. In Adams's presentation, these questions dominate the first part of *Utopia*, but the second part offers a set of "no less disturbing questions. For example, Can a community be organized for the benefit of all, and not to satisfy the greed, lust, and appetite for domination of a few? How much repression is a good society justified in exercising in order to retain its goodness? And finally, When we give some persons power in our society (as we must), and appoint others to watch them (as we'd better), who is going to watch the watchers? Can we really stand a society in which everybody watches everybody?"

10. For parts of the above account, see J. W., introduction to *Utopia*, v–vi, xii. Several famous sayings are recorded from the final moments of More's life. Thus, while ascending the scaffold, he told the executioner: "Assist me up, and in coming down I will shift for myself." And when his head was already on the block, he admonished the executioner: "Wait till I put my beard aside, for that has done no treason."

11. Cited in J. W., introduction to *Utopia*, xii.

12. Ibid., xiii.

13. Parel, *Gandhi's Philosophy*, ix–x. Under the rubric of justice and fairness, Parel also mentions some of the urgent reforms needed in India today: establishing "a balance between secularism and spirituality means, at the present time, the removal of the injustices under which the poor, especially the Dalits (the so-called Untouchables) suffer, the gender gap that still handicaps women, and the religious antagonism that still vitiates human relations" (x).

14. See K. J. Shah, "Of *Artha* and the *Arthashastra*," in *Comparative Political Philosophy*, 2nd ed., ed. Anthony J. Parel and Ronald C. Keith (Lanham, Md.: Lexington Books, 2003), 140–162; K. J. Shah, "*Purushartha* and Gandhi," in *Gandhi and the Present Global Crisis*, ed. R. Roy (Shimla: Indian Institute of Advanced Study, 1996), 155–161.

15. Parel, *Gandhi's Philosophy*, 7, 13. Parel finds similar impulses for restoring harmony in a number of recent or contemporary Indian philosophers, such as Daya Krishna, *Indian Philosophy: A Counter Perspective* (Delhi: Oxford University Press, 1991); Arvind Sharma, *The Purusharthas: A Study of Hindu Axiology* (East Lansing: Asian Studies Center, Michigan State University, 1982); R. Sundara Rajan, "The *Purusharthas* in the Light of Critical Theory," *Indian Philosophical Quarterly* 7 (1979–1980): 339–350, and "Approaches to the Theory of the *Purusharthas:* Husserl, Heidegger and Ricoeur," *Journal of the Indian Council of Philosophical Research* 6 (1988–1989): 129–147. See also Anthony J. Parel, "Gandhi and the Emergence of the Modern Indian Political Canon," *Review of Politics* 70 (2005): 40–63.

16. Mohandas K. Gandhi, *The Collected Works of Mahatma Gandhi,* 100 vols. (New Delhi: Publications Division, Government of India, 1958–1994), 44:80.

17. Parel, *Gandhi's Philosophy,* 24–26.

18. Ibid., 39, 50, 55, 63, 68–69. Compare in this context C. B. Macpherson, *The Political Theory of Possessive Individualism: Hobbes to Locke* (Oxford: Clarendon Press, 1962).

19. Parel, *Gandhi's Philosophy,* 90–91, 94–95, 121–122.

20. Ibid., 135, 163.

21. Ibid., 177, 183. For the autobiographical statement, see M. K. Gandhi, *An Autobiography, or the Story of My Experiments with Truth* (Ahmedabad: Navajivan Trust, 1992), x. The chapter on *moksha* also contains helpful comments on Gandhi's attempt to combine action with prayer and meditation. For Gandhi, "work was the sun, and contemplation and devotion were its satellites" (Parel, *Gandhi's Philosophy,* 191). The discussion should be read in conjunction with the book's section on "religion" (treated as a dimension of *dharma*), which touches on such issues as Gandhi's prayer life, his conception of "secularism," and his support of religious pluralism. See ibid., 99–116.

22. Parel, *Gandhi's Philosophy,* 197–198, 205.

23. Ibid., 204–205.

24. Sheila McDonough, *Gandhi's Responses to Islam* (New Delhi: Printworld, 1944), 83. See also my "Gandhi and Islam: A Heart-and-Mind Unity?" in *Peace Talks—Who Will Listen?* (Notre Dame, Ind.: University of Notre Dame Press, 2004), 132–151.

25. Parel, *Gandhi's Philosophy,* 57, 94–95.

26. M. K. Gandhi, *Hind Swaraj, and Other Writings,* ed. Anthony J. Parel (Cambridge: Cambridge University Press, 1997), 28–33.

27. Parel, *Gandhi's Philosophy,* 64–65; Bhikhu Parekh, *Gandhi's Political Philosophy: A Critical Examination* (Notre Dame, Ind.: University of Notre Dame Press, 1989), 123.

28. Parel, *Gandhi's Philosophy,* 55–56, 64–65. For the distinction between "average" and "heroic" resistance, see 122–123.

29. On this point, see my "Conversation across Boundaries: E Pluribus

Unum?" in *Dialogue among Civilizations: Some Exemplary Voices* (New York: Palgrave Macmillan, 2002), 31–47.

30. Parel, *Gandhi's Philosophy*, 100, 177. At another point, Parel comments somewhat ambivalently that, for Gandhi, "*purushartha* is the inner power by means of which humans overcome themselves" (23).

31. Parel's repeated criticisms of Buddhism, including "engaged" and "Navayana" Buddhism, seem off the mark to me. See *Gandhi's Philosophy*, 78–79, 200–202.

32. Ibid., 151. On this point, Parel cites *The Collected Works of Mahatma Gandhi*, 39:171, 254.

33. *Bhagavad Gita*, 52–53, 56–57 (Book 2, verses 47, 50, 55; Book 3, verses 7, 9).

8. Reason and Lifeworld

1. Daya Krishna, *Indian Philosophy: A Counter Perspective* (Delhi: Oxford University Press, 1991), 3, 6, 23–24.

2. Ibid., 14–15, 29.

3. Ibid., 32, 63, 164, 170. On the topic of Vedanta, Krishna's comments are most stern and uncompromising: "The search for the meaning of Vedanta leads nowhere. . . . The most haloed term of Indian philosophical thought connotes nothing. It is an empty shell, mere verbiage, an absolute nothing. . . . Let us be serious. Let us banish it" (170). In the concluding chapter, Krishna likewise deconstructs the traditional notion of the *purusharthas,* or goals of life, stating that the notion "has no place for the independent life of reason as a separate value. . . . This is a grave deficiency" (205).

4. Daya Krishna, *New Perspectives in Indian Philosophy* (Jaipur and New Delhi: Rawat Publications, 2001), 3, 5.

5. Ibid., 8–11.

6. Daya Krishna, *Prolegomena to Any Future Historiography of Cultures and Civilizations,* 2nd ed. (New Delhi: Centre for Studies in Civilizations, 2005), xii–xiv, 2. As he adds: "The deepest understanding of any culture or civilization relates to the role of consciousness in the maintenance, reproduction, and transmission of the symbols generated by it for conveying to other consciousnesses what it considers worthwhile and important" (2–3). In the text, I put quotation marks around "man" to indicate the intended gender neutrality. Regarding precedents of this outlook, see Immanuel Kant, "Idea for a Universal History with Cosmopolitan Purpose" (1784), in *Kant's Political Writings,* ed. Hans Reiss (Cambridge: Cambridge University Press, 1970), 41–53; Edmund Husserl, "Vienna Lecture: Philosophy and the Crisis of European Humanity" (1935), in *The Crisis of European Sciences and Transcendental Philosophy,* trans. David Carr (Evanston, Ill.: Northwestern University Press, 1970), 269–299. In the latter, Husserl elab-

orated the idea of Europe "as the historical teleology of the infinite goals of reason" (299).

7. Krishna, *Prolegomena*, 64, 80, 83. Applying these observations to the relations between West and non-West, the study remarks: "The encounter of all past civilizations with the modern Western one is bound to result in the unfoldment of new potentialities in the valuational projects and visions of those civilizations and radically modify them, just as a new metaphor unfolds hidden meanings that were unsuspected before the creative writer used it for the first time" (216).

8. Ibid., 84–85. At a later point, Krishna defines civilizational history explicitly as a history of consciousness: "The history of consciousness as it has evolved and changed and developed in 'human beings' has to be brought to self-consciousness and accepted by it, however reluctant such acceptance may be. This is, or should be, the real task of history and historiography as 'man' has to see himself as an 'essentially changing being' whose central fulcrum lies in his own consciousness as it can try to change itself self-consciously if it wishes to do so" (262).

9. Ibid., xi, 16, 262, 279. Compare this comment: "If the 'reality' of either the 'outer' or the 'inner' cannot be denied, nor the inter-relationship between them or the transformations and changes that these undergo all the time bringing radical changes in both the 'outer' and 'inner,' then how can one meaningfully talk of 'man's' identity or the truth about him? The truth, if any, is in the 'situation' itself which, however, is ever changing" (260).

10. Admittedly, the above presentation concentrates on a central strand in Krishna's work, while sidelining other dimensions or intellectual concerns. One such concern was the Indian tradition of *bhakti* religiosity, whose discussion was the topic of a learned gathering organized by Krishna, and whose essence he located in a subjective "inner" feeling of possibly universal significance. See Daya Krishna, Mukund Lath, and Francine E. Krishna, eds., *Bhakti: A Contemporary Discussion* (New Delhi: Indian Council of Philosophical Research, 2000), especially 65–70. A related concern that came to the fore mainly in his later life was aesthetics, with an emphasis on music (where, as far as I can see, Kant's *Critique of Judgment* remained canonical).

11. Ramchandra Gandhi, *Two Essays on Whitehead's Philosophic Approach* (Shimla: Indian Institute of Advanced Study, 1973), v, 2–3; Alfred North Whitehead, *Modes of Thought* (Cambridge: Cambridge University Press, 1938), 2.

12. Gandhi, *Two Essays*, 4, 6–7.

13. Ibid., 8, 18, 24; Whitehead, *Modes of Thought*, 5.

14. The later Wittgenstein famously defined the work of philosophy as consisting in "assembling reminders." See *Philosophical Investigations* (Oxford: Blackwell, 1953), 50. Regarding William James, Gandhi cites Whitehead's comments to the effect that "he systematized; but above all he assembled.

His intellectual life was one protest against *the dismissal of experience in the interest of system*" (*Two Essays*, 20).

15. Ramchandra Gandhi, *The Availability of Religious Ideas* (New York: Harper and Row, 1976), 3.

16. Ibid., 4, 9. Regarding ethics as a mode of communicative relationship, Gandhi adds: "Now an act of addressing has significant moral, and not merely metaphysical, features. In addressing you, I seek, solicit a communicative response from you, I do not merely casually interact with you. And I cannot solicit a communicative response from you . . . without exhibiting minimal care for you [echoes of Heidegger again?]. Thus, insofar as I think the communicative thought 'you,' I minimally value you. . . . And I cannot think the thought 'I' without casting myself as the object of another's caring communicative attention" (5–6).

17. Ibid., 8–9. Regarding "nothingness" as "nihilation" see Martin Heidegger, "What Is Metaphysics?" in *Martin Heidegger: Basic Writings*, ed. David F. Krell (New York: Harper and Row, 1977), 95–112. The idea of an "incomprehensible and yet ineliminable" notion finds a parallel in the work of Nicolaus of Cusa. In this regard, see my "Wise Ignorance: Nicolaus of Cusa's Search for Truth," in *In Search of the Good Life: A Pedagogy for Troubled Times* (Lexington: University Press of Kentucky, 2007), 58–79.

18. Ramchandra Gandhi, *Sita's Kitchen: A Testimony of Faith and Inquiry* (Albany: State University of New York Press, 1992), 18–19.

19. Ibid., 15–16.

20. Ibid., 9–10, 22.

21. Ibid., 13, 17–18. With specific reference to *bhakti*, the text comments: "The Babari mosque's medieval trespass into the kitchen area dramatizes the entry of Sufism into the corpus of Indian mysticism. Indeed, the cognateness of Abrahamic mysticism in general, and not only Sufism, with Hindu, aboriginal, and Buddhist mysticism is powerfully suggested by the continuity of the mosque's inner space of objectlessness with the void of the kitchen zone, which is continuous with the sphericality of the earth and with surrounding emptiness. And this continuity . . . is deeply evocative of *ahimsa* or non-violence, the virtue emphasized centrally by Jainism and savingly by Gandhi in our annihilationist age" (17).

22. A. K. Ramanujan, "Is There an Indian Way of Thinking? An Informal Essay," in *India through Hindu Categories*, ed. McKim Marriott (Delhi: Sage Publications, 1990), 46–49, 54–55. For my discussion, see "Western Thought and Indian Thought: Some Comparative Steps," in *Beyond Orientalism: Essays on Cross-Cultural Encounter* (Albany: State University of New York Press, 1996), 135–147.

23. Ramanujan, "Is There an Indian Way of Thinking?" 50, 52–53. On *jati*, see Harold A. Gould's essay "Toward a 'Jati Model' for Indian Politics"

in his *Caste Adaptation in Modernizing Indian Society* (Delhi: Chanakya Publishers, 1988), 171–185.

24. Maurice Merleau-Ponty, *Phenomenology of Perception*, trans. Colin Smith (London: Routledge and Kegan Paul, 1962), 46–47.

25. Ibid., 47–49.

26. Hubert L. Dreyfus and Patricia A. Dreyfus, translators' introduction to Maurice Merleau-Ponty, *Sense and Non-Sense* (Evanston, Ill.: Northwestern University Press, 1964), x–xi.

27. Maurice Merleau-Ponty, "The Metaphysical in Man," in *Sense and Non-Sense*, 93, 95–96. To underscore the difference between such inquiry and rationalist "system" building, he adds: "If system is an arrangement of concepts which makes all the aspects of experience immediately compatible and compossible, then it suppresses metaphysical [ontological] awareness and, moreover, does away with ethics at the same time" (94). It appears that the meaning of "metaphysics" here was borrowed from Henri Bergson, *An Introduction to Metaphysics*, trans. T. E. Hulme (Indianapolis: Bobbs-Merrill, 1912).

28. Gandhi, *Sita's Kitchen*, 18–19.

Appendix A

1. Lawrence Hass and Dorothea Olkowski, eds., *Rereading Merleau-Ponty: Essays beyond the Continental-Analytical Divide* (Amherst, N.Y.: Humanity Books, 2003), 13. See also Taylor Carman, *Merleau-Ponty* (New York: Routledge, 2008); Thomas Baldwin, ed., *Reading Merleau-Ponty* (London: Routledge, 2007); Ted Toadvine and Leonard Lawler, eds., *The Merleau-Ponty Reader* (Evanston, Ill.: Northwestern University Press, 2007); François-George Maugarlene, *Retour à Merleau-Ponty* (Paris: Grosset, 2007); James Hatley, Janice McLane, and Christian Diehm, eds., *Interrogating Ethics: Embodying the Good in Merleau-Ponty* (Pittsburgh: Duquesne University Press, 2006); Taylor Carman and Mark Hansen, eds., *The Cambridge Companion to Merleau-Ponty* (Cambridge: Cambridge University Press, 2005).

2. Diana Coole, *Merleau-Ponty and Modern Politics after Anti-Humanism* (Lanham, Md.: Rowman and Littlefield, 2007). In the following text, page numbers in parentheses refer to this work.

3. Maurice Merleau-Ponty, *The Visible and the Invisible, Followed by Working Notes*, ed. Claude Lefort, trans. Alphonso Lingis (Evanston, Ill.: Northwestern University Press, 1968), 272. Compare in this context Diana Coole, *Negativity and Politics: Dionysus and Dialectics from Kant to Poststructuralism* (London: Routledge, 2000).

Appendix B

1. Nikolas Kompridis, *Critique and Disclosure: Critical Theory between*

Past and Future (Cambridge, Mass.: MIT Press, 2006). In the following text, page numbers in parentheses refer to this work.

2. Martin Heidegger, *Being and Time,* trans. John Macquarrie and Edward Robinson (New York: Harper and Row, 1962), 330.

3. See my *Between Freiburg and Frankfurt: Toward a Critical Ontology* (Amherst: University of Massachusetts Press, 1991).

Appendix C

1. For some prominent statements in this debate, see Guo Qiyong, ed., *Debates on Confucian Ethics* [Chinese] (Wuhan, China: Wuhan Jiaoyu Chubanshe, 2004); *Contemporary Chinese Thought* 31, no. 1 (Fall 2007); Huang Yong, ed., "Symposium: Filial Piety as the Root of Morality or the Source of Corruption," *Dao: A Journal of Comparative Philosophy* 7, no. 1 (March 2008).

2. My discussion relies on and quotes from these two essays: Guo Qiyong, "Is Confucian Ethics a 'Consanguinism'?" *Dao: A Journal of Comparative Philosophy* 6 (2007): 21–37; Liu Qingping, "Confucianism and Corruption: An Analysis of Shun's Two Actions Described by Mencius," *Dao: A Journal of Comparative Philosophy* 6 (2007): 1–19.

3. Tu Weiming, *Confucian Thought: Selfhood as Creative Transformation* (Albany: State University of New York Press, 1985), 56. See also his *Humanity and Self-Cultivation: Essays in Confucian Thought* (Berkeley, Calif.: Asian Humanities Press, 1979).

4. Paul Ricoeur, *Liebe und Gerechtigheit/Amour et Justice,* ed. Oswald Bayer, trans. Matthias Raden (Tübingen: Mohr, 1990), 43–47. See also my "Love and Justice: A Memorial Tribute to Paul Ricoeur," in *In Search of the Good Life: A Pedagogy for Troubled Times* (Lexington: University Press of Kentucky, 2007), 220–235.

Index

absolutism, 8, 111
action, 140
  theory of, 182
Adorno, Theodor W., 176
Advaita Vedanta, 144, 146, 156
aesthetics, 134
Afsaruddin, Asma, 88
agency, 167–168, 170, 180
  political, 167, 170–171
agnosticism, 136
agonistics, 8
Alfarabi, 100
Americanism, xii
anarchism, 16, 48, 51
anthropocentrism, 175
anthropology, 31, 34, 43, 50, 59–61
Antigone, 189
antihumanism, 167–168, 170–172
apartheid, 137
application, 110–111
Arendt, Hannah, 180, 199n24
Aristotle, xii, 24, 33, 44, 64, 100–101, 110, 117, 187–189
artha, 130–132
asceticism, 135
assemblage, 152–154, 156
atheism, 48–49, 51
Augustine, St., 16, 52–54, 97
authenticity, 178
autonomy, 62–63, 123, 149
Avicenna, 100
Ayodhya, 157

Badiou, Alain, 38
Bakunin, Mikhail, 48
being, 112–113, 188
Benjamin, Walter, 181
Bergson, Henri, 77, 191n7
Berlin, Isaiah, 136
Bernstein, Richard J., 191n7, 193n13, 213n13
Bhagavad Gita, 81, 93–94, 135, 141, 143
Bhattacharga, K. C., 145
Blumenberg, Hans, 52, 202n11
Bobbio, Norberto, 199n22
Bodin, Jean, 25
Boff, Leonardo, 54
Boisvert, Raymond, 10
Bolt, Robert, 124–125, 128
Bonald, Louis de, 16, 31, 49–50
Bossuet, Jacques B., 31
Brahmanism, 131
Buddhism, 81, 92, 99–101, 116, 131, 140, 158
Bulter, Judith, 170
Bush, George W., 23–24

caesaropapism, 53, 62–63, 87
capitalism, 88, 209n24
  corporate, 88
Caputo, John, 76, 208n17
Catholicism, 49
Cavell, Stanley, 182
Chattopadhyaya, D. P., 148

chauvinism, 86
chiasm, 14, 168, 170
Christianity, 12, 52
  Eastern, 87
  Western, 87
Christian Right, 88
civilization, 148–151, 154
  clash of, xi, 2–3, 19, 104
cognition, 156
Cold War, 24
collectivism, 74, 127
colonialism, 116
communism, 127
  orthodox, 169
Comte, Auguste, 48
Confucianism, 99, 186–187, 189
Confucius, 92, 101, 185–186
Connolly, William, xiii, 6–7, 10–11, 77–78, 80, 193n18
consciousness, 112, 148, 150–151, 155, 163
  of self, 150–151, 159
  transcendental, 148
consensualism, 108
constitutionalism, 133, 137–138
contingency, 8
contradiction, 8
  performative, 8
Coole, Diana, 20, 167–174
Cortés, Donoso, 16, 31, 35, 49–51, 53
cosmopolitanism, xi, 29, 183
Counter-Reformation, 71
critical theory, 21, 176–179, 184, 186
Cromwell, Oliver, 31
culture, xi, 18, 148
culture wars, xi, 18

Dalits, 132–133
decision, 36, 49–51, 100
  sovereign, 47
decisionism, 37, 39, 51, 183

deconstruction, 37, 167
deism, 47
democracy, 2–3, 6, 39, 42, 47–48, 55–57, 97–99, 117
  liberal, 39
  modern, 3, 55, 57–58
democratization, 6, 16, 26
Deleuze, Gilles, 172
Derrida, Jacques, 30, 36–38, 40, 199n24
Descartes, René, 4, 10, 13, 20, 38–39, 106, 117, 151, 168–169, 175
Deutsch, Eliot, xiii
Dewey, John, 10, 44, 67–68, 77, 98–99, 117–118, 122, 193n17
dharma, 130–133, 140
dialogue, 11, 19, 49, 104, 108, 119, 121
difference, 5, 7, 13, 40–42, 58, 78, 107, 120
  dignity of, 78–80
  ontological, 61, 179
  symbolic, 61, 63
differentiation, 1–2, 11
Dilthey, Wilhelm, 105–107
diremptions, 123–124, 139
disclosure, 63, 153, 177–181, 184
  of world, 175–176
discovery, 153
disenchantment, 1, 72, 82, 191n1
disobedience, 129
  civil, 129
dualism, 1, 3, 9–12, 15, 39–40, 53, 63–64, 156–157, 165, 192n7
  essentialized, 15
  metaphysical, 63
Durkheim, Émile, 68, 72–74

ecumenism, 78, 118
emancipation, xii, 116
embodiment, 119, 121

Emerson, Ralph Waldo, 178, 182
emotivism, 111
empiricism, 4, 117, 162
emptiness, 65
Engels, Friedrich, 48
Enlightenment, 47, 50, 62, 68, 96, 175, 179, 186–187
epiphany, 63
epistemology, 8, 105–106
equality, 93
Erasmus, 126, 128–129
essence, 32–34, 39, 117, 149–151
  of politics, 39
essentialism, 4, 33, 35, 42
ethics, 97, 125
  interrogative, 179
ethos, 11
  pluralist, 11–12
  public, 11–12
Eusebius, Bishop, 53
event, 38
exegesis, 110
existentialism, 25
experience, 71, 77, 155, 159, 164, 168, 191n7
  perceptual, 161
  precognitive, 165, 175
  religious, 71, 91
exteriority, 62

faith, 74
  common, 67, 74
  postsecular, 67
Falk, Richard, xiii, 17, 81–82
fatalism, 132, 180
Fichte, Johann Gottlieb, 32
filial piety, 21, 185–188
finitude, 188
flesh, 41, 170–172
  of the world, 14, 16, 168–170
Foucault, Michel, 169, 171–172

foundationalism, 36, 69
fragmentation, 7–9, 15–17, 77, 123, 127, 136, 139
Frankfurt School, 168, 176
freedom, 49, 75, 93, 97, 160, 165, 178
  dependent, 176, 183
  religious, 67–68, 71–75
fundamentalism, xii, 123
fusion, 108
  of horizons, 108

Gadamer, Hans-Georg, xiii, 19, 104–118, 122, 213n13
Gandhi, Mahatma, 19, 44, 93, 98–101, 124, 129–141, 158
Gandhi, Ramchandra, 20, 143–159, 161, 164–165
genealogy, 171
generativity, 170
generosity, 11
  receptive, 11
genocide, 82
Gestalt theory, 161–163, 169
globalization, 3, 80–81, 114, 123
Grosz, Elizabeth, 170
Guo Qiyong, 186–188
Gutierrez, Gustavo, 54, 207n16

Habermas, Jürgen, 171, 175–177, 182–183, 206n2
Hauerwas, Stanley, 210n9
Hegel, Georg F. W., 14, 26, 31, 74, 113, 176, 197n14
Heidegger, Martin, xiii, 12–13, 21, 58, 73, 77, 106–111, 113–117, 121, 151, 155, 163, 171–172, 175–178, 180–184, 188
hermeneutical circle, 109, 115
hermeneutics, 18–19, 59, 103–116, 182
  of suspicion, 113
heterogeneity, 7–8

heteronomy, 62–63
Hewlett, Nick, 38
Hinduism, 81, 93, 133, 158
Hindutva, 88, 133
Historical School, 105–107
historicism, 112
Hobbes, Thomas, 2, 25, 31–34, 46, 111, 133, 165, 198n19, 202n4
Hölderlin, Friedrich, 181
holism, 2
homogeneity, 7
humaneness, 187–188
humanism, 105, 168, 171
  Renaissance, 105, 112
humanity, 30, 49, 188
Huntington, Samuel, 104, 191n4
Husserl, Edmund, 13, 20, 106, 148, 151, 162–164, 169
Hutten, Ulrich von, 128

idealism, 3, 13
identity, 120, 149
  cultural, 149
  exclusive, 158
  human, 150
immanence, 12, 36, 48, 64, 85, 172, 194n22
immanentism, 156
imperialism, 28, 30, 65, 95
incommensurability, 104
individualism, 17, 90–91, 133
  modern, 17
  new, 72–74
Indology, 59
industrialization, 26
infallibility, 50
injustice, 91, 99, 139, 185
intellectualism, 4–7, 10–12, 161–162
intentionality, 172
intercorporeality, 121
interpretation, 103, 112–113, 116

intersubjectivity, 119, 170–172, 177
Islam, 88
  political, 88
isolationism, 97

Jainism, 131
James, William, xiii, 3–7, 9–13, 17, 20, 69–74, 77, 82, 91, 154, 165, 193n15, 206n4
Judaism, 79
Jung, Hwa Yol, xiii
jurisprudence, 105
justice, 37, 85–86, 90, 93–95, 97–101, 131, 186, 190, 199n25

kama, 130–131
Kant, Immanuel, 10, 15, 20, 87, 111, 147–148, 151, 164, 169, 175, 184, 189
Kantorowicz, Ernst, 56, 72
Kautilya, 131
Kearney, Richard, 76, 208n18
Kelsen, Hans, 25–26, 47–48, 53
Kierkegaard, Søren, 37, 91
King, Martin Luther, Jr., 98–99, 101, 211n16
Kissinger, Henry, 24
Kompridis, Nikolas, 21, 175–184
Krishna, Daya, 20, 143–151, 153–154, 159–161, 164, 217n6, 218n10

Lefort, Claude, 3, 16, 24, 40–46, 55–59, 119, 200n31, 204n19
legality, 68
legitimacy, 52, 57, 68, 73, 83
  ethical, 74
  global, 83
  legal, 68
  public, 78
  traditional, 68, 70
Leibniz, Gottfried Wilhelm, 46

Levians, Emmanuel, 30, 40, 173
liberalism, 16, 27, 30, 33–36, 68, 97, 169, 198n19
   bourgeois, 51
lifeworld, 169–171
Liu Qingping, 186–188
logocentrism, 7, 175
Lutheranism, 91
Lyotard, Jean-François, 7–8, 10, 192n12

Machiavelli, Niccolo, 25, 32, 55, 124, 169
MacIntyre, Aladair, 214n1
Magna Carta, 125
Maistre, Joseph de, 16, 31, 49–50, 56
Mandela, Nelson, 137
Manicheism, 86, 83–95
Marcuse, Herbert, 181
Marx, Karl, 48
materialism, 169
Mauss, Marcel, 169
Mawdudi, Abul-'Ala, 88
McDonough, Sheila, 137
Mencius, 101, 186, 189
Merleau-Ponty, Maurice, xiii, 13–16, 19–20, 40–41, 58, 77, 118–122, 161–164, 167–174, 192n7, 194n21
metaphysics, 62
   modern, 106
   Western, 62
methodology, 106–107, 110
Metz, Johann Baptist, 54, 204n17
Michelet, Jules, 56
militarism, 28
Mill, John Stuart, 178
Mirandola, Pico della, 126
modernity, 1, 63, 67–70, 123, 130, 160, 169, 171–173, 176, 191n1, 202n6
   Catholic, 74
   Western, 1, 151, 168–169, 175
modernization, 160
moksha, 130–134, 139–140, 145–146
Moltmann, Jürgen, 54, 204n17
monarchy, 41–42, 52
   divine, 53
monasticism, 90
monism, 3–6, 9–10, 12, 15, 64
   radical, 17
monotheism, 52
Montesquieu, Baron de, 43
moralism, 169
More, Thomas, 124–129, 136–139
Morgenthau, Hans, 18, 24, 96–97
multiculturalism, xii, 36, 126
Muzaffer, Chandra, xii, 92, 99

nation, 135
   civic, 135
nationalism, 98, 118
naturalism, 33–34, 162
nature, 1, 4, 148
   human, 31, 34, 43, 50, 96, 120
   state of, 120
negativity, 170
neutrality, 67
   liberal, 78
Newman, Cardinal, 49
Niebuhr, Reinhold, 18, 94–96
Niebuhr, Richard, 89
Nietzsche, Friedrich, 76
nihilism, 16
nondualism, 146, 156–160, 164
nonviolence, 129–131, 134, 139
nothingness, 156, 171
   radical, 170

obscuranism, 61
omnipotence, 17, 47, 87

ontology, 21, 106–107, 110, 163, 168, 170, 172
  dynamic, 117
  existential, 163
  negative-positive, 170
ontonomy, 62–64
  cosmotheandric, 63
optimism, 101
orthodoxy, 67
orthopraxis, 67
otherness, 7, 31

pacifism, 27–28
paganism, 52
Panikkar, Raimon, xiii, 5, 11–12, 17, 46, 59–65, 192n10, 205n24
pantheism, 48
Parekh, Bhikhu, 138, 214n26
Parel, Anthony, 9, 124, 130–141
parochialism, 188
particularism, 79, 186–188
particularity, 8, 176, 187
patriotism, 118
peace, 43, 85–86, 90, 99, 118, 131
Peirce, Charles Sanders, 161
perception, 169
  primacy of, 169
pessimism, 34, 86, 101
Peterson, Erik, 52–54
phenomenology, 12–13, 43, 106, 161–162, 168, 175
  existential, 105, 119
  genetic, 169
  hermeneutical, 12
  narrative, 43
philology, 105
philosophy, 3, 59, 143–145, 147, 154, 162–163, 179–180
  analytical, 144
  Chinese, 185
  critical, 147, 151, 175

  German, 175
  history of, 179
  Indian, 144–147
  modern, 106, 184
  nondualist, 144
  of religion, 76, 154
  pluralistic, 10
  political, 6, 40, 49, 58, 77
  practical, 19, 105, 112–114, 117
  speculative, 152
  systematic, 152–154
  Western, 3–4, 13, 144, 150
Plato, 4, 33, 38, 100–101
pluralism, 2, 6–12, 15, 26–27, 36, 136, 159, 164, 176
  deep, 8, 80
  integral, xii, 2, 8–9, 15, 18–21, 136
  social, 27
  thick network, 11
plurality, 9
pluralization, xii–xiii, 2–3, 15, 17
  political, 40–42
  concept of, 23–32
politicization, 18
  of religion, 86
politics, 38, 64
  essence of, 39, 96
  international, 95–96
positivism, 40–41, 47–48, 58, 117, 169
post-Confucianism, 186, 188
postmodernism, xii, 7, 36, 39, 175
postsecular, xii, 68, 73–74
poststructuralism, 21, 167–170
power, 96–97
  struggle for, 98
pragmatism, 117, 175, 179
praxis, 111–114, 117, 172, 179, 182, 187
  political, 121
privatization, 17–18, 75, 86
  of faith, 77, 86

proceduralism, 179
progressivism, 33
Proudhon, Pierre-Joseph, 48
psychology, 69
purusharthas, 130–135, 139–140

Qutb, Sayyid, 88

Rajchandbhai, 140
Ramanujan, A. K., 160–161, 164
Rancière, Jacques, 38–39
rationalism, 4, 7, 12, 47, 50, 96, 117, 161, 168–169, 175, 179
rationality, 8, 67, 153, 175
  communicative, 176
  pure, 164
realism, 24, 96
  international, 24, 96
receptivity, 180, 182
recognition, 117, 180–183
reconciliation, 123, 130, 135
Reformation, 2, 17, 62, 70–71, 90, 112
relativism, 6, 8, 48, 53
religion, 19, 64, 67, 70–72, 82, 85–87, 140, 154
  of mastery, 69, 76–77, 80
  of service, 17, 68–69, 80, 82
  personal, 70, 73–75
religiosity, 5, 67, 74, 78, 128, 136, 154
  pluralistic, 5
  postsecular, 68, 73–74
  pure, 92
Renaissance, 62, 112, 126
republicanism, 133
  civic, 133
responsibility, 167
revolution, 56
  French, xi, 56
Ricoeur, Paul, 17, 75–76, 82, 117, 190, 207n14
rights, 134
  fundamental, 134
Romanticism, 105, 112, 181
Romero, Bishop Oscar, 101
Rorty, Richard, 8, 10
Rousseau, Jean-Jacques, 47, 178

Sacks, Jonathan, xiii, 17, 79–82, 208n23
Sartre, Jean-Paul, 170–171
satyagraha, 19, 93, 129, 134–137, 139–140
Saussure, Ferdinand de, 169
Schleiermacher, Friedrich, 105, 109
Schmitt, Carl, 15–16, 23–40, 43, 45–48, 54, 71, 95, 118, 195n2, 203n12
Schrag, Calvin, xiii
Schwab, George, 245
science, 106
  modern, 47, 175
  natural, 52
scientism, 48
secularism, xi, 59–60, 68, 78, 130, 135, 216n21
secularity, 60
secularization, 59–63
Segundo, Juan Luis, 54
Shah, K. J., 131
Shankara, 144, 146
skepticism, 180
socialism, 127
society, 133
  civil, 133
Socrates, 128, 145, 151
solicitude, 180, 182
solipsism, 177, 183
sovereignty, xii, 16, 45–48, 55, 57, 60, 86, 90, 196n4
  absolute, 88
  monarchical, 41
  of state, 50

Spinoza, Baruch, 182
spirituality, 75, 135, 159
Stahl, Friedrich Julius, 31
state, 26–27, 196n5
  civil, 34
  coercive, 139
  law state, 2, 47, 68, 72
  liberal, 67
  modern, 73, 138–139
  nation, 72, 133, 137
  of war, 34
  theory of, 45
St. Augustine, 16, 52–54, 97
Strong, Tracy, 196n5, 197n15, 201n1
structuralism, 20, 167–168, 170
struggle, 139, 180
subjectivism, 106, 168, 183
subjectivity, 110, 113, 121, 168, 170, 177
  transcendental, 151
Sufism, 219n21
syncretism, 12

Taylor, Charles, xiii, 17, 68–75, 80, 82, 89, 122, 206n6
technology, 175
temporality, 61
terrorism, 23
terror wars, xi, 23, 30, 81
theocracy, 52, 62–63, 87
theology, 45–46, 50–105
  apophatic, 58
  Christian, 25, 89
  death of God, 90
  liberation, 16, 54, 76
  new political, 54
  political, 16, 45–46, 49–54, 60
  Protestant, 105
Tocqueville, Alexis de, 56
Tolstoy, Leo, 189

totalism, 3
totalitarianism, 7, 63
totality, 156
tradition, 109, 111, 147
traditionalism, 6
tragedy, 189
transcendence, 12, 36, 48, 64, 85, 182, 194n22
transcendentalism, 156
triumphalism, 89
Tu Weiming, 189

universalism, 6, 147, 150, 182–183, 186–188
  rational, 176
universe, 9–10
  pluralistic, 10
untouchability, 133
utopia, 127, 181, 183

validation, 179
Vedanta, 146
violence, 30, 37, 91–93, 98, 134, 137, 159
virtue, xii, 111, 133, 139, 187
  civic, xii, 11
  ethical, 100
  moral, 134
  pluralist, 11

Wang Yangming, 187
war, 28, 30–33, 43, 98
  civil, 27–28
  culture, 2
  of all against all, 2
  preemptive, 89
  terror, 1, 30
Weber, Max, 15, 68, 70–72, 168–169, 173, 191n1
Weimar Republic, xii
Westphalian system, 27

Whitehead, Alfred North, 20, 144, 151–154, 165, 192n10, 207n15
Wittgenstein, Ludwig, 7, 39, 73, 77, 104, 151, 154–155, 218n14

xenophobia, 86

Zhu Xi, 187

www.ingramcontent.com/pod-product-compliance
Lightning Source LLC
Chambersburg PA
CBHW022007220426
43663CB00007B/996